MiraLAX® Dissolves in Vodka, Ya Know
Empty Nesting, Migraining, and Menopausing

by
Sarah Berardi

Copyright © 2012 by Sarah Berardi
All rights reserved

ISBN: 0615707769

ISBN 13: 9780615707761

Library of Congress Control Number: 2012918594
CreateSpace Independent Publishing Platform
North Charleston, South Carolina

*Dedicated to Auntie Mim for a chuckle now and then.
Love, the Good One*

*And a special thank-you to my friend Joanne, who read each and every one
of these dumb old stories*

Introduction

I started writing a blog after my two kids urged me to try to keep busy. They thought that if I spent my time blogging, perhaps I would call them less frequently while they were away at college. Instead, I called them every day, asking, "Did you read my blog today? No? Let me read it to you."

So here is my story. I titled my blog *Empty Nesting, Migraining, and Menopausing*, simply because that's what my life entailed at the time.

My friends and family expected me to crumble and pretty much expire when I officially became an empty nester after both my kids went to college. After all, I was one of those annoying "perfect" mothers who had raised two "perfect" children. Now what would I do?

I had officially retired and had a new lease on life. I took a whole year off, reading everything and anything from my cozy bed. After a year of reading, I had this little party in my head I called a "breakout, breakup, breakdown, breakthrough, or newfound stuff to do." Turns out I really hated being so "perfect" all the time, and I was really a wannabe "havefunner." I think I discovered this by having that year of non-uptightness and lounging around. Now I'm out in the world not so much as "Mom," but as myself, which is humbling, blessedly imperfect, humorous, and zany.

Alas, newly developed migraines and the typical woes of premenopause often sidetrack my days, but I still manage to get myself into some unimaginable predicaments. One friend commented on the blog, "Sarah, do these things *really* happen to you?" They do, and I hope you can laugh and commiserate with me as my dendrites shrink in front of you faster than a speeding bullet.

You might find this list of characters helpful as you read:
Marty: My husband
Chris: My son (Lawyerboy)
Andrea: My daughter (Sciencegirl)
Goose: My brother's wife
Betty: Big Belly

❦ MiraLAX® Dissolves in Vodka, Ya Know ❦

Freddy: Fat Chin
CoD: Crack of Dawn (Lawyerboy's girlfriend)
Libbylicious: NYC travel gal pal
VT: Heather, the Viper Tongue
THWIV: The Hospital Where I Volunteer

Herein lies a compilation of some of my blog entries

AUG 2009

You Might Be Mistaken Just Which "Sarah Berardi" This Is (I'm the Batshitcrazy One)

I've noticed out there on the big old World Wide Web that a few other Sarah Berardis exist. I am not an Italian jewelry designer. I am not that teenager who tweets inane things about Hollywood stars. Let me enlighten those of you who don't know exactly which one I am.

- A. I spell my name S-A-R-A-H, with an *h* at the end. This is important to me. Sara and Sarah have totally different connotations. Although I may have been friends with or worked with them for years, and I may have corrected them repeatedly, certain people still can't manage to put that *h* on the end; just like my second-grade teacher who didn't believe I had an *h* at the end of my name and made me bring a note in from my mother. Nope, haven't forgiven her either. That's forty-four years of grudge holding.
- B. I lack pigment in my legs, and I hate to do grocery shopping, cooking, or cleaning anymore. I was a perfect mother for twenty-two years. I am officially burned out from perfection.

C. My tolerance level is low. I deal with migraines, anxiety, and depression. So OK, my tolerance level is *very* low. I admit it. I'm perfectly fine as long as you are polite, intelligent, empathic, and/or interesting. Or, on the other hand, if you're a special needs person, I will love you to death right off the bat and take you under my wing. But the normal people who just choose not to enlighten themselves or take their blinders off? They can bugger off. Perhaps I shall start wearing this on my forehead.

SAYS: IT'S NOT THAT I'M NOT A PEOPLE PERSON, I'M JUST NOT A STUPID PEOPLE PERSON

D. I think I can readily admit my mistakes. At least at work I do. ("Work" is a term I use for my volunteer positions. It makes me feel better.) I fess right up. I don't care for people who blame others, not one bit. Cowards. I don't care for cowards of any kind. Grow a pair.
E. I'm severely independent, so when I ask for help, I really need it. Don't blow me off, please. It took a lot for me to ask for help. I've already grown a pair; I just need your pair to help out.
F. This Sarah is at a stage in life where she had a little party in her head deeming herself retired after putting the kids in college. So there. This is my time. This Sarah loves her bed, and she would love to go back to Italy and Paris.
G. Passive-aggressive people should all go to hell where sulfur does wonders for your hair, my friend Priestieboy has told me. I have no trace of passiveness in me. I've worked and worked and worked on passiveness with a therapist. I've been drugged and drugged and drugged to be

passive. It surfaces now and then. I am, however, aggressive pretty much 24/7. That's what the *other* drugs are for.

H. This Sarah will cut your tongue out if you lie. No lie.
I. OK, time to go take that pill in item *G*. (P.S. Hormone therapy ended today. Praise somebody.)

Ah, but wait—maybe I should wear this in order to show my humility:

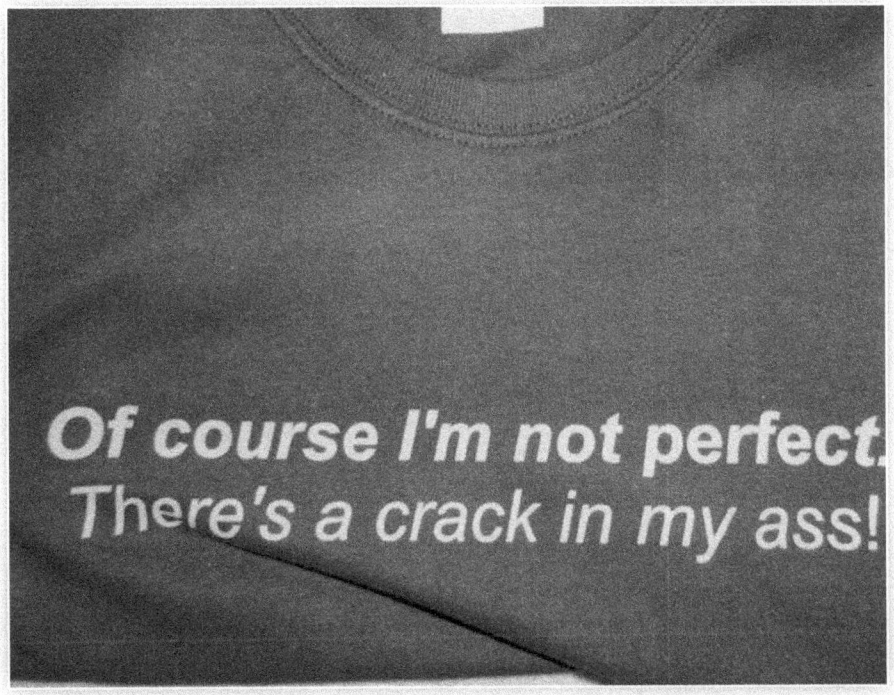

"OF COURSE I'M NOT PERFECT, THERE'S A CRACK IN MY ASS" FUNNY T-SHIRT

J. I get migraines. They suspiciously started after one dumbass sibling decided he wasn't "happy" in life. So he decided to do something about it. Just so happens he went about it in a dumbass way. I'm not saying this caused the migraines to start, but I am saying the stress and tension sure did contribute.

They started slowly, creeping up on me in the middle of the night, making me hold my head as I writhed in pain, and then run to the bathroom to retch, which for some reason gave me enough relief to get back to sleep. I'd wake up the next day feeling hungover, saying, "What the hell was *that* last night?"

After a few months of that, the migraines decided to camp out in my little head, which is the heaviest part your body, you know. It's got a lot going on in there. As you continue reading, you will see that I have pursued doctors and clinics inside and outside of our sometimes blessedly ignorant insurance company's reach; I have traveled wherever I needed to, read incessantly, tried proficiently, and refused to give up, all in order to just get my ass out of bed. The migraines have literally taken over my life.

And please know they are not "headaches." It's a neurological disease, thank you.

If you would like, watch this: http://www.themigraineproject.com/#section3. My friend Libbylicious sent me the link, and the video made me cry. One of my favorite authors, Joan Didion, speaks in it, and one of my doctors, Dr. Carolyn Bernstein from Boston, also makes an appearance.

Migraines put my marriage in prison. That's what Marty, my husband, says. Almost every day. When Marty comes home, I'm often in bed in a dark, quiet room. This has gone on for three and a half years now. Obviously, I take a lot of drugs that enable me to get out of bed when I have to. But all the drugs, and the weight gain that comes with them, can't help but bring on a little good old-fashioned depression—just saying. It's a vicious circle for *all* involved. Events get canceled. The fridge goes empty. The laundry piles up. Showers are skipped. The bed never gets made since I'm perpetually in it with my sunglasses on. (I can still remain fashionable, but that's not why I wear them. Andrea, my daughter, calls me Paris when I wear them inside the house or when she takes me to doctors' offices, referring to the pictures of Paris Hilton in her heyday.)

So I print this link for those who don't understand that popping two Tylenol doesn't help. I want to make it known that when you call in sick with a migraine to your volunteer job and you still get e-mails from them asking you to do things—since they don't understand that you are likely vomiting, having the runs, and believe there is no possible way your blood vessels are not going to burst and that you are, therefore, dying—maybe they'll finally get it. Migraines make you want to die. They corrupt your vision, they fog your brain. They force you to give yourself shots in the thigh and your husband to bring you ice packs. If he's in town.

As this book progresses, so do my migraines. But I refuse to give up. I'm a bitch like that.

{ Sarah Berardi }

Football Hall of Fame Trip

Marty and I just got back from the induction of Ralph Wilson and Bruce Smith (and others I didn't know) into the Football Hall of Fame in Canton, Ohio. I thought I would be bored stiff, as I don't give a fiddler's fart about football, but I ended up laughing a lot and having a blast with friends. The speeches were great. I have to say that the old Ralphie-boy is a funny guy! He's in his nineties, and he comes up with some good ones.

I spotted lots of "old" Buffalo Bills from quite a few years back, when I followed them a bit—Andre Reid, Daryll Tally, Will Wolford, and Jim Kelly. I went up to Marv Levy and asked him if he'd let me have my pic taken with him. I told him I had written a small editorial in the *Buffalo News* a while back and had used one of his famous sayings. He asked which one. I told him I had called myself an "over-officious jerk." (Bills fans will remember that quote.) He got a hearty chuckle out of that, claimed he'd never call me an "over-officious jerk," and we took the pic.

THING IS, I AM AN OVER-OFFICIOUS JERK!

migraines

Whoa, did I have a mother of a migraine yesterday. A huge storm rolled in while we were driving home. I took as much of the migraine "rescue drug" Treximet as I could, and then slept for about five hours. I woke up with the headache somewhat diminished, but not by much. I resorted to my next and last hope: I took an Imitrex injection and my trusty old Xanax, and went back to sleep. Relief came upon waking this morning.

For those of you with migraines, you can understand how debilitating they can be. My journey fighting these damned things started with local neurologists who diagnosed me with migraines but were too damned busy for me to ever see again. You don't mess with me, so off I went to the Diamond Headache Clinic in Chicago. Nothing but the best for me. I stayed in the hospital there for one week and came home feeling much better. I had a blast flying back and forth to Chicago during my maintenance appointments because I would stay in a luxurious hotel on the Magnificent Mile and window-shop (and maybe do a little actual shopping). Unfortunately, the upkeep of that regimen proved difficult for obvious reasons.

So I switched to a local neurologist here in the suburbs near Buffalo. He's been pretty aggressive in my treatment—see?

It's called a sinus nerve block. I numb the inside of my nose with a nasal spray of lidocaine. Then the doctor comes at me (very kindly) with these ten-inch-long Q-tip things that have been dipped in some liquid that looked like water, but I'm sure was lethal in some sort of way. He sticks them up my nose just about to my brain for thirty minutes. I'm going to do this for five days in a row. It helps the facial pain. I also get nerve blocks (injections) in the back of my neck every eight weeks. This numbs the nerves that contribute to tension headaches. Infusions are also on my menu of rescue treatments when I'm down deep with a migraine. This is when they start an IV on you and pump you with a concoction of great drugs and antinauseants. Hey, a girl's gotta do what a girl's gotta do.

As for the cause of these spur-galled, hell-hated migraines, they say menopause and barometric pressure changes can bring them on. I can predict the weather better than Accuweather. And now so can my poor husband. (I sort of feel sorry for him as I'm such a load, but don't tell him so.)

Napoleon and Chipmunks

For those of you who've been asking me who that pirate is in my picture, it's not a pirate—it's Napoleon, you ninnies. Granted, he's a bit tall, but he was handsome. I love a man in uniform. I found him dressed up and waiting for me in a little corner gift shop in Paris last month. I asked him if he was for sale, as the other things were. He said with a sly smile, in his French accent, "It depends. Where do you live?" I told him New York. "Ah, yes, then I am definitely for sale." I furthered my description of where specifically in New York I live, and confessed it wasn't New York City, but Buffalo, near Niagara Falls. (I knew what he had been thinking.) He then declined the offer.

The Never-Ending Chipmunks

Today, I've been procrastinating. Badly. I've wanted to put our "Have-A-Heart" animal cage up in the attic again to catch those nasty varmint chipmunks, but I've decided that there are a million other things I could or should do instead. I hate going up there. So those critters in the attic that I hear at night will be playing beer pong again tonight (at least that's what it sounds like they're doing).

When I catch the varmint "chippies," I put them in the car (still in the cage, of course) and take them to the local ballpark. You see, if I take them to the ballpark, they can still stay together as a family (except the one I accidently ran over while backing up). Sometimes this requires four or five trips to the park. I have lots of chippies up there. And I've noticed that if I hear the trap go *kerplunk* late at night, and I bring it down from the attic and put it in the garage for an early morning run to the park, the little guy will unfortunately be dead in the morning. Maybe from shock? I don't know, but rigor mortis will have set in, the poor things.

{ Sarah Berardi }

NYC, Letterman, and Sarahlicious

For three or four years now, I've been going to New York City with my friend, Libby. We laugh the whole time we're there and drink ~~a lot~~ a little. Well, I drink. We see two shows, do a walk down Canal Street for kicks and giggles, and have fun lunches and dinners. We see shows on Broadway that are make-you-cry divine or shows where I am dancing in the aisles and singing along with the cast. (I'm not supposed to be doing that.) We eat and stay at places I read about in my New York magazines, trendy places, 'cause I'm a happenin' kind of gal. Sometimes we are so hungeryhungry, though, we stop at the nearest dive. I could even eat a hot dog from a vendor (yum), but Libby refuses. Her loss.

Libby works out in the mornings while I sleep (this is a pattern with me). Libby likes to take the subway; I like to take cabs or limos, whichever comes at the doorman's first whistle. I have to say, my favorite taxi ride was with a driver who kept turning around and smiling at me while he was driving. He asked me my name. "Sarah," I said. After a few more blocks of him smiling and looking at me, he said he decided my name should be "*Sarahlicious*." Libby, of course, jealously told him he was just trying to get a big tip and that I wasn't really all that good-looking. Whatever, it worked… I gave him a big tip, a hug, and got a picture of the two of us. Made my day. Ha-ha, *Libbyjealouspoop*.

Every time we go to New York, we try to get into the *Letterman* taping. And every time, we fail. One time we called the ticket hotline, answered the trivia question correctly, and were told we were numbers twenty-one and twenty-two. We were instructed to show up at the theatre at NBC Studios and stand in a numerically ordered line. Off we went as directed, with high hopes this time. Guess what—they took numbers one through twenty. We were so disappointed, we hung out backstage on the stoop with the paparazzi. We saw Richard Branson (Virgin Airlines), Ciara (a singer we had no clue about), and Dane Cook (comedian). Then Biff came out. He gave us a big smile and waved at us. We felt pleased with ourselves and decided we were on a roll, so we went over to Rupert's Deli for lunch. We're pathetic.

On another trip, we went straight from the airport to the studio for tickets, only to find it closed with a sign saying they were not taping due to the writers' strike. We're trying again this October, so cross your fingers. And from now on, Libby shall be referred to as "Libbylicious."

The Miracle Bathing Suit

Yesterday I decided I would go to the club pool for a bit. This obviously required me to put on a bathing suit. So I hesitantly pulled out my suit from last year. Mind you, I've gained at least ten pounds in the last year. In fact, I have put quite a few things in my daughter's closet that don't fit me anymore. (They shrank, OK?) So trying on the bathing suit was going to be F.R.I.G.H.T.E.N.I.N.G. But at the same time, I had a little hope. It is, after all, a brand called "The Miraclesuit®." It's called this because it literally squeezes you and holds you in place. It is a true miracle. So I wish I could say I "slipped" it on, but I didn't. You never can slip on a bathing suit, right, girls? I squirmed, contorted, twisted, and jitterbugged into it. Then I apprehensively went to the full-length mirror. There I beheld a true miracle. I had squished into the thing, and it didn't look bad! Wow, maybe I should start wearing this under my clothes instead of my Spanx®. As I turned to search for my sunscreen, I caught a glimpse of my back. Yikes! I had *back fat*. Back cleavage, as my daughter would say. (Politely, though. She never hurts my feelings.) The suit that had performed a miracle on the front of me had just squished all my fat to the back. Darn it all, what kind of miracle is that? So I learned that I need a new Miraclesuit® that is either a larger size or that doesn't have an open back. Right. Off to the store I go.

P.S. I heard the chippy trap go off. I must have set it wrong—he just went in, ate my sunflower seeds, and happily went on his way to play more beer pong.

A Nine-Out-of-Ten Headache

Those damn chippies. I hear them up there. It sounds as if they are scurrying about, gathering together, laughing down at me in bed, and then scurrying about again. Haven't caught one yet. Last night I had a wicked migraine. In the migraine world, you rank your headaches on a scale of zero to ten, with ten being the worst. My husband, Marty, came home and (after I *told* him I had a bad migraine, which he should have known since the room was dark and I looked dead in bed) proceeded to make as much noise as possible. Likely this wasn't the case, but it sure seemed like it, and since this is my blog, that's what I'm saying. When I have a migraine, I'm incredibly sensitive to light and sound. He proceeded to close closet doors and drawers as loudly as possible. Then he *plopped* down on the bed where I lay prostrate with my hands covering my eyes and vomit rising in my throat. He nonchalantly started to read his newspaper. Every single turn of the page was amplified to me. I finally said, "Please stop with the paper!" He was oblivious. What's that book? *Men Are from Mars, Women Are from Venus?* He's the king on Mars.

Chippie the Tooth

OK, Dr. Dentist, I believe you now. I *must* grind my teeth at night. I've chipped that front tooth again for the fourth time for no good reason. Darn it all. But I still don't want to wear that mouth-guard thing. I have enough problems sleeping. The last thing I need is to have something in my mouth obstructing my nightmarish screams.

Marty's getting used to those nightmares. They are quite often physical in nature. Half the fun of waking up in the morning is having Marty tell me who I screamed at the night before and what I said, and, usually, how I flailed away at him.

Anyway, I'd better get my tooth fixed before I see Chris (our son) next week. He loves to call me Cletus the Slack-Jawed Yokel when it's chipped.

The Kidney Stone

I like to refer to our family as the Griswolds, you know, from those National Lampoon movies where everything Chevy Chase does goes wrong? We're sort of like them in that everything we do goes wrong. I sign our Christmas cards, "Love, the Griswolds." Our vacation house has a *G* on the welcome mat instead of a *B* (they were out of *B*s).

Here's one instance to illustrate the similarities. My urologist told me it was time to get the darned kidney stone out of my right kidney. It had been in there for about two years gathering moss. It would bother me now and then, but not too badly, so I had been ignoring it. Plus, I had passed stones before, and knowing the exact source of the pain is half the battle. But this stone had been too big to pass on its own from the start.

The procedure, called lithotripsy, smashes the kidney stone with ultrasound waves. They do this by locating the stone via the X-ray machine (this part is key), then putting a water balloon-type thing between your kidney and the sound-wave blaster. The blast breaks up the stone. You are then put on narcotics for three days while you pass the bits and catch them for analysis. Fun. Get a visual of that, 'K?

First, they connected me to IVs and anaesthetized me. (My favorite, favorite part. I love drugs that make me relax.) Then they threaded some stuff into "places" and turned on the X-ray machine. That's when the machine bloody well broke. I was in a very expensive, drug-induced sleep, mind you. Mission aborted. Swell. The mortified doctor walked out to tell my husband that they couldn't complete the procedure due to an equipment failure. This was a Griswold adventure.

Interestingly enough, after the next procedure I was able to hand over my bits of stone for analysis. The urologist told me to cut back on my cola and tea consumption. When I couple that with my neurologist telling me to avoid citrus, stress (my extended family), nuts, aged cheeses, stress (my extended family), MSG, artificial sweeteners, and stress (my extended family) for my migraines, that cuts out a lot of foods and beverages. I asked the neurologist if he would agree that I should just start drinking vodka at 9:00 a.m. every day. He said no. Partypoop.

Toilet Paper Can Be Useful in Any Situation

One of my favorite cities to visit is Chicago, because I can't get lost on the Magnificent Mile. It's just a straight shot up or down. I know which block I'm on by which store is on the corner. Now, whatever city I'm in, I always visit the art museum. And while I'm a tourist, I like to dress to the sevens so I don't look like a sloppy tourist. (Not to the nines. If I could reach a nine, I'd *so* be a nine.) So I was on my way to the Art Institute in Chicago, which is all the way down at the other end of the Magnificent Mile from my hotel, when I stopped to get my coffee and go to the ladies' room. Marty was going to meet me on the steps of the museum after his conference finished. So I walked leisurely down the Mag Mile window-shopping (and looking pretty good, sevens and all) until finally reaching my destination. I waited on the steps for the husband, enjoying some people watching. When Marty arrived, I stood, and he quickly said, "Sarah, *sit down*." Sheesh, simmer down, I thought. Turns out, I had a good twelve-inch strip of toilet paper sticking out of my skirt for all the world to see. Now mind you, I'd just walked down the whole bloody street—I'd say about fifteen blocks. Do you think some kind woman could have pulled me aside and said something? Ugh. Griswold?

The Buffett

I had the opportunity to meet Warren Buffett about two years ago. Marty didn't give a fiddler's fart, but I'm a stalker and a gawker when it comes to famous people (embarrassingly so). I've always been fascinated with his mind and how he picked his investments. I even read a huge doorstop of a book about him. So I told Marty to RSVP to an invitation from the *Buffalo News,* which Buffett owns, to see their new printing presses.

I put on my suit and waited in a very short line to shake his hand. Most of the people in line were in the publishing business or were some type of bigwigs in Buffalo. When I got up to the front, I introduced myself. "Hi, I'm Sarah Berardi," I said. "I'm a nobody. Just wanted to meet the man behind the curtain."

"Well, hello, Sarah," he said. "Are you married?" (He asked this simply because in our conversation he discovered the man I was standing with at our introduction was not my husband.)

"Yes, my husband is over there somewhere." I pointed in his direction.

The Buf said, "Give me a call if he ever dumps you," or something like that. He gave me a little smile, and I was speechless. Yes, Sarah Berardi was speechless. How does one respond to that?

Anyway, I was still starstruck at the end of the evening. Our picture hangs on my Wall of Fame upstairs.

PHOTO COURTESY OF THE *BUFFALO NEWS*

DC

My friend, Lynn, and I have taken a few trips together. We get along great, laugh a lot, learn a lot. So she was a good choice to invite on a trip to DC for a personal tour of the *Washington Post*. Please do not read anything political into this. Politics suck on so many levels. I simply love the journalism aspect of any newspaper. Thank you.

When we landed in DC, I couldn't get the overhead luggage compartment open. So who helps me open it? (Mind you, it's a trip from Buffalo to DC.) Olympia Dukakis. (Remember how starstruck I become?)

"Oh, thanks," I said. "It even says 'Push.' I should have known." She just gave me a sweet, understanding smile (you fool, she's thinking). Then I turned and said, "Are you who I think you are?" She said she was. So I walked down the gangplank or whatever that walkway is called, waited for Lynn, and said, "*Oh my God*, Olympia Dukakis helped me with my luggage thing." So when Ms. Dukakis reached us in the terminal, Lynn gave her our copy of a very complimentary *Buffalo News* article about a talk she had given the night before. She was thankful and grateful to us. (Well, to Lynn. She's the one who read the *Buffalo News* on the way down. I read *People* magazine.) Ms. Dukakis asked us what we were doing in DC. We acted like two country bumpkins. "We're here to get a behind-the-scenes tour of the *Washington Post* with a Pulitzer Prize-winning journalist!" we both bleated.

"Oh," she said sweetly, "are you two journalists?"

Lynn said, "No, we're housewives."

She actually laughed out loud.

Anyway, we spent the rest of our trip trying not to get lost. We couldn't even walk in the right direction off the elevator at our hotel half the time. We went around the block thinking we couldn't get lost, but somehow that darned block was octagonal or something and, indeed, we got lost. I asked my kids if I was always this stupid. They both said yes. Thank goodness, or I'd be a little worried about dementia.

⁌ Sarah Berardi ⁍

Annual Doctor Appointment

So I visited my doctor for my annual checkup. I asked him to explain why the cardiologist said he could not pass me with flying colors, but rather "just colors," after my treadmill stress test. So the doctor read the letter attached to my file.

"Aha," he said. "You could barely finish the minimum, such as an elderly, smoking patient would do."

Yikes. I've never smoked, and I'm not elderly! I remember telling the girl while on the treadmill, "OK, I'm dooooone." But she kept saying, "Surely you can do more."

Um, no, I can't. And don't call me Shirley.

So my internist suggested I take up the exercising I used to do before my migraines hit. I asked him if throwing in a little hop, skip, or jump on the way to the mailbox counted. He said no. My daughter's boyfriend suggested I get back to it as well. I hate it when men are right. It doesn't happen that often, so I don't worry about it much.

So we'll see if I get back to my walking or swimming routines. I think tennis is officially out. Oops, I hear the mailman. Must go. Good time to start. I'll skip all the way back and forth to the mailbox!

P.S. Dumb chippies are ignoring my trap. I'm giving up. Maybe they've been enjoying the outdoor weather.

I Smell Things

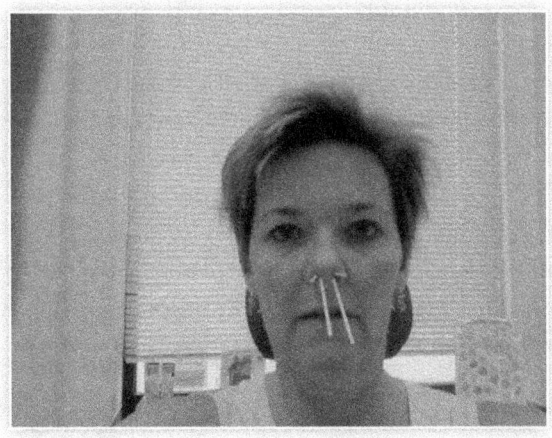

❦ MiraLAX® Dissolves in Vodka, Ya Know ❧

OK, compare this picture of the sticks up my nose with the first picture of the sticks up my nose. (Egad, check out my Freddy Fat Chin.) I went to my ear, nose, and throat (ENT) doctor yesterday for my sinuses. Some of my migraines settle in my sinuses. The neurologists say it's called a "facial migraine" (remember this), which leads to the occipital migraine, and finally to the rest of the migraine that makes me vomit and not see clearly. Anyway, I told the ENT that the neurologist has been giving me sinus nerve blocks. Well, he was *not* to be outdone. With a flick of his wrist, he had two sticks up my nose—with *no* lidocaine like my nice neurologist gave me first—and for good measure, to prove he was better at it than my neurologist, *two more* little sticks. I was choking and pushing his arms away. He just came at me, man! He certainly showed me who was boss. My entire face and jaw went numb. He strutted away like a peacock while I dabbed at the tears running down my cheeks. There they sat, those tusks up my nose, for thirty minutes. By the way, today I have about a "four" headache (out of ten), and it's bloody early yet. I only went to him for a dumb refill on my nasal spray. Anyway, if he can fix me, go for it.

When I texted our kids a pic of this, Chris replied, "Kookookachu."

I texted back, "?"

He replied, "I am the Walrus" (The Beatles). Did you know there is controversy on the web about whether or not it's "koo koo kachu" or "goo goo g' joob"?

Since we're talking about nose stuff, I appear to have a highly developed sense of smell. Ask anyone close to me. It drives them crazy. When our friend Brian spent the night here, he said, "Did I hear you get up in the middle of the night?"

"Yes," I said. "I was still hunting for that smell."

"There is no smell!" he said.

Yes, there was. I just *had* to find it. I can usually find the source, whether it's a rotten potato stuffed in the back of the pantry or a dead frog in the garage. I've had this gift of highly sensitive smell ever since I got pregnant. I smell body odor miles away, I smell gas leaks when they're so minor that the gas company knows me by my first name. So how could my sinuses be blocked?

Must go. Land surveyor is here, then I'm catching a plane to New Jersey to visit my brother and his girls, and still have to skip to the mailbox.

Don't Pass Gas

Two Rants for the Day:
1. People who pass gas on the airplane. (Sort of fits in with my smelling abilities, no?)
   Someone passed gas on my flight yesterday. It had to be someone sitting quite close to me. Now I know the proper etiquette for that: ignore it. Well, sometimes, *I don't feel like being proper*. Because I have *enough* problems flying. So I loudly put my book down and, disgusted, looked around with my stink eye at everyone in the near vicinity. Was I expecting someone to own up and say, "Sorry, that was me"? I just wanted the gasser to know that I knew they did it. I don't know why. It's a problem I have. Well, one of many.
2. People who say *truly*. It's such an easy word, but people who use it think they're using a big word. Get over yourselves.
   Thank you.

Drive-Through Problems

One of my kids' favorite things to mock me about is my problem with ordering at a drive-through. I was at Tim Horton's one day, waiting, waiting, waiting oh so patiently for the person in the speaker to say, "Welcome to Tim Horton's, may I take your order?" After what I thought was a reasonable wait, I said, "Hello?" No response. So I repeated my "hello" about three times, each time getting a little louder and a little angrier. Finally I rudely yelled, "IS ANYBODY THERE?" (Mind you, there were people in cars behind me watching this.) I suddenly hear a faint, "Could you pull up please, ma'am?" I realized I was screaming into the garbage can, which looked amazingly similar to the speaker.

SEP 2009

Snoring

The other night at book club, my girlfriends and I were talking about how our husbands snore. Some of us wives choose to pick up and go to another bedroom. Some of the guys give up and go to the other room after continuous pokes from angry wives. Now, there's obviously a difference between sleep apnea and snoring, so I insisted my husband go to the snore and headache doctor, and I naturally tagged along to tattle on him. Based solely on my description of his snoring, the doctor decided that Marty is just a normal snorer and that he does not have apnea. He just kind of said, "Yup, he snores." I'm OK with that deduction, but is he the one trying to sleep next to my husband? How did this solve the problem? I already *know* he snores.

So as I read in bed a few nights later while my husband slept—snoring *really loudly* next to me; so loudly, in fact, that I kept having to read the same paragraph over and over—I had a great idea. I picked up my cell phone from the table next to me. I hit "record," stuck it near his face tucked into the pillow, and just let it sit there for sixty seconds.

The next day I played it for him.

"What is that?" he said.

"Are you serious?" I asked. "You really don't know what it is?"

"No," he said. "Is it a dog?" *Really?*

An Undershirt?

I noticed something folded neatly on top of my dresser the other day. I asked my husband what it was. He said it was a pillowcase—the pillowcase he had taken out of his undershirt drawer and tried to put on that morning. Can you see him pulling it over his head and finding no holes for his head or arms? I can't stop laughing at that mental picture. It was the type of pillowcase made of jersey, and it was white, so it looked just like an undershirt, in my defense.

How many times has he found weird things in his drawers among his clothes? He's found panty hose stuck inside his shirt sleeves while sitting in meetings. He's found dryer sheets sticking out of his shirts while golfing. He's even attempted to wrestle into my trouser socks, which look very similar to his, but only go up to about his heel. Whatever, at least he's got clean, ironed, and neatly folded clothes, right?

Belly Fat

So you know all the hoopla you see now and then about plus-sized models? Those models have what we in my family call a "Betty Big Belly." Yes, that's right, my belly fat has a name. I have to say, I am always so pleased to see it in pictures, and I do *not* find it offensive or gross. Do you? After all, those pictures of plus-sized models are similar to those gorgeous paintings hanging in Le Louvre or gracing the Sistine Chapel ceiling, right? You can even *tell* that the Mona Lisa had a Betty Big Belly. Maybe that's what she's been smiling about all these years—that we can't see her Betty.

Having a Betty is real life. It's age. It's having babies. It's having surgeries that cut the abdominal muscles down there. It's having a "menopot." It's when you start wearing empire waist dresses and shirts to cover the Betty. Do I wish I didn't have a Betty Big Belly? You bet. But I do. Do I fret about it? Absolutely. Do I have the same figure my mother had? YES! I also don't starve myself, I don't barf after eating, and I don't exercise. I eat movie popcorn with butter. I eat oatmeal cookies. Sometimes I even have a hankering for Starbursts. And Jiminy Crickets, I put both butter and sour cream on my baked potato sometimes. Bad Betty.

Attack Mother

So I *might* be known in my family as "crazy Aunt Sarah." I'm also known as "Cruella" (fondly, I'm sure), and some other terms of endearment that my own kids and husband call me. As for the sign on my door in the garage that says, "Attack Mother," I am known among family and friends to have a list. Yes, a *list*. For instance, there was a nasty girl in my daughter's high school who was particularly piggy to her. Actually, two girls. They are on my list. A kid my son knew as an undergrad is on my list because he was drug dealer scum. This might be called a grudge list. You may call it whatever you want, but I like it. When people are rude to me—say, at a cocktail party—I just look at them and say, "Don't you know I have a *list*?" They have no idea what I'm talking about, of course, so I just walk away.

I remember when my daughter brought a friend home who told me a story about how some colleagues of his stole one of his ideas. I patiently listened to his story, hearing how unethical it was, and calmly asked him, "What are their names, those colleagues?" My daughter quickly said, "No, don't tell her, she has a list!" Her friend just looked quizzically at her, a little frightened I might add, and said, "What?" So my daughter explained. He still won't tell me their names, but I'll find out. Naughty people.

You have to know that you shouldn't mess with my family. They're *my* family. I am their protector, you see. My list protects my family because I like to see that what goes around comes around. Then I can take them off my list.

As for my sign, an undergrad friend of my daughter's who's from India took a picture of it to show his family back home. He was quite humorously confused about it.

Migraine

I am a diet-cola-aholic. I drink about four or five a day. I just realized the fake sugar is a trigger for my migraines. Oy vey, that's going to be a big change.

Exercise

OK, these are my sneakers. Notice how white and clean they are. Notice where I keep them—way up high in my closet. In other words, they get *no* use. I got them when I bought a new treadmill. My daughter just recently suggested that for exercise I should get back on my treadmill. I told her I didn't have a treadmill.

"You just bought one," she said.

"When?"

"About eleven months ago," she said. "It's in the basement workout room."

Oh. I also have no idea why there is a stray sneaker up there by itself.

Idiocy in Winery

We're still in California. Today we booked three winery tours. Now, I don't drink red wines because of the migraines. When we got to our first tour, they said they didn't make whites. No problem. I walked the tour with the group of young well-to-doers (who thought quite highly of themselves) with my wine goblet full of water. I enjoyed smelling my husband's red wines, though. When the winery's idiot tour guide asked me why I wasn't drinking, I told him I was afraid it might trigger a migraine.

"Oh, all you have to do is pop a Benadryl," he said. "And if it doesn't work, the worst that could happen would be you might get a little headache."

What a bleepin' idiot. I wanted to kick him in the crotch and pull his dumbass ponytail. Not only was this guy an ignoramus, he was just plain raunchy and rude. His favorite word was *dude*. He kept bragging about his great selling, big-dealing himself (I don't care for people who aren't humble). Then he started to get crude, speaking in sexual terms to our group. Now, I realize that my husband and I were by far the oldest couple in the tour group, surrounded by successful, younger couples—attorneys, a pathologist, a pharmacist, etc.—who were clearly impressed with this forty-five-year-old tour guide. Well, I clearly was not. When the tour guide acted crude, I mentioned to my husband that, if he really loved me, he would speak up or punch the guy or something. He just said, "OK, I don't love you. Plus, I have a rule never to punch anyone on my birthday." (It *was* his birthday.)

The CIA

Had dinner tonight at the CIA. No kidding. The Culinary Institute of America in Napa Valley, commonly known as the CIA, is beautiful and the service excellent, as was the food. I had the yummiest roasted chicken with lemon, white wine, and capers that melted in my mouth.

However, we shared the dining room with an obnoxious table of about thirty people celebrating a birthday. They had obviously been drinking heavily. They added so much to the cacophony of noise in the restaurant that I felt the need to go over and remind them that there were other people in the restaurant (who just *might* have bloody headaches—not migraines) who were trying to engage in conversations but couldn't hear one another over their cackling and whistling.

My husband wouldn't let me, though. He claims he has a rule that he doesn't throw punches the day *after* his birthday.

Recap of My Cali Trip

Little do you know, but I have quite an illustrious history as a fearful flier. I am *not* a good flier. (Stories of my trips to and from Germany while we lived there could be a book in themselves.) So this trip to California was a big one for me. My fear has turned into something on a lesser scale now, thanks to Prozac and a little Xanax here and there.

I really wish this state didn't have those dreaded earthquakes; otherwise, I'd pitch a tent and live here. While here, we stayed in a villa and rode our bikes to eat, spa, swim, and sun (shade for me). Yes, we ate at Bouchon—divine! I learned a lot about wine making, but won't bore you with it, other than to say that rosé is making a comeback—can you believe it?

Things I have learned on this trip about flying (that I may or may not have already known):

1. Obviously, people talk *way too loudly* on their cell phones while waiting for the plane. I have sticky notes that say, "You're talking too loudly," but Marty won't let me give them out. Partypoop. I suppose he has some rule about not throwing punches at airports.
2. The old ashtrays on the restroom doors on airplanes do not open them. You must push to open the restroom doors, like the signs say.
3. You should hold your stylish maxi dress up so that it does not get caught in the escalator, getting all greasy and stretched out on one side and

causing you to freak out in fear that it will rip right off you. (Marty could have cared less.)
4. When you land at the San Francisco airport, the runway appears to be nowhere in sight. I was scared shitless that we were landing in the water until Marty calmed me by explaining the runway comes out onto the water.
5. I never want to fly anything but first class again. Marty has created a flying monster.

That Ain't No Chipmunk

Holy crap. I've been up since about 5:00 a.m., jamming a plastic hanger up at our attic cover. It's now 6:00 a.m.

I was awakened around five o'clock by a noise that sounded as if a branch full of leaves fell on our house. I didn't much care, and tried to go back to sleep. Until, that is, some pesky, large-sounding critter started playing up in the attic, the attic door being just a few feet above my bed. What in the world is he making all that clatter with? I'm picturing a squirrel with a pickax, hardhat, and work boots on up there. He's gnawing away at my fan wires, I can hear him. And he's thumping up and down on something to get his leverage. *I can hear it. I can picture it.* There is a fan switch right above where Marty's suits hang, and I can hear him gnawing *right there*. So I wake up snoring Marty by banging on the attic door with a plastic hanger. It only deters the large critter for about five minutes. I keep doing it every time he resumes, and now it doesn't deter him at all. At this point, Marty is up and awake, telling me to relax.

The last thing you should *ever* do is tell me to relax. Ticks me off. Probably any woman, right? He told me to put my earplugs in, take a couple of Xanax, and go back to sleep. I said, "A couple? I won't wake up until seven this evening!"

"Then take three," he said.

So here I sit, with my fluorescent pink earplugs in, fuming, knowing that damn creature is gnawing away up there, and Marty's downstairs reading the paper, drinking his coffee. So no phone calls this morning to our house, because I can't hear the phone ring. But if you do call and a critter answers, call the trapper, as I'll be asleep at least until 7:00 p.m.

Chippiayyaaayyy

Can you see him in there? OK, so he wasn't the Loch Ness Monster like I thought. He was a chipmunk. But he was a *hefty* chipmunk, you have to admit. In trying to escape from the trap, he pulled through quite a bit of insulation (*that's* what created all that racket up there). No worries, you animal lovers. I took him to the local park to let him go. Now I just need to find out how the hell they are getting in. Winter's coming, so they'll be searching for a nice, warm home. Although their home is already set up in my attic, beer pong and all, I'm sure. Damn. They're on my list.

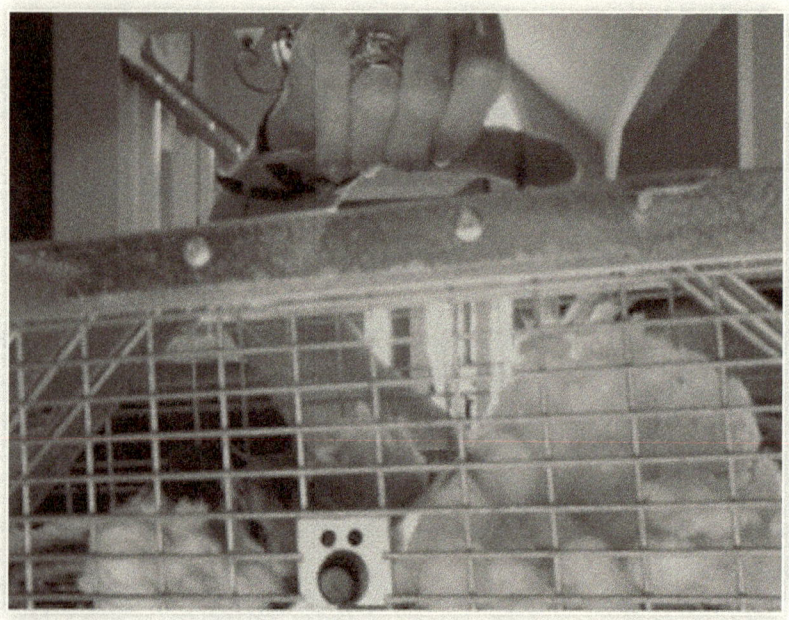

Morbidity

Since I'm flying again in a few days (on an airplane, obviously—keep your broom comments to yourselves), and due to my intense fear of flying (and, of course, being the good mother that I am), I decided to tell my daughter that my dying wishes have changed from what's stated in my will. And I thought it important that I pass this pertinent information along to her *now*.

I told her that if I die, I no longer want to be cremated. I'd prefer to be in an inexpensive coffin, lying straight as a pin, toes pointed, with my arms crossed across my chest.

"Like a mummy?" she said.

"Yes, exactly!"

"Eewwww, Mom," she said. "You're freaking me out. Stop."

"Well, this is important to me," I said, "so I have to tell someone in the family who *will remember* what I've said."

Then I told her not to burn her daddy either, when the time comes.

I've given her instructions for my eulogy, being the ever-controlling bitch that I am, suggesting she can tell mourners (yes, people will mourn) about all the funny (aka embarrassing) things I did to her and her brother.

"Stop!" she finally said to me. "You are not having a funeral. I am getting your ashes, throwing them in a Dumpster, and calling it a day."

Goin' Huntin'

During one lunch with three friends (they are my "lunch friends"), I mentioned my abundancy of chipmunks; how they seem to be having a carnival or beerfest on my lawn, darting in and out of my huge landscape rocks. They've become very bold, as if they own my place, acting as if *I'm* the intruder. They are no longer afraid of me. I have to admit, the one on my front porch started out as adorable, but the cuteness phase ended when they all invited their extended family and friends to join their beerfest on my property. My "Have-A-Heart" cages and trips to the local baseball field are getting tiring. It seems endless. They're laughing at me. So I told my friends that I wanted to purchase some type of gun—just to scare them, mind you. I live in a wooded area, so I thought I could do it. Not a *real* gun. Just something to scare those dratted rat-looking critters out of my place.

One of my friends explained to me the types of harmless guns I could use—water guns, marshmallow guns.

Then I said, "Hey, couldn't I use those water guns or marshmallow guns in the car when someone cuts me off or doesn't let me merge?"

He said calmly, "Well, no, that would be considered harassment." Oh.

Come to find out, when two of those friends got into their car after lunch, the one said, "The *last* person who should own *any* type of gun would be Sarah."

⁌ MiraLAX® Dissolves in Vodka, Ya Know ⁍

P.S. I have severe road rage at times (which they know), so watch out for me on the road. I will follow you if you make me mad, no matter what you look like.

Goin' to See My Sciencegirl

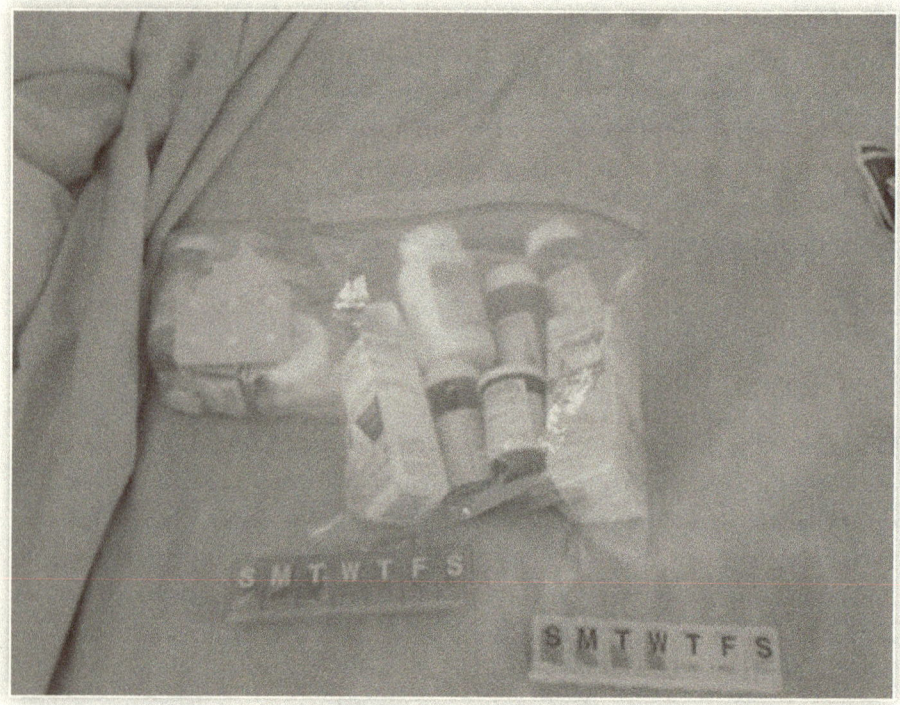

These are my bags of migraine drugs I have to travel with. A small zippy and a large zippy. So this means I have a total of three zippy bags to be screened, because I have all my regular lotions in the one zippy that I didn't picture. My lunch friends and I call it my Michael Jackson bag of drugs.

This was my adventurous trip down:

Good Lord, I'm sitting in the new JetBlue terminal in JFK, on my way to visit my little Andrea (aka Sciencegirl, who's getting her PhD in biology, for your future reference). Marty said he didn't think I would like the new terminal. I see no reason why I wouldn't, since there's a bar every six gates or so.

There are alarms going off all over, blue lights flickering, TSA people and police running to and fro. It's all getting to be a bit much for me, making me a little anxious. They've changed my gate. So I pack up my gear, find the new gate, reboot my computer, and try to relax again. Three birds sidle up next to me on the floor. Sparrows. I follow their flight path, since I'm not feeding them, and see them bathing and slurping in the water fountain behind me. Yuck. Note to self: My mother was right—don't ever drink out of those yucky water fountains.

The man behind me must have TB. Correction, it's a woman. She's coughing, or should I say hawking up a lung, right down my neck. A man just passed me wearing a suede skirt. Not a kilt, mind you. This is all too much for me.

Oh...*now* I see why so much security. An airplane just took off in front of me that said, "United States of America." Humph.

I think flight attendants should be trained to give massages.

University of Virginia

I have to admit, this was our second shot of this photo in Target. The first one showed our "Freddy Fat Chins." In writing this, it makes me realize my family must have a thing for putting names to unsightly parts of our bodies (Betty Big

Belly, Freddy Fat Chin). Sciencegirl said we had to look up into the camera to make our chins disappear. Voilà.

We've been doing a bunch of things that she hasn't had time to do. I taught her how to make a nice bead of caulk after having her sliding glass door fixed. As we sat in the waiting room at the car wash drinking coffee (this is how I taught her to get the inside and outside of the car washed—paying for it with Daddy's credit card), I picked up a local paper. A picture of her condominium building dominated the entire front page. The story: "The Husband, the Wife, and the Hit Man." Crikey, on the floor just above her, this was all going on. For real! Do you see why I don't sleep?

Flight Confessions

Confessions of a menopausal, not-quite-with-it flyer (variant of flier):

I never looked very intently at my itinerary for my connecting flight from Buffalo to JFK. And I have a ritual before flying that I have to be at my gate about one and a half hours before boarding to sip my tea, plug in my relaxing music, and read. So for this trip I arrived at the security podium in Buffalo at 11:43 a.m. for my…WHAT?…11:45 a.m. flight? I thought it said 1:45 p.m.! I knew I should have gotten that eyeglass prescription updated that's been sitting in my purse! I went through security (asking kindly if I could jump ahead), ran (urine leakage) the three gates up to JetBlue, and watched the gate door shut. I screamed, "Oh wait, please, oh please, oh please!"

The gate guy said, "We've been paging you."

"I'm here, I'm here. Can I still get on? I have a connection to catch." Only every other word was audible since I couldn't breathe. He let me on. The flight attendants were just chatting up there, but the people strapped in were giving me the stink eye. Problem averted. Just a little urine leakage, a pounding heart, and lungs gasping for air.

Then, on the way back, I arrived at Richmond my required two hours early with Sciencegirl rechecking my times for me. Went through screening fine. Stopped at a little store to get my bottled water while still hanging onto my laptop and sweater instead of jamming them back into my carry-on bag or putting my sweater back on. While paying for my water, the poor checkout girl looked horrible, with one eye almost shut.

"Oh my gosh, you have a migraine, don't you?" I asked.

Sarah Berardi

"How did you know?" So we had a quick conversation, during which I put my laptop and new J. Crew sweater (so you can envision the price) on top of the candy shelf. After our talk, *I left them there*. After about, oh, twenty-five minutes, I realized I had left them, ran back (urine leakage), asked for them, but they had just turned them in to security.

Long story. Got both back, and had many delayed flights. Marty wonders just how the hell I can travel alone. I'm beginning to wonder that myself.

So now back safe and sound. Blaaaah.

Off to volunteer at the local cancer hospital—from here on in to be known as "THWIV" (The Hospital Where I Volunteer)—where all of the stuff above just doesn't matter.

Followers

I think, perhaps, that my original blog title *Life of a Terrace Lane Housewife* might have had a different connotation to some than it did for me. I think this because of the picture that accompanied the first follower I had. The picture was of a man holding up his shirt, exposing his nipples. Another male friend of his was tweaking one of those nipples.

When I first opened my blog, I was sitting next to Marty, and I said, "Oh, I'm so excited, I have a follower, I have a follower! That was so quick. I have a follower!" He didn't give a fiddler's fart, but feigned slight interest by replying, "Oh, good." I looked at the picture closer, then closer with my bifocals. I said very quietly, "Um, could you look at this picture and see if you see what I see?"

He put down his paper (he does *not* like to be interrupted in his paper reading), took the computer, and said, "Where am I looking?" I showed him. "Oh, that's just great, Sarah," he said, and gave it back to me. This confirmed that he saw what I saw. (Marty has this way of "yelling" at me and the kids without ever raising his voice, we shudder and really don't care for this at all.)

I texted the kids with the picture of my first follower.

Sciencegirl texted back, "Eeeeeeewwwww, BLOCK HIM!"

Chris (our son) texted, "OMG, stop making me laugh, I'm in class!"

It took me a few hours to figure out how to block him, but block him I did.

NOV 2009

Nothin' but Class, Baby

Well, *so what* if, when I took off my coat at a local women's fund luncheon, the back of my dress was tucked into the top of my panty hose?

Would you expect anything less of me?

My Reading Light

When I wake up in the middle of the night, as many women my age do, I sometimes pick up a book or watch TV with the volume very low. Marty has always been someone who can sleep as soon as his head hits the pillow and usually stays asleep unless purposefully woken up.

When I would read at night, I found that those little book lights were too small and just not bright enough. They ticked me off. (Surprised?) I kept having to adjust them to the proper spot on the page. Nuisance. So I switched to a regular flashlight I'd lay on my chest. This actually worked fine, but it, too, dimmed too fast. Then one day I was in Home Depot and saw those headlamps that you slip over your head with a piece of elastic. Not those huge ones for mining, but of the smaller variety. I thought this would be great!

It was. It was so incredibly bright. The light covered the whole page. It was easy to turn on and off. It was perfect (like me). But in the middle of the night, I must have been making way too much noise doing something (eating in bed?), which woke Marty up. He propped himself up on one elbow, turned, and looked at me (while I was looking straight ahead at my book, reading with my headlamp on), and he anxiously said, "What's wrong, what's going on?"

I turned to answer him, forgetting I had my mega-bright headlamp glaring in his eyes, and said, "Nothing."

He screamed, "Crap, what the hell is that? What's that blinding light?" He covered his eyes.

I kept staring at him, still forgetting I had the blasted headlamp on, saying, "What are you talking about? You must be dreaming."

"Get that out of my eyes!" he screamed.

"Oh my gosh, it's my reading light. Sorry."

He lay back down to go to sleep and said, "Jeez, I'm seeing lights, like in the old days when those camera flashbulbs would go off."

Being of Sound Mind...

Dear Kids,

Here is another update for my will. I'll make the official changes later.

This is in addition to being placed ever so gently into an inexpensive coffin with my toes pointed and arms crossed upon my chest as if I were a mummy. I would like you to donate my body to science. This is new, this donation part. However, I would like you to *get the results of any research* they do on me. I would like you to find out the following:

1. Why oh why does my Madame Bovary (my name for my right ovary, which has been removed) keep bothering me? What's in there? A critter? A chippy? A left-in-there surgical instrument? Another rogue ureter? (I have three; you're only supposed to have two.) There is no more Bovary! "It haunts me," as Edith Piaf says when introducing her beautiful song, "Padam." My Madame Bovary is haunting me. Haunting me, I tell you.

2. What's up with that third ureter? Is it just hanging out in there? And how's that sponge kidney? Do I have any more stones gathering moss in there? Let's get some researchers on that situation.
3. What the hell is up with that gaggle of nerve cells up there in that huge brain of mine? There are some *terrible, serious* misfires going on up there. Research needs to be done on how to fix those misfires. For the good of the people, you know...
4. While up there in my huge brain, they can research all that migraine trouble.
5. Build a very large monument with a statue of me in high heels, reading a book, probably lying in bed. This can then be placed in Forest Lawn Cemetery.
6. Have them frame the size of my heart, 'cause it's big.

Thanks, man. Yours in morbidity,
Love, your mother.

DEC 2009

My First Christmas Present for the Season

Tonight I attended my book club dinner with four of my girlfriends. On the ride over, my friend Karen gave me my first Christmas present of the season. Isn't she so naughty? She reads my blog every day, so she thought this was appropriate. I love it. It's a little journal. Sometimes I think people are afraid to say things to me now because they say, "And *don't* put that in your blog" a lot. Which, of course, is the kiss of death, because there's a good chance I will (though I would never if asked not to). In fact, one friend of mine would never, ever speak to me again if I put anything in the blog about her (big ol' baby). She once said in an e-mail to me, "Blog me." Which, if you think about it, wasn't very nice. But pretty darned funny. (She wasn't telling me to write about her.)

Tomorrow I'm going to the doctor to see about my "one more pill," since so many friends keep hinting that my anger might require a little bump in the old Prozac. As I told the receptionist when she inquired why I made the appointment, "Well, some people think I have a little problem with anger, but I personally think they can all go to hell." She burst out laughing and told me she'd get me in to see the doctor ASAP.

Yet Another Doctor

Humph. Since so many of my friends have been saying I need "one more pill," today I went to a neuropsychiatrist. The neurologist for my migraines made me, 'K? It kills me to admit it, but I'm going.

I was pretty apprehensive going in. I just didn't feel like having to go over the whole sordid family history thing. We are the picture you see in the *Encyclopaedia Britannica* under the subject heading, Dysfunctional Family. Not my current family, I mean the one I grew up in. You all do know that my current family is perfect, right?

So as we got to talking, I found myself blurting out all my stuff, dropping the f-bomb, telling him about my list. In other words, I gave him full warning. He actually turned out to be a nice guy, even though I thought he was going to be a real bastard—somehow male therapists of any kind rub me the wrong way; they're a little pricky, arrogant. (He told me I could say that. Actually, he said I should say he was a Cuban bastard.) I told him I thought he'd be an arrogant prick and was pleased he wasn't.

I mentioned to him some of my recent problems, such as the Fruit-Belt incident. I got out of my car in a notoriously dangerous neighborhood—you know, shootings, muggings, drug deals—in the city of Buffalo, located in what is historically known as the Fruit Belt (for the fruit trees German immigrants planted in 1839) to try to catch the thug who threw a rock at my car. I told him about my fogginess when going through Tim Horton's and talking into the garbage can instead of the speaker. And I told him a few other good secrets. I told him I thought I have the same problems everyone else does. I got no reaction out of him on this statement, which made me worry a little.

I asked him if he thought my husband had anything to do with any of my so-called problems (since I don't have any).

"Um…is he writing the check for this appointment?" he asked.

"Yes."

"Then I have no comment," he said.

P.S. He thinks I'm perfect.

P.P.S. One of my migraine prevention drugs, an antiseizure (no, I do not have seizures), actually causes brain fog—not kidding.

Humor in Death?

Today at "work" (THWIV), I talked on the phone with a nice lady whose husband recently passed away. We cried together for the first five minutes or so, but ended up laughing hysterically for the next ten. I found she had an incredible sense of humor, which I find, even in these horrible times, is what gets me through.

Some of my friends cringe at my sense of humor in bad times. Everyone except my friend, Anne. She and I can go back and forth with morbid cracks about death, even our own close, personal experiences with death. While A and I laugh hysterically, we feel the looks of others in our group and know they're thinking, *What heartless people*. And sometimes we are.

I hate to say this so publicly, but my father passed away during the hanging-chad debacle. So right when I imagined him "going toward the light," I screamed into his ear, "BUSH WON," even though we didn't know yet who would be declared the winner. Just thought he might want to believe that on his way out, since that was his last worry.

Or my poor mother. When I flew in from Germany to see her before she passed away, she wasn't conscious. So I screamed in her ear everything I had to say to her. It wasn't until later that a kind hospice worker told me that they believe the patient can still hear you just fine. So her last remembrance of me was, *I wish to hell Sarah would quit screaming in my ear!*

P.S. That nice lady I talked to at work said, "When God closes one door, he opens a window, but in my case, I wouldn't fit, so I hope he's opened another door."

New Follower on Blog

I have a new follower as of last night. A friend e-mailed me and asked, "I was wondering whether the Cuban bastard is your new follower? Do you think if you rant one day in your blog, he'll call you up and change your meds? If it's him, he's a special kind of bastard!"

Wouldn't it be great if my fancy, new neuropsychiatrist—*it's for my migraines*—is indeed my new follower? Or maybe it's the student he had following him for the day. Now I'm worried about how often I've talked about death. It's all in good humor, you know.

And, did I tell you he guessed my weight to be fifteen pounds over my real weight? Humph.

P.S. Sciencegirl is now calling me "Crazy" instead of "Mom."

Indian Wells, CA

Yesterday Marty woke me up at five o'clock to catch our flight. Being that I had just fallen asleep around 1:45 a.m., I was my usual happy-go-lucky self. We were flying to Indian Wells, California, where Marty had a medical conference. I got to tag along by using his free airline miles.

On our drive from the airport to the hotel, I couldn't help but notice the proliferation of wind turbines:

{ Sarah Berardi }

Jeez. It was almost sci-fi creepy driving through them all. And as for the freeways—Buffalo has found its mate in horrible roads. I, to date, had never traveled on roads worse than Buffalo-area roads. But I applaud the turbines.

I was *starving*, and I find that if I skip a meal, I'll get a migraine. All those IN-N-OUT BURGER® signs looked so tempting. But I hadn't had ground beef since I saw *Food, Inc.* Michael Pollan made in impact on me. At the same time, I wanted to see what all those women at the Golden Globes went to eat after starving themselves for a week in order to fit into their dresses. Conundrum. Exit after exit, I saw those IN-N-OUT BURGER® signs. That was my choice. Finally, I felt so hungry I was ready to eat cardboard. I caved.

Yummy. It was soooo good. The toasted buns were thin, not fluffy, and the beef was well done. No pink. And it came with onions, lettuce, and tomatoes, with "special sauce."

Next we checked in, and I assumed my normal position for the day. Never mind it was three o'clock in California. Or, never mind it was only six o'clock my time.

❦ MiraLAX® Dissolves in Vodka, Ya Know ❦

SPECIAL POSITION

Then, for a little reading to put me to sleep, I thought I'd browse through the hotel spa brochure, but came upon this first:

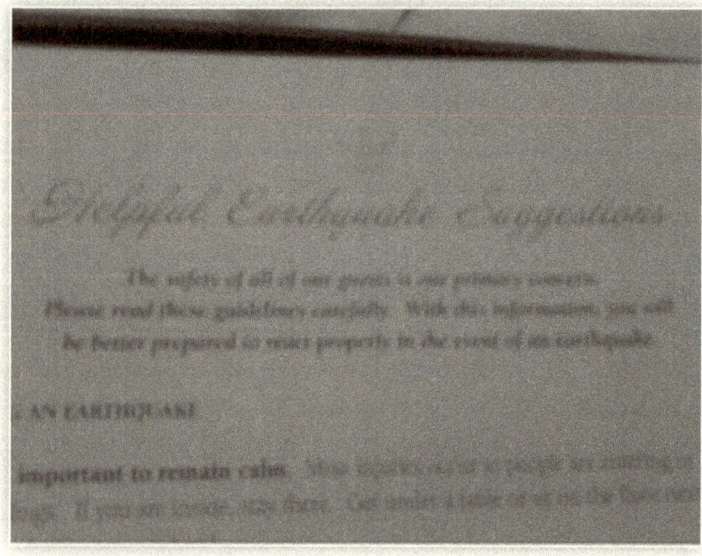

HERE'S TO SWEET DREAMS.

Going Home ☹

Traveling home today. Sitting in the LA airport with the sun shining in. Sun makes a big difference on one's disposition, no?

On our ride from the Palm Springs area to LA yesterday, I swear the Balloon Boy family passed us on the freeway in their van. I saw three boys fighting, unbuckled in the back, and I know it was the mom in the passenger seat.

We stopped for lunch at a marina before checking into the hotel. A particular item on the menu caught my eye:

Therefore:

❦ MiraLAX® Dissolves in Vodka, Ya Know ❧

GETTIN' MY DRINK ON

The next day, upon returning our car to Hertz at the off-site return, the gentleman there asked us if we'd like a courtesy ride to the airport instead of taking the shuttle to the bus. Now, Marty's been doing this car rental stuff for thirty years, and never—I repeat, never—has he been asked this. He said, "Sure." Then he said, "I'm just curious, but why are you offering this service today?"

I butt in (who, me? butt in?), "Is it because I'm so good-looking?"

The nice fellow burst out laughing and said, "Yes, ma'am, it sure is!" What was he laughing at?

Then we went to get our boarding passes. Mine came out of the machine just fine. But Mr. Traveler's did not. He had to see the attendant. Apparently his said he was traveling with an infant. I immediately became indignant and declared that I knew I was a pain in the ass to travel with, but he didn't have to claim me as a bloody infant.

It's tiring being here in California where people mistake me for a movie star, in my big sunglasses (that help prevent my migraines) and my leopard-print coat. I was working it the whole time and loving it.

{ Sarah Berardi }

Stink Eye

Is this a picture of me:
- A. Giving the stink eye to somebody sitting near me in the airport who was talking way too loudly on her cell phone, or
- B. An advertisement for someone who needs her roots done?

If you answered both A and B, you are correct.

Udders

I first decided to get a cell phone in 1996, after we moved back from Germany. Being ever so efficient (perfect—do you hear that, Dr. Cubanbastard?), I shopped around at different stores. When I stopped at Sprint®, I asked the salesman if I would get good reception out where I lived. He asked me where I lived. When I told him the town, which was out in a fourteen-house subdivision surrounded by farmers, he said to me, "Oh, I'm sorry, ma'am, we don't build cell towers for cows."

And I was supposed to put commission in this guy's pocket? I was livid. When I came home and told Marty, he said, "You should have lifted your shirt, showed him your udders, and left."

Weight Management Vitamins

My sister-in-law, Goose, and I frequently give each other things that we've purchased for ourselves but find are really not suited for us. Sometimes they're free samples that we know the other would use or enjoy. Sometimes it's a blouse that just doesn't look as hot on as it did on the hanger.

I always give Goose all those free samples of eye-lift creams I get, since I don't need them; or the wrinkle repair stuff, you know, along those lines. Well, one day she gave me a large bottle of some type of vitamins made specifically for women that supposedly help maintain and control weight. It was a well-known brand. She said she just didn't like them. Fine. So I took one the next day along with my other morning pills, did a little cleanup around the house, got in the shower, and barfed.

After I realized what the heck happened, I called the vitamin company, laughing. I told them I could see how the vitamins helped women maintain their weight because they made them barf! The lady said, "I'm sorry to hear about that, ma'am. To compensate you, we'd like to send you three coupons for one dollar toward this product."

I said, "Are you kidding? I just barfed them up! I'm not going to buy them again." She tried again with the same offer, but just wasn't getting it or seeing the humor in it. "Never mind," I said.

I called Goose and told her. She burst out laughing.

"What was it that you didn't like about them?" I asked.

"They upset my stomach." Biatch. I think she did that on purpose.

Mall Etiquette

Things you should and should not do while in the mall:
1. If you're walking at a pace other than my pace, stay out of my way.

2. When entering a store, don't stop at the entrance to decide which direction you want to head. Someone (*me*) might want to get in behind you.
3. When exiting a store, look both ways (as if crossing a street), so as not to pull out into oncoming traffic, which would cause an accident resulting in personal injury.
4. Please do not exhale your anxiety in close proximity to my face at any time. You may have bad breath. I know I may have bad breath, so I don't go around breathing it at people.
5. Hang around Lee Nails and inhale for a quick fix. I love that smell.
6. If you are window-shopping, please move in toward the windows so others can pass you.
7. No walking more than two abreast. Nobody can get around you. It's aggravating. You have miles of people you're blocking who are trying to get by while the three, four, or five of you giggle and preen for your boyfriends and girlfriends with your pants dragging.
8. Please don't be cheery and tell me what you have on sale today as soon as I enter your store. If I want help, I'll ask for it.
9. If you are in a greater hurry than I am, and I can A) hear your heels coming scarily up on me, or B) feel your anxious breathing down my neck, I will be happy to move over, plaster myself against the nearest wall, and let you pass.
10. Please stop staring at me as if I'm a movie star when you see me. I know I look like one with my sunglasses on, but if I have them on indoors, it means I have a headache. And I know I look like a movie star because I'm so beautiful, but that I can't help.

EEG

Yesterday I had a 7:30 a.m. appointment (yuck, on a Saturday) for an EEG for my migraines. I've seen them done before with my nephew, so I knew it would be quick and painless.

When I first got to the medical building, after rolling out of bed, brushing my teeth, and washing my face (no need for a shower, I was headed straight back to bed), I found an Out of Order sign on the elevator. Great. I was still half-asleep, and now I had to walk up four flights of stairs. By the second flight, I was in trouble deep. Remember that blog about my treadmill stress test that I barely passed? Well, I wasn't doing much better on the stairs. I gasped for a few minutes on the second-floor landing and proceeded on up.

I finally made it, and was taken straight in for the setup. I snapped a quick pic for my nephew, as I had taken one of him when he had his first EEG, so I figured tit for tat.

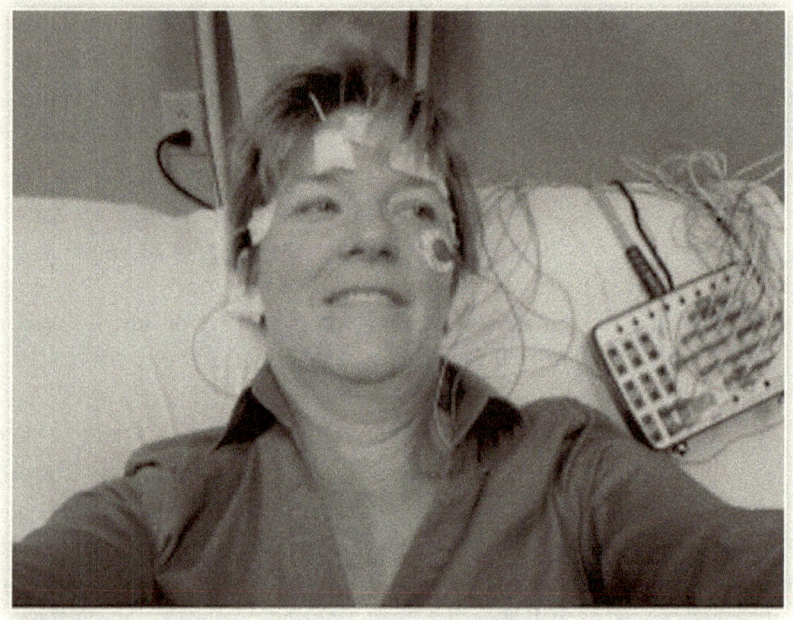

FREDDY FAT CHIN

(I remember being at a dermatologist/Botox-type doctor who said he could get rid of that lump of fat under my chin. I said, "What lump of fat?" So he kindly pointed it out to me. Now I'm pointing it out to you all. I obviously kept it—the lump of fat, that is.)

So the session started, with the technician leaving the room and turning the lights out. I closed my eyes and lounged in a recliner, just letting those nubbins do their work. Then the technician announced through a speaker that the strobe light would start, and that I should keep my eyes closed. After that finished, he asked me to take rapid, deep breaths for what seemed forever. Again, I was in trouble deep. Maybe somebody should check out my lung capacity problems instead of my brain stuff.

Then he instructed me to relax for the next ten minutes while the nubbins again recorded their data. While "relaxing," I realized that I had booked an annual Christmas gift exchange dinner with friends at their house on the same night Sciencegirl was coming home. I immediately became anxious that I would have to move the dinner to my house instead so that we could welcome Andrea home. In addition, now I would have to cook! YIKES! What would I cook? Now I would have to go to the grocery store to buy everything, figure out a menu, plan. How would I fit that in before Wednesday night? All these things raced through my head until I heard through the speaker, "Sarah, could you unclench your teeth, please?"

It's no wonder I have migraines. This was my "relaxed" state. I'm quite sure I go through the whole bloody day, every day, with my teeth clenched. All I need is a whopper-sized Valium every day. It's so simple, isn't it?

Christmas Decorating

What do you say when your ever-so-kind husband offers to decorate that eyesore of a bare tree that's been standing naked in your living room for a week? You say, "Oh my gosh, I'd love it! Thank you so much." And relief and newfound respect wash over you. But when you come back downstairs, you see it and say, "Are you done?"

He says, "Yes."

You say, "But where are all the ornaments?" (You see only about twelve or so on the tree.)

He says, "You had too many, this is enough."

So you say, "OK, thanks a lot." And you leave it.

If men are from Mars and women are from Venus, why are my guys from Pluto?

Holiday Cooking

Family togetherness. Yay. It started on the twenty-third of December with my pork roast dinner, which began auspiciously. I bought a new roast pan, just because I wanted to. I took a picture from my Betty Crocker® cookbook of

MiraLAX® Dissolves in Vodka, Ya Know

the type of pork roast I wanted, showed it to my large grocery-store meat guy (Wegmans® is a great large grocery-store chain), and asked him for "one of these" (not knowing the proper name for the cut of pork—it's a center-cut pork loin with the bone in). He told me they only had the prepackaged ones, and I'd need four separate ones to feed the amount of people I needed to. Humph. I said, "Please, oh please, don't make me go to Federal®, your competitor. Can't you cut me something fresh and pretty for my new roast pan?" Voilà, magic word: Federal®. He amazingly found some in the back, and I left Wegmans® happy. Well, as happy as I get.

I started preparing the nine-and-a-half-pound roast. I oiled and spiced it in my beautiful new roast pan. Then I walked over to my preheated oven with it and found that my shiny new pan with pork didn't fit in my oven. I tried to unscrew the handles, but they were soldered on. I reverted to my old, ugly roasting pan.

My roast tasted divine, if I must say so myself. I even used my antique salt dishes with the little spoons when I set the table, which provided an hour of fun for the youngest of my guests, after Marty spilled his and Will made piles of and wrote things in Marty's spilled salt.

Just remember how much I hate cooking. Here's the reason I don't cook—I make a horrible, undeniable mess. I even use the floor as if it is a countertop.

{ Sarah Berardi }

Goofy Gifts

I like to give goofy gifts, and who better to give them to but my freaky family who enjoy those goofy gifts? This is proof. The first picture is on Christmas morning, when Chris and Sciencegirl are testing their blood to find out their blood types. Sciencegirl's been so obsessed (where does she get *that* from?) about finding out what blood type she is, I was ecstatic when I found this do-at-home kit. The problem presented itself early on with Butthead (Chris) and Scaredy-cat (Sciencegirl) taking their tests. Chris had to redo his, for some reason, so it was lucky I had an extra. It was also lucky that Andrea has good pipette skills, being a scientist and all.

Then it was time to get Sciencegirl's blood. She wouldn't prick her finger. I understand it's hard for some people; it's hard for *me*. She also can't—*cannot*—do tongue depressors. (She's scarred for life on that one.) So she sat there whining, "Mommy, I can't prick my finger. Mommy, I can't do it," for about five minutes, with me, Chris, and Marty trying everything we could come up with to convince her to just go for it. Chris had already done his finger prick, no problem. She just couldn't do it. So I grabbed the pricker thing, tackled her on the floor, and pricked her sanitized finger. Done. Her boyfriend sat there slack-jawed, watching.

This next picture is of Marty in his coonskin cap from the *Daniel Boone* days (he used to watch that show incessantly as a kid). I had gotten one for Chris's godson. While I was wrapping it, Marty saw it and commented that he had *always* wanted one of those caps, ever since he was little. So I went back to the store and got him one. It might have been his favorite gift. He kept singing the theme song from the *Daniel Boone* show all day, driving us crazy.

{ Sarah Berardi }

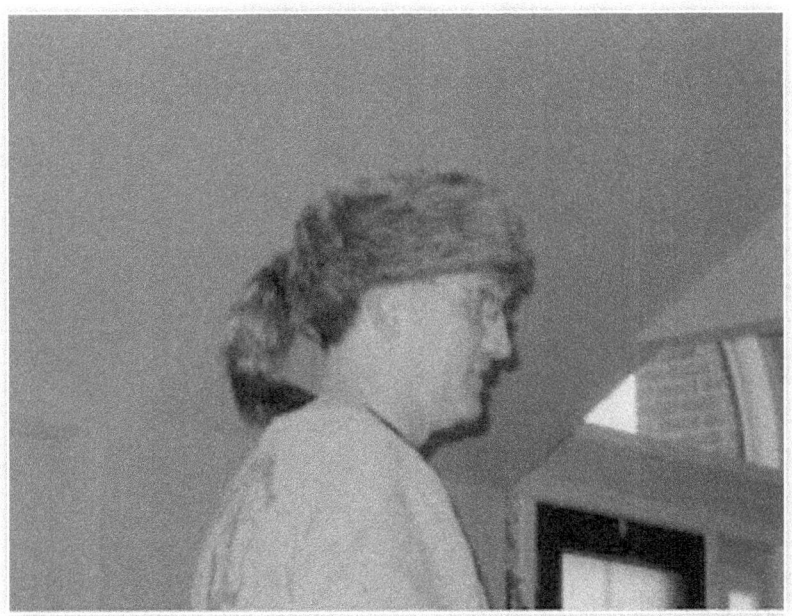

I Am Formidable?

Chris introduced himself a few days ago to the new headmaster at his former high school. The headmaster said to him, "Oh yes, I've heard of your mother. I understand she's quite formidable."

Upon hearing this, I decided that before I had my gut reaction, I'd better check out the proper dictionary definition of *formidable*.

Main Entry: for·mi·da·ble

Function: *adjective*

1: causing fear, dread, or apprehension; 2: having qualities that discourage approach or attack; 3: tending to inspire awe or wonder: impressive.

Back when I was in school, I remember learning that when using the dictionary, the most common definition was listed first, then the second, and beyond. So, as you see, the first two definitions that are most widely used and understood by the general public are *not* flattering, are they? Poop.

I quite like the third definition, but I have a wrenching feeling he wasn't aiming in that direction.

{ MiraLAX® Dissolves in Vodka, Ya Know }

I know I have a reputation that when I take on an assignment, I get it done. And I can usually do it 100 percent (although while trying desperately to dot all my i's and cross all my t's, I'm rarely perfectly successful). Does this make me formidable? Perhaps. Or was I being labeled as formidable as my nephews define me: "Don't mess with Aunt Sarah." He could have meant either. *C'est la vie* and *das ist leben*. (I can speak French and German today.) And here's the English: I am formidable, and I love it.

Back to School?

THIS IS A PICTURE OF MY FAVORITE WINE STOPPER THAT I USE ALL YEAR BECAUSE IT REMINDS ME OF ME.

Did I tell y'all I signed up to audit a course at the University at Buffalo? I'm pretty excited. I've never been to proper college. I *only* went to a two-year business school for my two-year degree in secretarial science.

I decided to just audit this class (as opposed to participating properly for a grade) at University at Buffalo for two reasons. First and foremost, I don't want to do any homework or study for tests. Second, I travel with my man, so I don't want to be freaking out about missing classes and having to get somebody's notes to copy. So I e-mailed the prof (college slang I'm getting into), and he said he'd love to have someone in class who just loves to learn. That's me! Barf.

I felt torn on which class to take. I've always wanted to take a class in literature so I could learn more about what I read, particularly the classics. I've also always been interested in world religions. But Sciencegirl suggested (perhaps because of the dysfunctional family I grew up in) that I might take a class in psychology. So I ended up signing up for Psych 101. I'm a little afraid the prof might make me his subject matter.

Funnily enough, when I had to purchase magazines from my niece a few months ago (which I had forgotten about), I apparently ordered *Psychology Today*. See how weird my brain is? And I just received the first issue today—how serendipitous! I'm a little afraid to read it. Here are the topics listed in this month's issue: 1) "Getting Even—Stories of Sweet Revenge"; 2) "Who Cheats and Why"; and 3) "What I Learned from a Terrible Mom." This magazine might be feeding my insanity, no?

(I'm currently getting even because I grew up with two alcoholic parents and have some family members who are naughty. I might be taking revenge on them for their general betrayal. Naughty people. Naughty.)

JAN 2010

I Have a Lisp?

We had the bright idea of trying to build credit for Chris by putting our family cell phone service in his name. This meant that the bills came to my house (he doesn't live here) for me to pay, but it was under his name. It also meant that when anyone in our family called anyone from one of our cell phones, it showed up on their caller ID as "Christopher Berardi." My friends would wonder, *Why is Chris calling me instead of his mother?*

After a few years of this, it got to be a pain for various reasons, and we decided to just shift it back into my name. Since we thought it would save time to do this over the phone while driving (therefore speaker-phone quality), we did it that way. Both of us had to be there to say, "Yes, I agree to pass over the liability of payment to Sarah...blah, blah, blah," and, "Yes, I accept...blah, blah, blah." It took over an hour. Very frustrating, to say the least. It would have been so much quicker to just run into the store, wait our turn, and have someone switch it over on the computer right in front of us.

After the long hour, which felt like two, I received my first phone call from Andrea, using the phone on our family plan. Voilà! Instead of saying "Christopher Berardi," it said... "Farah Berardi"? NOOOOOOO!

I'm so sensitive about the way I say my *s*'s. I've gotten so much mail from people addressed to Farrah Berardi over the years, and it makes me spittin' mad. When I was in fourth grade, the teacher decided I needed speech therapy for my "lisp." The speech therapist pulled me out of class and made me say, "Sarah has six silly sisters." But I said, "Tharah hathz thix thilly thithterth." *I had a million teeth missing.* I did *not* have a lisp! (Not that there's anything wrong with it.)

Another thing I'm sensitive about is the *h* at the end of my name. When I was a new kid in a new school in second grade, the teacher called me up in front of the class several days in and said—out loud, in front of everyone—"Sara(h), you're not spelling your own name correctly. You're putting an *h* at the end of your name, and you don't have an *h* at the end of your name." I told her that I did. She said that, according to her records, I did not, and I'd have to bring a note from my parents. Which I did. But she had so humiliated me. Did she read my mom's note out loud to everyone to prove I was right? No. (Am I a grudge holder? Yup, formidable.)

So, now our phones all say "Farah Berardi." At least there's an *h* at the end. And I should tell the buttheads that Farrah has two *r*'s.

Filter? Screw That.

As I sat in the neuropsychiatrist's office again—but this time talking with the nurse practitioner instead of the Cuban bastard—I was telling her how intolerant I was of people and how I just couldn't get my bum out of bed in the morning. I told her how my nephew said I reminded him of Sandra Bullock's character in *The Blind Side*. (Is this a bad thing?)

This is what she said:

"First of all, your B_{12} is on the low side. We really like to see it much higher than it is. Let's start you on over-the-counter supplements at a thousand micrograms per day. This could be contributing to your inability to get out of bed in the morning, your wanting to take so many naps, and your wanting somebody or something to 'crank you up.'

"Secondly," she continued, "your EEG came out normal. Thirdly, do you think you might…sometimes…lack a…filter when you say things?"

Wow, she hit the nail on the head. But I stammered, "Well…if you…well, I mean…not like…um…yes, actually. That must be why my family cringes when I say things in public that they deem I shouldn't say."

But I should have said, "*You* should have a filter," shown her my udders, and left.

Unfortunately, she said there is no pill to create a filter. Perhaps my college psychology class that starts next week will touch on Filtering 101.

I think of "filtering" differently than the nurse practitioner does. I think of it as being practical, cutting to the chase, not mincing words, saving time, putting on your big-girl panties, and dealing with it. It's not like I say to the hostess at a dinner party, "These potatoes suck, man." I wouldn't go up to a lady at the mall and say, "That hat doesn't suit you well" (like a German lady did to me in Germany). I would, however, say to my sister-in-law, Goose, "You need to cover up that zit before we go out," or I might say to Chris, "Your hair is too long, can you get it cut this weekend?" I find this latter advice endearing and practical, and I do it out of love. I certainly wouldn't want Goose to go out without covering up her zit. And I certainly wouldn't want Chris to go out with shaggy-looking hair. See? See? I don't need a filter. FILTER THIS: @#$%^&.

On the way home I couldn't help but think this girl was all of perhaps twenty-seven years old. She lives life looking through rose-colored glasses. She has a built-in filter at this age. Just wait. When she turns fifty, has two kids in grad school, has been married for twenty-seven years, and has perhaps grown up in a dysfunctional extended family, her rose-colored glasses will have turned to black-colored glasses, and she will lack a freakin' filter. That filter naturally disintegrates all on its own. Mark my words.

Ever hear of those song lyrics, "Pushing an elephant up the stairs"?
Pertinent comment to this post:
"Your filter may be disintegrating more rapidly than others. That 'whatever you want' thing usually kicks in around sixty-five or seventy. You may have EARLY ONSET FILTER DISINTEGRATION."

College at Forty-Nine

I don't know where to begin. I'll start with: I took my nighttime medications at 3:00 p.m. today, which means I needed to chill and relax a good five hours earlier than normal. Today I went to University at Buffalo (UB) to get all the paraphernalia needed to audit my class. This meant I needed to:

1. Find a parking spot somewhat near my destination. It's a huge campus, especially for someone as anxiety-ridden as I am. Where the hell was I going?
2. Put quarters in the parking meter. I had no quarters.
3. Find the required buildings to:
    A. Get my ID card. After walking through five buildings and finding the proper office, I found I was the only one there (school was not yet in session). A kindly woman helped me as I confessed I'd never been to college, it was a bit overwhelming to me, and I needed a cup of coffee (decaf for migraines, of course). She told me where all the coffee places where. I told her that, being almost fifty, I would probably be the only one on campus who would add a fiber supplement to her coffee. She laughed and said, "Well, if you go to Starbucks®, it's pretty strong. You probably don't even need that supplement!"
    B. Get my audit form. Totally different building. I walked, walked, walked, and walked. Why do students need to work out? I might cancel my membership to the Y.

THE CLICKER

C. Get my books. What the hell? I paid over two hundred dollars for this? And what the heck is a "clicker to answer with in class"? What happened to raising your hand? How the heck does it work?

D. Get my IT info "swiped." I don't have anything worth swiping, but I figured UB must think I have something. The poor nineteen-year-old boy who didn't have anything else to do had no chance with me. I saw him looking bored, sitting at his help desk. I needed help. He did his duty by giving me my IT info. I asked him to watch me sign in, go to my page, etc. He helped me navigate this (to me) unknown region. He laughed a little while trying to be respectful. The poor guy.

E. Get my parking sticker. I gave up. Too overwhelmed, overloaded. I had actually walked back and forth three times, passed the same classrooms six times.

That evening, my little Sciencegirl remotely took over my computer so she could see on her screen what I was doing (how did she do that?), and so patiently helped me. I can see why she gets good reviews as a TA at her university. She is a good prof. She's incredibly patient, and she could see my frustrations on the screen and how things just didn't work smoothly.

I still don't understand why I can't have a bloody textbook. That's the best part of going to school! So as I sit here typing, I'm printing three hundred or so pages. I need them. I can't read online. I'm old. Not new. And I paid $847 for the privilege of this course, plus over $200 for this weird clicker and the rights to view this e-book. I don't get it.

But here's the best part…guess who's on the first page of my e-book: *Tiger Woods*! And remember, this is Psych 101. (I'm making a reference to his recent headlines.)

Prepping for First Class

Things I've done while reading my first chapter in Psych 101 (which I haven't finished yet):

- Called my sister-in-law, Goose
- Texted Sciencegirl three times
- Went to the bathroom
- Ate an apple
- Whitened my teeth with those strips for thirty minutes
- Looked up a psych term (glial networks) on dictionary.com, and then decided to watch two YouTube videos about it
- Called my sister-in-law again
- Texted Chris
- Read an article in *Time* magazine
- Took a nap
- Made dinner
- Wrote a blog
- Read some other blogs

I hope I get to the ADHD/ADD chapter pretty soon. Update tomorrow on how my first proper college class went.

❦ Sarah Berardi ❧

First Day of College for a Fifty-Year-Old

I never went to "real" college before. I have my two-year associate's degree. There are two reasons I didn't go to a four-year college. The main reason is because I was too scared. *Scared to death.* They used to called it "shy," but nowadays, in the *DSM-V* (Google it; I've blogged about it long ago), they call it "social phobia." I would have *real* panic attacks. In other words, I'd crumble and worry so badly that it paralyzed me with vomiting and the runs just thinking about college: 1) How would I find my way around campus? I'll never be able to. 2) How would I ever find someone who would like me? What if my roommate didn't even like me? 3) Who would I hang out with? 4) How would I do in classes? I'm not smart. 5) Whom will I sit with in the cafeteria?

So off I went to the Bryant and Stratton Business Institute where we had lockers, just like high school, and the bells rang, just like high school. I graduated second in the class (I'm not bragging, it was a small class), so I clearly had made a good choice, and I could support myself right out of school.

After *years* of having this "social phobia" and panic attacks for any gathering (large or small)—PTA meetings, my husband's office functions, small coffee get-togethers, exercise classes at the Y, the kids' plays at school, etc.—I started about eight years of silly old therapy (on and off) and various anxiety pills. Those of you who know me would be startled, to say the least, to know that I was "shy." See how hard I've worked? And people now call me formidable?

I pulled into the university parking lot. Not a spot to be found. (Chris had warned me of this, as well as warning me to turn my cell phone on silent. Do you love him? You can't have him, he's mine. I deserve him. Plus, both kids were on standby for my needs.) I parked alone in a snowbank. The way I saw it, the plows should have plowed farther, as there was a whole row of parking spots sitting under that bloody snow. Goofballs. So I parked my huge "mom" station wagon half up on a snowbank. Tickets be damned. When I came out, seven cars had joined mine. But they were much smaller cars. Hybrids probably. Liberal college kids. (Not that there's anything wrong with that.)

I went to sit in front of my classroom early. I felt as if everyone was staring at me. If they were, they were probably wondering why this old lady was sitting there among them. But I was trying to be "hip," reading on my laptop, then on my Kindle.

❧ MiraLAX® Dissolves in Vodka, Ya Know ❦

The doors to the classroom opened. Music came blaring out. The music was *naughty* music, I tell you. I texted Sciencegirl some of the lyrics. She just laughed about it. I had also previously texted her that I might have some serious stomach issues before class due to my anxiety, and I might need to take half an anxiety pill. She kindly said, "You can do it, Mom." Do you love her? You can't have her, she's mine. I deserve her.

So I entered the huge room, prepared for three to four hundred kids in there. I decided to make my way to the back, which happened to be *up*. Up, up, up, up, pant, breathe, pant, breathe, pant, breathe. *Sit*. I got my notebook out where I'd printed the first two chapters of my e-book. Nobody else had done this. *Nobody*. Chris had warned me of this (my need to print the e-book). Then some kid walked behind me and whacked me in the back of the head with his huge backpack, unknowingly, I guess. What did formidable Sarah do? Shrank in her seat, thinking everyone was looking at her, when in reality nobody gave a shit. Ah, where were those drugs? Buck up, girl. I looked like one of those people on *America's Funniest Home Videos* where a kid gets whacked in the head with a football when he's not looking. But I wondered if the kids were looking at me, thinking, *Ha, that Goody Two-shoes old bat who has her notes all printed out got her head bashed*.

Then the professor introduced himself, and declared straight on that he cusses. Well, I have a mouth like a truck driver, I can handle that. He claimed he will say ass, damn, shit, and effity-eff-eff now and then.

When the real lecture started, I was seemingly the only one taking notes. Loser. I was also one of the few getting all the answers right during the first ten questions (via show of hands; not everyone had their clickers yet—slackers). I had based my answers strictly on my life experience, which the younger kids did not have.

Time to leave. I went up to introduce myself, shake his hand, tell him I need his signature to allow me to audit. (I don't want to study, take tests, do homework, and I'm already missing seven classes due to travel.) He immediately looked like a dog with his tail between his legs. Was it the music he was playing? Did I look like his mother? Was it his cussing? To make him feel at ease, I told him I didn't much care for Freud either (he had mentioned it earlier). And I don't.

{ Sarah Berardi }

End of day. Need a martini, and need to start reading chapter two.
Cheers, Sarah, Psych 101 PhD
P.S. My shingle will be hanging out in front of my house by the end of next week for consults.

The Head

Crap, so much for happiness. But I loved having seven whole days of it. My migraine came back on Thursday night. Oddly enough, Chris, who has them infrequently, had a doozy. And a friend of mine also had his very first migraine; it sent him to the ER. All of us on the same night. Barometric pressure must have been horrific.

It's amazing how this stupid migraine stuff can make my mood horrible. Marty (and I) enjoyed seven days of me cooking dinner every night, washing laundry, putting laundry away, picking up after myself. I didn't lose my keys for seven days in a row. I caught up on my paperwork at my desk. I paid my bills, stacked my stackables, and threw away my throw-outables.

Now I am back in bed. Maybe tomorrow will be a better day. You who know me know I'm a "glass half empty" girl until proven otherwise.

Dr. Urologist, Pleeease!

I'm sitting at Starbucks® on Saint Simons Island, Georgia. We have a little place down here, and now and then I like to come to make sure it's still functioning properly, not leaking anywhere, etc. I also like to sit on the beach, no matter how cold it is, and read. I have a winter coat down here, which enables me to even take a brisk walk on the beach. I love it. This is the place I don't have to be anybody. No makeup (YIKES). No special hair—usually a baseball cap I wouldn't be caught dead in at home unless I'm at the Y (we all know how often I'm at the Y).

So I woke up yesterday morning to come down, took my time getting ready (no packing, I have everything down here). No problem on my first flight. I looked for the terminal for my next flight and started the *long* walk to the tram. I turned on the new pedometer application on my iPhone (so cool). However, darn that urologist who says I don't have a weak enough bladder to do the corrective surgery. I peed my pants a teeny-tiny bit every fifth step! This is not normal.

You know, I think I need a female urologist. Do you think my current doctor pees his pants every fifth step or so if he's had a small decaf on the flight before he has to walk to the bloody tram? Does he dribble? Bet he doesn't. Do you think his wife dribbles?

My iPhone Pedometer

Crapity-crap. I thought I was doing really well for my brain functionality with my new iPhone. So far I had used my map application to find a house our friends rented down here in Saint Simons Island. Then I took pictures of the house with it. I downloaded them to the computer. That's three things, if you're keeping count. (Aside from the normal texting, e-mailing, and calling I'm handling, so let's count those, too, to make me look good—six.)

Then, after taking a migraine pill (boy, I wish I could take one of those every day, but I'd be dead), I had a burst of energy. In actuality, it was just that my blasted headache disappeared. So I put on my sneakers, my friends—I know, relax, but it's true. I went down to the beach. I had turned on my new pedometer application (seven things, keep counting). Turned on my iPod function (eight). Started walking. Then I got a phone call. Holy crap, now what? I have two other apps running. Will it work? I answered the phone, but our conversation had to be cut short, as I was somehow pressing a button that kept beeping, beeping, beeping, and beeping in our ears, and I was afraid to touch anything for fear of cutting off my pedometer. I wasn't going to waste those steps without counting them! We had to laugh as I told my friend I couldn't handle my new phone. She understood, and we hung up.

So I continued on my incredibly fast-paced, be-boppin' and scattin' walk, swinging my bum as much as possible without falling over so that the pedometer would feel each step (I actually tip over a lot with the stupid migraines; Doc claims it's normal). I also sang out loud (I don't care), and occasionally played the air drums (again, I don't care). I was on an endorphin high, baby. I felt so exercised, that I was seeing stars by the time I got to my front porch again. Sweating. I took my iPhone off the holster, checked the pedometer. It read zero steps. Help me. It was the best part of my day, awaiting the results of how many miles (quarter of miles?) I went and how many calories I burned. You see, it just doesn't count if it doesn't record.

Fuggetaboudit. Going to bed after my coconut rum.

I Want Jury Duty

Hey, how come Obama, Bush, and Clinton all got called for jury duty and I haven't? I'd love to get called for it. Don't you think I'd be great, being so formidable and all? I'm rule-abiding, honest, I say it like it is...I'd be the *perfect* juror.

I actually was summoned once, while living in Germany. I sent my response back, stating that I was living abroad, blah, blah, blah, with my expected year of arrival back in the States. Same thing happened to Marty. But he's been called twice, I think, since we moved back years ago. I haven't been asked since.

Seems so many of my friends have gotten the summons. Do you think they've heard about me?

I'm Losing It, Baby

Dang it all, I've lost something, again. I don't know how many times I've done this. Nor does Marty. I've even succumbed to the embarrassment of asking him to help me look for that something that I've put somewhere—in a special place, so as not to forget where I've put it. (He's so good to me, he usually finds it.) This time I've misplaced the charger to my computer.

I was out to dinner the other night with a couple of friends and one admonished herself for not bringing the papers her friend had requested. She said, "I printed them out just for tonight, for you, but I couldn't find them when I was leaving. I looked all over for them, but I was going to be late, so I just gave up. It makes me so mad when I do that."

I said, "Check the fridge when you get home."

"But I never went to the fridge," she said.

"It doesn't matter," I said. "I never go to the fridge either, but somehow that's where my stuff always ends up." We chuckled.

I told them how I once had a missing soft-shelled taco. Long story short, I accused Marty of eating my taco. He vehemently claimed he did not eat it. I looked in the pantry (please don't let it be in there, it required refrigeration). Wasn't there. About four days later, Sciencegirl called from college to say thank you for the care package she had received from me. "But why did you put this taco in here? Remember, I can't eat gluten?"

"Eeeeeewwwwww," I yelped, "that required refrigeration about six days ago, and I do, of course, know you can't eat gluten! I wondered where that thing went." I confessed to her that I had accused her father of eating it and not fessing up to it.

Poor Marty.

My Dearest Auntie

My Auntie Mim inspires me so. Remember this as I tell this short story.

The old lady is getting up there in age (she's about 165 now, I think), so I like to send her a nice, glossy, hard copy of my blog for her to read at her leisure the good old-fashioned way. She loves to write, read, and to write poetry as well. She's my biggest fan.

We laugh a lot when we talk on the phone. I told her that I was taking a course at our local university and I reminded her that she'd read about it in the blog book I sent her. She asked me why I had picked psychology. I said, "So I could figure out how my whole family went to hell!" speaking of my family I grew up in, of course. We got a good guffaw at that one.

Then, as I warned her that I had not proofread any of my blogs before sending them to her, she said, "I figured. You've always done things half-assed."

I was shocked, and peed my pants laughing. I said, "Crikey, Auntie, you're going straight to hell." She didn't miss a beat and said, "See you there."

Dumber and Dumber?

I've often asked the kids, "Have I always been this stupid?" One of them always says, "Yes, Mom, you have." I always argue back, "No, I haven't, you can go to…"

So I'm watching my e-book for my psych class (Get that? Watching my e-book—what a hoot), and there's this particular video that says (I'm paraphrasing):

As estrogen levels decrease, dendrites either don't form at all or don't form well, which prohibits chemical absorption from the synapse.

AHA! See? All my chemicals are just floating around up there with no place to go. I have bad dendrites! I was right all along; I am dumber now than I used to be. What a relief!

Moral of the story is that estrogen keeps us on our toes and mentally sharp. That darned hormone. I'm blaming estrogen and sticking with it, as many women have for years. Game on.

FEB 2010

I Smell Nice

Doesn't every girl want her husband or boyfriend to say that she *looks* nice/pretty/beautiful? Doesn't every girl want him to also say she *smells* nice after she's just doused herself (I spritz) with perfume? I know I, for one, do. I live for it. So now that I think of it, I shouldn't be alive. My husband (do not feel sorry for him) just doesn't seem to notice.

Yes, it's true, most women dress for women, but first and foremost I dress for my husband. It just "stinks" he doesn't notice. (Ha! I crack myself up.) Or, maybe he does, and he doesn't think I look nice and is being polite by not saying so? My girlfriends, one of my "lunch friends," and my son's *creepy* neighbor always tell me I look nice. Why can't my husband?

So one night I come downstairs to where Marty's patiently waiting for me for a dinner date with another couple. I think to myself, *He's absolutely going to have to say something because I know he likes this type of dress*. Nothing. So I say, "Could you at least say I look nice, smell nice?"

"You look nice, and you smell nice," he says.

"It doesn't *count*, because I asked you to say it," I whine.

So we meet up with our friends at the bar, and the first thing I hear out of the male half of the couple is, "You look beautiful." He kisses me hello, then adds,

¶ MiraLAX® Dissolves in Vodka, Ya Know ¶

"Ohhhh, and you smell great, too." I look over at my husband, stick my tongue out at him, and say, "I told you so."

Accountability

If someone "wrongs" me (intentionally hurts my feelings, lies about me, or misrepresents me—my definition has too many examples to list), should I hold them accountable? Or should I roll over, let them use me as a doormat, accept it, and let them do it again?

I did that for the first thirty years of my life. I don't do it anymore. I just may be a little abrasive in holding accountable those who wrong me. There's nothing wrong with that, because what goes around comes around. Just so you know who's writing this book.

NYC

Just back from the big city, New York. Our hotel gave us a free upgrade to a suite, I think because I am so good-looking. Our main goal on this trip (I went with Libbylicious again) was to try to get on *Letterman* as we've tried for the last four years. Well, since he's recently made headline news, he's on vacation this week. So no *Letterman* for us. But no worries, we had a blast anyway.

We saw two shows. *Billy Elliott* made me cry *a lot*. I was very hormonal, OK? It was such a beautifully historical, emotional story…and very funny. Makes me want to read the history of Margaret Thatcher breaking the unions back then. What an unimaginable upheaval. Disclaimer: This is not a political statement, it's a historical statement.

We also saw *Steady Rain* with Daniel Craig and Hugh Jackman. I'm pretty sure I saw both men wink at me. Libbylicious must have missed it, since she doesn't believe me. It's just an intense, two-man show. Really, really great.

We went ice skating in Rockefeller Plaza, which means I cackled (it's how I laugh, please help us all) all the way around! People who were watching clapped for me just for standing up. Libbylicious had to hold my hand. She was showing off turning backward.

OK, saving the best until last: we ran into some guy, Bret Wilson Michaels from Poison. (I don't listen to what I consider Naughty Music, but Libbylicious knew him because she obviously does.) With him (and the person I noticed first), was the *Take Home Chef* guy. I didn't know his name, but I pointed at him and screamed, "I know you, I know you, I just saw you on TV an hour ago this morning. Can I have a pic of you for my blog?"

He said he couldn't, as they were doing a special charity event at noon, but we were welcome to come for a pic with him there. TV cameras rolled the whole time as I gushed over him, saying how gorgeous he looked in person! (I'm almost fifty, and I was embarrassingly starstruck—hey, I'm from Elma.) We said good-bye, and I blew him kisses. Then a guy came up and asked us to sign waivers to be used on TV. We signed, losers that we are. Libbylicious behaved very civilly. I was the only one who made a jackass out of myself.

Come to find out, they were filming for *Celebrity Apprentice*, as Sinbad, Darryl Strawberry, that Blogdonovich (?) guy, and some other guys were there, too.

I SAID I NEEDED A HAT, AND MENTIONED I WAS FROM BUFFALO. THIS IS WHAT SHE RECOMMENDED.

THIS IS ME ON CANAL STREET—I DON'T BUY THE KNOCKOFFS, JUST THE REAL STUFF

﹃ MiraLAX® Dissolves in Vodka, Ya Know ﹄

HORRIFIC SENSIBLE SHOES

CHEERS—SARAHLICIOUS AND LIBBYLICIOUS

{ Sarah Berardi }

LIBBYLICIOUS, SHOWING OFF

THIS WAS A STRUGGLE FOR ME

{ MiraLAX® Dissolves in Vodka, Ya Know }

I MAKE FRIENDS WITH EVERYONE

Sarah Berardi

OY VEY

My Bed Is Nice

OK, I fess up. I've been in bed for quite a few days. Crabby doesn't describe the mood, but there's a cartoon from the *New Yorker* where a Santa says, "I don't care who's naughty or nice anymore—I only keep track of who's crossed me." That cartoon pretty much sums me up. I keep thinking that tomorrow I will get back to blogging and feel funny. But I don't yet.

I've noticed in talking with my gal pals that certain sayings keep being said: "*Karma*, Sarah, *karma*," or, "Let them walk a mile in your shoes, then they can criticize," or, "He'll come around," etc. But what the heck do I do while I'm waiting for the karma and all the rest? I'm waitin' on the karma, man. Life is so much easier in the basement bedroom!

Costa Rica

I made the flight. Poor Marty, sitting next to me with all my flying quirks. He's used to them, though, and tries to cut them off at the pass by warning me ahead of time that it will be bumpy because we're landing in a valley, or because it's a windy takeoff, or whatever.

Our original flight was cancelled due to the weather, so we had to reroute, and darn it all, the only seats left were in business class. I think we'll have to cash in stock to pay for my ticket. Crikey. So what? I love that first class/business class stuff. All those quirks (I rock back and forth while plugging my ears and humming) are easier to deal with when I have more room. I told Marty if he didn't fly me back business class, I wasn't coming back. He said, "Fine, stay in Costa Rica."

For the last few months, I've been calling this Costa Rica trip the Puerto Rico trip. Marty would get mad and say, "*Oh my gosh*, Sarah, it's *Costa Rica*, for the last time." I'd say, "Same thing, whatever." And I have to say, it sure looks the same, weather-wise. Geography's not my forte, 'K? Not that I have a forte.

As I sat down at the pool to read after arrival, I realized that I fit in nicely with my white legs (they lack pigment, remember) and my Betty Big Belly. The best part was seeing a very pasty-white man in a Speedo. Frightening as it was, I couldn't take my sunglass-concealed eyes off him. I envied his total lack of embarrassment at his appearance. Or his ignorance, perhaps? Did I envy his ignorance? Or his bravado? Self-assurance? While I'm trying desperately to cover up my bits and blobs, everyone here lets their blobs hang out, seemingly without care. Can't do it. I have a pic of him, but I'm afraid I'd get sued. His fruit salad was hanging out.

Buenas Noches

Friday night: OK, I was the Dancing Queen tonight. Or so I thought, until they started playing the native music. The Costa Ricans "feel" the music. I was so jealous at how beautifully one girl danced, I asked her to teach me how to dance like she danced. She said in her broken English that she just danced. "You have to feel the music." She was sensual, without being naughty. She was simply beautiful.

Let me tell you, that Costa Rican band started playing Michael Jackson and all the Americans…well, we got up on that dance floor and cut the rug. We were gettin' down. Trippin' the light fantastic. We had such a blast! I, of course, was the Dancing Queen, but my Ralph Lauren shoes were killing me, despite the fact that they received a gazillion compliments. (They are stunning.)

Tonight I learned to salsa, tomorrow I learn to ride a zip-line.

Adios, Costa Rica Und Mia Nuevos Amigos

Poop. No zip-line today. I'm so disappointed. One of the two other girls I planned to go with got a flu bug last night, so they cancelled. I would have gone by myself, but I wasn't really given the choice. When will be my next opportunity to zip-line? Over Niagara Falls, just a mere forty minutes from my house, perhaps? I don't think so. Somehow I think falling to my death into the rain forest would be better than falling into the Falls.

Heading home tomorrow. Not looking forward to the flight or the weather back in Buffalo. Nor am I looking forward to the BS dysfunctionality (I made up that word) of life back at home. Much nicer staying somewhere where a nice girl (whom I tipped heavily) comes in, straightens my room, and makes my bed every day.

Those Costa Rican Long Island iced teas are helpful, too.

Pertinent comments to this post:

- *Just catching up on your posts after a week away. What's up with this? You can't drive across the Grand Island Bridge, yet you're willing to zip-line in Costa Rica? Have you stopped to see the irony in this? Have you done any kind of risk analysis here?*
- *Well, we are looking forward to having you back, brightening up Buffalo. As for zip-lining, maybe we could hang a clothesline in my backyard and fly over the koi pond.*

Hmm, maybe I should have stayed in therapy a little longer with the Cuban bastard and asked about that risk analysis. That is weird, isn't it?

Not a Good Packer

Marty just informed me that I've been brushing my teeth here in Costa Rica with his toothbrush. Eeeewww!

I also forgot my face lotion, so I've been using the little freebie bottle of "orange zest" stuff they have here on the counter in the bathroom with the free shampoo and conditioner. But now my face smells like sushi.

The "sunscreen" I packed might not be sunscreen. It was white stuff in one of those clear travel jars, unmarked. I thought I had put sunscreen in it on my last trip. Well, my face and neck (where I applied it), have been exfoliating for the last twenty-four hours. So maybe it's not sunscreen.

And the little bottles for the shampoo and conditioner provided by the hotel look the same, so I have to ask Marty to come in and read which bottle is which, since I don't shower with my glasses on. Do you? I have to remind him to put the shampoo in one corner and the conditioner in the other. Not that I'll remember which corner is which.

And what's up with some bellboy dude knocking lightly on my door, not hearing me say, "Yes?" and opening my room door with his key while I am lying in bed reading in the middle of the day? He just bloody well walked in! I said, "Can I help you?"

"Oh, sorry."

Oy vey.

Class Today

I was *fly* today in class, especially for a fifty-year-old. First of all, the topic appealed to me. It focused on alcohol and drugs, and what they do to your brain. (Have I mentioned my upbringing? I was raised by a set of parents who liked to get their drink on.) Secondly, we had a teaching assistant (TA) do the lecture instead of the professor. He clicked with me. So far, I haven't given a fiddler's fart about most of the topics, you know, about the cones and rods in your eyeballs and why some people are color-blind—that's Psych 101.

When the TA started teaching, I thought he was cute. He's a third-year PhD student with his research in alcohol in college kids. He walked a little funny as he paced back and forth from the lectern—I couldn't figure out if he had a load in his pants or if he had a little "bounce in his step." Didn't really matter, as I had zeroed in on his topic.

I actually asked a question in class. (Chris told me *never* to do this in a 101 class of three hundred, but I did, as this TA was so inviting.) I asked, "Since cocaine prevents dopamine from being taken back up in your brain (which gives you the 'high'), why don't doctors give cocaine abusers trying to kick the habit NDSIs (norepinephrine dopamine reuptake inhibitors)?"

The TA said that I had a great analogy, a great question, and that he didn't know the answer since his research was in alcohol versus cocaine, drugs, etc. An example of an NDRI is Wellbutrin, which many of us take because it prevents the reuptake of both norepinephrine and dopamine (whereas an SSRI is just a serotonin reuptake inhibitor). I was just so proud of myself that I *got it*. You all know that I'm usually dumb as a stump and can't even find my car in the parking lot. It's the shrinking dendrites and my antiseizure drugs, I tell you!

❦ MiraLAX® Dissolves in Vodka, Ya Know ❧

The NYC Debacle and Chris

Chris is living in New York City for his internship of his last semester of law school. This required him to find a place to live from February through mid-May. However, he explicitly asked me to "stay out of it." I left it to him. *Totally*.

So he had found his place through a nice property management woman who deals with short-term leases. After he moved in, I asked him to send me pictures of the place. Twice I asked him, but he was being passive-aggressive. After those two times, I gave up—I've had enough therapy to do this giving-up crap, thank you very much. But I knew something was up—I've had enough therapy to know this, too, thank you very much. But after two weeks of him living there and not saying much about anything, I finally "butted into his life" by asking about his apartment, *again*.

"Well," he said, "it's pretty sketchy, come to find out. There are sneakers hanging on the wires right in front of my apartment building, there are wrappers all over the sidewalk, and 'deals' going down all night." (For those of you who don't know, sneakers hanging from overhead wires are drug talk for "buy drugs here.")

STEPPING OUTSIDE CHRIS'S APT.: CAN YOU SEE THE INFAMOUS "BUY DRUGS HERE" SNEAKERS?

By nine o'clock the next morning, I was on the phone with Dalia, the property management woman whose name he wouldn't give me. I combed through all Marty's paperwork and found it. The first thing she said to me on the phone was, "Oh my God, is he *lost?*"

"No, no," I said. "He's fine, but—"

She blurted in her Israeli accent, "You want to move him, don't you? I told him a *million times, your mother no want you to live here*." But she never told him why. The "why" involved needing a hand cannon with him at all times.

Long story short, he's booked to move this weekend to a different neighborhood. He reported back to me that this is what Dalia said to him on their walk back to the office: "Your mother and I, we talk, mother to mother. I have three boys. You her baby. You dating anyone? Well, let me tell you, your mother would pay for this advice I tell you, just like she pay for your apartment since you still in school... you can have many wives, many wives, I tell you, but *only one mother*. Don't you ever forget that, you hear me?"

She is going to get a very large gift basket from Dean and Deluca from me. And you know what? Guess who I'm calling if he's ever in trouble down there? She's my new best friend. She said to me, "Oh, your boy, he so cute, I just looooove him, he sooooo nice."

Pisspot Girl

I went in Delta Sonic, a local car wash chain, to purchase a gift certificate for someone who was kind to me. Kindness needs to be rewarded nowadays.

So here's my conversation with the teenage clerk behind the counter:

Me: Hi, I'd like to purchase a gift card or whatever gift certificates you might have to offer.

Girl who couldn't care less: We have these three options, which can be purchased in books of two. (She points to paper under the counter and gives me a very fast, wordy spiel.)

I read it.

Me: I'm sorry, did you say I have to pick one of these three categories for a wash/detail as listed here, and then multiply by two, therefore giving two gift certificates to the person?

The girl repeated the same spiel, just as fast and just as quietly (she was a *low talker*, I tell you).

⁋ MiraLAX® Dissolves in Vodka, Ya Know ⁋

Me: Oh, OK, sorry. I needed that confirmation. I'm a little slow on the uptake.

Girl: ………………………… (Nothing—total blankness.)

Me: So you have nothing else along the lines of gift cards/certificates, such as a simple cash card?

Girl: Well (talking low and fast), we have a twenty-five-dollar gift card that can go toward three brushless, basic car washes, or two car washes plus an interior, or toward a detail, or toward an interior.

Me: Oh my gosh, how much was that gift card? (I'm only hearing the options I have to decide on at the end of the sentence—by the way, it has been proven that we quite often only hear the beginning and end of a sentence.)

Girl (eye roll, really disrespectful, fed up with me even though nobody is behind me in line): We have a twenty-five-dollar gift card that can go toward three brushless, basic car washes, or two car washes plus—

Me: I'm so sorry to bother you, I'm on an antiseizure drug (truth—for my migraines), which is notorious for making one daft. (Also true; it's in every side-effect list of the drug—tough on short-term memory, and can't remember certain words, which I've learned today in Psych 101 is actually part of long-term memory.)

Shitpot Girl: Oh, it's no problem, I don't mind, whatever I can do. (In other words, she felt uncomfortable, as I did earlier in my daftness.)

Remember what my nephews say? "Don't @#$% with Aunt Sarah."

And I said nothing but the truth. How about a little kindness and respect from a little snot? But what if I were an eighty-year-old man or woman with a cognition problem? Would she have been so snotty? I only hope that she learned the lesson I was trying to teach, that not everyone has the same capacity to absorb what one is saying at the same level, no matter what they look like. Poophead. If only that countertop were flippable.

Beerface

I haven't had a glass of beer in ages. I usually have to take my inhaler after I drink one. Must be the hops. But when I visited Sciencegirl, she had a birthday party to go to and invited me to go along. Ever the partier, I said I'd love to go! It was at a brew house-type place. All the beers on the menu had long descriptions about their brewing processes and their bouquets. I was overwhelmed (easy to do) with my choices. Thank goodness they had a "sampler" listed at the bottom of the menu, which gave me six little glasses of beer.

The last ones claimed to have a chocolate taste or to contain chocolate (?), so I was afraid to try them because chocolate is a migraine trigger for me, so I gave them away. I have to admit, 'em beers tasted better than Corona. And I had no need for the inhaler, but did have a need for a boiled bratwurst.

Giving Proper Change

When the kids were young and played in Little League, every parent was supposed to take a turn in the candy stand. Of course, the same parents always worked, as the other lowlife parents couldn't be bothered being responsible. *Arschloch loser parents*.

But when I had my turn, I always felt so nervous. You see, I'm horrible giving change out when I'm on the spot. I can't do the math that fast. Consequently, when the kids would see me in the stand, a long line would always form at my checkout versus the other parents' checkouts. I fancied myself the favorite "cool mom" among them. Finally I heard one kid say to another, "No, stay in *this* line. Mrs. Berardi always gives out too much change." Humph. And I did, not wanting to gyp the kids or have their parents come back and point it out to everyone.

Since my cash drawer was always sure to be short at the end of the shift, I'd get a ten-dollar bill out of my purse on the way out and throw it in the pot. It always cost Marty money for me to volunteer at the candy stand. Come to think of it, the same thing happened to me when I was the "cookie mom" for Girl Scouts.

Vision Test at the DMV

She said, "Read line seven out loud to me, please."

I said, "Which line is line seven?"

I thought I was in trouble deep at the Department of Motor Vehicles when I got the affirmation that my paperwork was, indeed, correctly filled out and I could proceed to the next step, which was the dreaded eye exam. It was worse than I thought it would be as I realized I couldn't even distinguish which line was line seven. Yikes. I hesitantly blurted out letters and numbers. On the last letter, my intonation had a definite lilt in it, as if there was a question mark at the end of it. She looked at me and said, "You passed, but *just*."

The thing is, all of a sudden my distance vision has gotten a lot worse. But if I had worn my current glasses to renew my driver's license, I would have had to wear them all the time in case I ever got stopped by my "friendly" policeman or policewoman. Bummer. I think it's time to try those progressives again.

P.S. I also put on my new license that I was three pounds heavier than I am so that I could feel skinny, all day, every day. I'm pathetic. Oh, and I'm an official organ donor, as I'm going to make some research scientist very happy when I'm dead.

MAR 2010

"You Gotta Shut Up Now"

OK, so today I finally did what you all have been shocked that I haven't done already.

During Psychology 101 at UB, the professor rarely tells people to "shut up," "be quiet," or (my mother's favorite) "pipe down." It aggravates the hell out of me. I can't stand it when the teacher's method of getting the class to be quiet is to stand there and just wait for everyone to be quiet. This is so lame. So...weak. I understand the professor might think that if the student fails because he's talking, it's his problem, but what about the student who's sitting next to him and can't hear? That's *not* fair, and it's the professor's responsibility, right?

The kids in the class, as a whole, talk *incessantly*. Last week in class, both the cute little freshman sitting next to me and I turned around and gave the guy behind us the stink eye at the same time since he so blatantly talked loudly during the whole lecture. We couldn't concentrate. She said she couldn't believe he was talking in his normal voice instead of whispering. I was so pleased that someone else in the class cared.

So today, after the professor did his usual "stand there and wait for quiet" (the chatter started up about ten seconds after he began talking, as usual), I couldn't help myself. That *same* kid sitting behind me was still talking, talking,

talking. This time I turned around and said, in *my* normal voice, "Excuse me, I paid eight hundred and sixty-seven dollars for this course, and I'm sure your parents did as well, so could you shut the hell up?"

He just looked at me and said, "What?" So I repeated myself. He repeated *himself*. I realized he was messing with me. So I very sternly said to him, "Don't $%&# with me."

It was quiet in the row behind me after that.

After class a woman who appeared to be a mom like me smiled at me. (*I made a friend at school!*) I had noticed her a few times before, sitting up front like me. I asked if she heard what I said. She laughed and said no, but she's not surprised. She said she had transferred over to UB from NCCC (a local community college) where it was just as loosey-goosey, where the kids had no respect for the professors, but the professors didn't ask for the respect, either. Hmm. We shared our belief that the chattier kids who were so naughty and snotty and disrespectful were probably the same kids who would get the As.

Interestingly enough, the professor himself even brought up in class today that he heard that another psych professor with 328 students had his teaching assistants walk up and down the aisle and throw out the kids who were talking. I thought that was a great idea.

I also liked my friend's idea that you should have to pay in cash for the course on your way in the first day.

P.S. I ran all the way to the parking lot afterward, afraid that kid and his posse would come after me.

Fifty Schmifty

So today I'm the big 5-0. It really doesn't matter to me. I have great kids, a *very* understanding husband (although one of my gal pals said his life would be really boring without me—she's right), and the best of friends (some of whom gave me a Tiffany charm for my bracelet, which is oh so gorgeous).

I spent the week so far getting my third or fourth colonoscopy. Then had my first mole removed for biopsy. In four weeks I get my leaky bladder fixed—YAY! I've had three hot flashes today already. I've bought myself a new outfit, but no new shoes. I spent so much time on the phone with Dell customer service during the last three days I now speak with a permanent Indian accent. Not that there's anything wrong with that, but I'm not of Indian descent, to my knowledge. (Those Dell technicians are *liars* anyway, I tell you, *liars*.)

I've spent most of the day going through four days of mail I've been putting aside, and cleaning up my desk. This was my favorite find in the pile:

Pay It Forward

I volunteered today at THWIV. As I stepped into the elevator, a girl already inside asked what floor I needed (I had a huge pushcart that took both hands to maneuver). She pushed my floor number button for me.

Girl: I love your jewelry, your earrings, necklace, belt. It makes you look... so happy? So approachable!

Me: Well, I'm not.

Girl: Then you'd better take off that necklace, girl!

We had a good laugh between us, happy with the fact that we were so funny.

Me: Actually, some of my girlfriends just gave me a charm for my bracelet that says "happy" so that I can be happy this year (instead of abrasive).

Girl: Then go for it and be happy!

Me: I'm trying, I'm trying, and so far, so good.

We shared a few other fun things and went our separate ways.

At the end of my day, I logged out. On my way to the parking lot (already dialing a number on my cell, checking my to-do list, etc.), I heard "Hi" somewhere beside me. I looked to my right and saw the sweetest older lady sitting in a wheelchair. Her face was clearly ravaged from cancer of some sort, and she had an eye patch over one eye. She seemed to have been medicated pretty well. A guy sat next to her looking discouraged and down, perhaps her son.

I stopped, since she had greeted me, stooped down closer to her, and said, "Hello." We had a short conversation. She was thrilled to be going home that day. I was thrilled for her. She put her hand out for me to take. I took it and I told her how warm it was, and that I had been chilly in the office all day, and how good her hand felt in mine. She said she was glad to warm me up.

So you see, I am happy when I want to be, and I am approachable. If you're not a poophead, I'm nice to you. I'm just not outwardly or overly nice to people who don't deserve niceness. Being civil is one thing, being nice is another. Is that wrong?

The Chapel

Today I visited with my friend's family while her mom had surgery at THWIV. I sat with them all before and after my hours. When I left them in the morning to go "work," "M" (one of the family members) asked where in the hospital I worked. I said, "Pastoral Care." Well, this cracked everyone up. You see, I'm not one whom you might find in Pastoral Care.

While I "worked," I asked one of the deacons to go say hello to them for me during his rounds. When my deacon friend introduced himself to the family, "M" said, "Where's Sarah now?"

The deacon said, "She's back at the office, at the chapel."

"M" quipped back, "You left her alone with the wine?" I'll kill him.

Wheelchair or Radio Flyer Wagon?

I'm finally having my stupid leaky bladder fixed in April! Yay! No more ads on the side of my blog for bladder incontinence. However, while they're doing some fixin', they're going to do some other work, sort of an overhaul. No, I'm not having a sex change (scandalous), but I will require four to six weeks off work. Pardon me, did I hear you say, "You don't work"? Surely you jest—and don't call me Shirley.

I'm supposed to sit around, avoid walking, stairs, lifting, vacuuming, etc. So how can I go see my nephew's lacrosse games?

I thought maybe I could have Goose push me in a wheelchair. Um, no. She will tip me over with the first shove onto the grassy surface. So then, what if I fit into my red wagon I still have from when the kids were little? She could pull me! I think she'd tip me over in that as well. Plus, my nephew might be embarrassed, but he's used to it. All his friends know me as "Crazy Aunt Sarah" anyway.

Piggyback?

APR 2010

Los Cabos

I get around, huh?

I'm sitting here at the infinity pool in Los Cabos. Most of the gang is golfing, which is not my forte. Not sure just what my forte is, or if I even have one for that matter. I've brought no books to read, only a huge pile of magazines that I need to catch up on.

The water's edge here on the beach has such a precipitous drop on the Pacific side, the undertow is dangerous. No swimming in the ocean! The drop itself looks scary. I don't mind, as I don't even swim in the ocean at our place in Georgia. Because of critters. Well, I sort of swim in the ocean. I lie flat on a surfboard-type floaty in ankle-deep water and push my way out. Then I paddle with my arms. I stay afloat the whole time. This way my feet never have to touch the ocean floor where the critters are. Can you imagine how ridiculous I look? One neighbor saw me on the beach one day, eyeing my surfboard floaty thing, and asked if I had little kids down visiting with me. I said, "No, it's for me."

Be My Witness

Today when I went into the office to volunteer (I know, I know, I don't work), I asked two of my office mates to witness my signature on my new will. (Surgery coming up, taking no chances.)

Bill: Wait a minute. It says here that I'm signing claiming that you are of "sound mind." I don't think I've ever seen you "of sound mind."

Me: This is as good as I get. Sign it.

Mary: What am I signing, now?

Me: You're just verifying that it was, indeed, me who signed each page and that you watched me do it.

Bill: I think we're signing to agree that she has the right to take any organ she wants from us.

Mary: Which organs are you taking from me?

Me: Your heart.

Bill: And from me?

Me: A kidney and a lung. Then I won't get kidney stones anymore, and I won't have to take my inhaler.

Mary: But why do you need a heart?

Me: Hello? I'm formidable?

Bill: As long as they don't take your sense of humor, we'll all be fine.

There will be profound silence every Monday in the office. They will miss me like crazy. They will be bored. They will chuckle, but they will not laugh. They will miss my colorful high heels. They will miss my *faux pas* while setting up the chapel for Father. Who will look up the soup of the day for Father? Who will transfer the calls without disconnecting them? Who will call IT every Monday to ask them to "unlock" her so she can try again with her login?

They will miss me for four to six weeks.

The Brand-New Pharmacist

What do you do with a fresh-out-of-pharmacy-school pharmacist who loves her job too much? Actually, I'm thrilled that she loves her job; I just need her not to be a loud talker when she's giving me new medications. (My editor told me I just wrote a split infinitive, sorry.)

Every time Marty or I get a new prescription, we have to flip a coin on who's going in the store to get it. Because when the scrip is a new one, it has a label on it that says, "Pharm Consult." This is actually a great idea, medically speaking. But this girl does not pull you around to the side to tell you about the drug and its side effects, she blurts them out while a line of ears, attached to people, stand behind the HIPAA rope.

Not only is this pharmacist a loud talker, but she's also a slow, deliberate talker.

Pharm: Now, are you familiar with this new medication?

Me: No.

Pharm: Well, it has numerous side effects. First of all, you should not drink alcohol with it. Nor should you drive while taking it until you see exactly how it decreases or enhances your reaction time. It will probably constipate you, so you may want to increase your fiber intake. It also has a side effect of drying out all your mucous membranes...

When she finishes with the first embarrassing part that I could have read myself online without my whole town hearing exactly what's going to happen to me after I take these pills, thank you very much, she gets to my second new prescription.

Pharm: Now, are you familiar with this second new medication?

Me: Yup.

P.S.: Thank goodness MiraLAX® dissolves in vodka.

Fall from Heaven

I fell out a second-story window.

I was about three years old, I'd say. It's one of my earliest memories. My older sister and I were leaning against my parents' bedroom window screen in the early morning hours. We were observing the goings-on, apparently. To tell you the truth, I don't know if I actually remember this or if it's been told to me so many times that I think I remember it.

My mother was pregnant with my brother at the time. She was lying in bed, as it was, like I said, early morning. As my sister and I were pressing our faces against the screen to see out, the screen gave way, and out I went.

Apparently, our sweet, elderly neighbors right next door saw me from their kitchen window (can you imagine?), hurtling from my parents' bedroom window to the garden sidewalk area on the ground. They came running at the same time my mother yelled to my father, "Bob, Sarah just fell out the window!"

I only recall being carried in my father's arms as he ran through the halls of the hospital. From the stories my parents tell, I had landed in the loamy soil where a few flowers were planted, about three inches from the cement sidewalk. "No damage done."

My current family begs to differ.

The Screechin' Freak

I have a scary propensity to scream—and I mean really scream—in my sleep. The screams come from night terrors, nightmares, call them what you like. I've had them for years, much to Marty's delight.

One of the first times I had one of these horrible dreams, I vividly remember screaming and shouting, "EAT SHIT," really, really loudly. About five minutes after that, my alarm went off for the morning school day. I got up, shook it off, and woke up my little Chris. (He was about eight years old.)

Chris: Mama, did you just scream, "Eat Shit," really loudly?

(I'm a loud talker, can you imagine my scream?)

Me: Oh, I'm so sorry you heard that. I guess I did.

Chris: I know who you were screaming at, Mama. Boy, were you ever mad!

Me: Yup, and apparently I still am.

I walked into little Andrea's room to wake her up. (She was about seven years old.)

Andrea: Mama, did you just scream, "Eat Shit," really loudly in your sleep?

Me: Yeah, sorry, lovey, didn't mean to have you hear that.

Andrea: You scared me. You were so loud.

Me: Scared me, too.

Needless to say, "eat shit" is not something I wanted to teach my kids at that age. I didn't even let them say *stupid* or *hate*. (Remember, I was a perfect mother.)

So let's move on to Marty. Can you imagine sleeping next to me? Jiminy Crickets! I can't believe I haven't given the poor guy a heart attack. Many, many, many nights, whether he's in town or not, I will suddenly jump up, having a fistfight with someone (it's usually the same person in my dream). But if Marty's there, he gets the brunt of it. Can you imagine it? Poor guy. He frantically swoops in to grab my wildly flailing wrists, settles me, tells me I'm dreaming. I apologize, and then go back to sleep. He does as well, although we're a bit shaken up.

Just last night I fought with my ghosts and swooped everything off my bedside table. I am now not allowed to have any open containers anywhere near me at bedtime. I found my phone under the bed, pills scattered all over the carpet, the clock on the floor, Tums across the room, etc.

So when I recently spent the night in the hospital, I thought it best to forewarn my poor roommate that I was a potential scary screamer in the middle of the night. I also warned the night nurse not to come running if she heard me screech, and told her that she had permission to ignore me.

She asked me if I've ever had that looked into. Yup, I have. She just looked at me, quite puzzled. (I offered no more information.)

Do you see what a freak I am? Do you see how bored Marty would be without me? Do you think I will end up on *20/20*? I could be a TV star for my freakiness. I could show all of my freakiness and fill a whole damn episode. I could be famous. Do you see why I took Psych 101?

Naughty Kids

I wasn't going to blog this, as it was just too…too…naughty for me. So instead, I sent it to a few of my friends via e-mail. But one comment on this e-mail back to me was so darned funny I just had to blog it.

I was listening to my police scanner on my iPhone. (I know, I'm a loser, just *let* me, 'K? It's blog fodder.)

"Bailey and Kensington Avenues. Indecent exposure. Two white teenagers, male and female, having sex in public. Male has pants open. He is wearing white pants."

And this was the comment to this post: *White pants? Before Memorial Day?*

Signs That Spring Has, Indeed, Arrived

1. My neighbor has been shirtless for the last week. The shirt won't be back until the snow flies.
2. Time for lawn cleanup—not at my house, but Goose's. (This was done BS—before surgery.)

❡   MiraLAX® Dissolves in Vodka, Ya Know   ❡

3. I notice an increase in stray doggie doo-doo on my lawn.
4. Ladybugs appear out of nowhere buzzing through my kitchen.
5. Allergies, allergies, allergies.
6. A new Miraclesuit® must be purchased.
7. My neighbor's lawn once again looks better and greener than mine.
8. I can hear the high school gym classes running track beyond Buffalo Creek behind my house (I love it).
9. My UB class is over. :((But no more parking tickets.)
10. The AC is humming in preparation for those 24/7 hot flashes.
11. Cocktail hour starts promptly with that five o'clock breeze.

Sensory Overload

Jiminy Cricket, I can't figure out my new car. There are *way* too many gadgets.

Sarah Berardi

Remember how we used to roll our eyes at our parents because we thought they were so daft since they couldn't figure out how to work the VCR? Or the remote control for the new TV? Cell phone? Well, now I'm the idiot who can't even figure how to get *into* my own car!

I stood there pressing any and all buttons on my new keyless remote. Instead of my car door unlocking, the hatch popped up. Then I couldn't close it manually. Come to find out there's a simple button on the hatch itself that closes it automatically. Then the next time I tried to get into my car, it was somebody else's car, so *none* of the doors would open. (Thankfully!)

One very kind soul pulled up next to me the other evening around nine o'clock, rolled down his window, and motioned for me to do the same. He said, "Be very careful, you have no lights in the back of your car."

"Oh my gosh," I said. I turned the light button on a different pictured position—you know, the one that indicates "lights on." I asked, "Are they on now?"

He checked for me, said they were, and I confessed that it was my first time driving my new car at night. In other words, I confessed that I was a moron.

My senses are overloaded and there is fluff coming out of my ears. I can't stuff anymore fluff in my head, you see. I have navigation, telephone, and radio/Sirius all controlled with the same joystick. I haven't figured out how to answer the phone yet. I did manage to turn on the rear windshield wiper, but then couldn't figure out how I did it, therefore couldn't turn it off (for weeks).

I WAS MUCH CLEVERER IN PSYCH CLASS.

Auto-Correct

I blogged once about how I had trouble texting on my phone due to what I called "fat thumbs." I thought it was funny that someone linked a page back to me about how Koreans use Slim Jims to text since these have the same texture as our fingers and are the perfect size But now I not only have a problem with my fat thumbs, I have a problem with the auto-correct. Here's a perfect example of how the iPhone auto-corrects, without me noticing before I hit send:

Sciencegirl: I'm making Gramma's special German Apple Kuchen.

Me: I'm too fat for lichen

Sciencegirl: Probably not too fat for lichen

Sarah: Kuchen, gd this correction thing

Sciencegirl: Do you know what lichen are?

Me: Not off top of my head.

Sciencegirl: Google image it—it's a specialized mutualism between a fungus and algae, it's that crusty stuff that grows on rocks.

(She's not a nerd; she's a biologist/scientist.)

Me: Yum. I would probably have room for a few spoonfuls of that vs. kuchen

MAY 2010

Sciencegirl and Chris

Tons of people—OK, just my "editor"—suggested I give a more expanded view of what Sciencegirl and Chris are like. SG and LB will not like this one bit. I will keep my secrets and give you a vbv (very broad view).

Sciencegirl is my peacemaker. Calm, cool, and collected. She is *just* like Marty. So he clearly did have an influence despite his traveling. She is the voice of reason. However, she can sometimes be a bit of a sloth. We have found her in her room, thinking she was quietly doing her homework, only to find her lying on the floor hitting her head repeatedly with the cardboard tube from a roll of used-up wrapping paper. She has this uncanny ability to zone out. A couch and TV help. She gets that part from her father. She keeps to herself and minds her own business and is always professional when need be.

Lawyerboy is different. He's like me. Poor kid. We are either laughing hysterically together or cussing at each other. There is no happy medium between us. He is proficient and verbal when he wants to be. *Very* verbal. He's a Star Wars geek and has been from the age of six. I think instead of boutonnières at his wedding there will be Star Wars figures on the lapels. At the same time, he's very protective of me.

MiraLAX® Dissolves in Vodka, Ya Know

They are not "close" as in calling each other every day, but they're there for each other when I piss one of them off. Damn. They also both do that thing when I tell them to do something and they say, "OK, Mom." I know they're both just pacifying me and will do whatever they want.

❦ Sarah Berardi ❧

My New Progressive Lenses

I have to say, Marty has been very good to me with my surgery, *this time around* (he usually schedules himself a business trip the next day). He's still doing the laundry, grocery shopping, and unloading the bottom of the dishwasher. I still can't lift more than a gallon of milk (eight pounds). He claims he likes doing the laundry. "It's no big deal while I'm watching golf/football/hockey. I just go get it out of the machine during the commercials."

See, that's the difference. When am I (or any of you reading this) ever just sitting there for six hours watching TV? Ha! (I know, it's his day off...)

So anyway, that's not my subject matter today. He was so tired of trying not to laugh at me with my literal "four eyes" on, that he insisted I try progressive lenses again.

MY VERSION OF PROGRESSIVE LENSES

Chris actually blurted out in the middle of a conversation not too long ago, "Mom, take those off. I can't take you seriously like that!" As if he ever does?

❡ **MiraLAX® Dissolves in Vodka, Ya Know** ❦

Not only that, but the doctors at UB MiniMed School would actually pause in the middle of their lectures and do a double take. (I'm worth a second look, glasses or no glasses.)

There's also that time I walked into Wegmans, forgetting I had both pairs of glasses on, and people gave me weird looks. What?

So off I went to get my new progressive lenses today. I quite like them. I had to endure TalkALotMan at the optician. Sciencegirl and I know he's good at what he does, but boy, do we dread him. I drove home wearing the new lenses, and did OK, but I'm pretty self-conscious in my new frames—do they look OK? Do I look like a dork? After all, they're straight from France, and I don't live in France.

So I sent off a Photo Booth pic from my Mac to the kids, asking, "Do you like my new specs?"

One replied: Fun!!

The other: Sure

What the hell does "sure" mean?

I don't think that was very nice.

Ding-Dong

Poor Marty. I've been having fun at his expense, again.

My cell phone ringtone is a doorbell. Since Marty's rarely with me when my cell phone rings, he had never heard it before we went to Cabo together about five weeks ago. We stayed as guests in this beautiful house where we were expecting the group to gather for cocktails before dinner. My cell phone started ringing, which sounded like a doorbell repetitively ringing, as if somebody outside was repeatedly, succinctly, persistently pressing the bell—ding-dong, ding-dong, ding-dong, ding-dong, ding-dong! Marty obviously thought it was our expected guests. Now, he doesn't walk fast, but he was getting ticked, saying, "I'm coming, I'm coming," which turned into, "I'm coming, damn it, settle down!"

Meanwhile, I was searching for my phone in my purse while sitting on the couch. It clicked with me as he was opening a door to…nobody…what was happening. Ha! I explained to him that it was my cell phone ringtone. Well, he didn't think it was very funny. I thought it was freakin' hilarious.

But it didn't stop there. It continued as he was so kindly taking such great care of me while I was convalescing. Five weeks later, he would hear my cell phone ring and hurriedly get up from his recliner, scamper to the door, and cuss. Then he'd come up to me and cuss a little more and say, "Change that blasted ringtone."

"OK," I'd say.

But it was so much fun, and still is, watching him scamper to the door, that I refuse to change it. He falls for it each and every time.

DMV Day

I got in my newfangled car. I tried, tried, and tried, mind you, to enter into my navigation thingy the DMV at 160 Pearl Street, Buffalo. I finally had to pull over on my way to the thruway. I tried everything. You see, I've been lax. My proper MMwhatever (information) book is still laying (Lying? Laid? Lied? Whatever) on my footstool in front of my fancy sleigh bed, waiting to be read, cover to cover. I pressed every button. I gave every voice command, including, "go blankety-blank." Nothing worked. It kept saying, "Call Peter?" NOOOOOOOOOOOOO.

So, I called my Chris, as he knows downtown better than I do.

Me: Chris, where's the Rath Building downtown?

Chris: Pearl Street?

Me: Yeah, I got that, but I don't see it, and my navigation thingy says, "You have arrived." But I don't see it.

Chris: Use your iPhone.

Me: I did, I can't read the map. I need it to talk to me. Doesn't it talk to me?

Chris: No, Mom, you have to read the map, like the good old days, and walk.

Me: Oh. Never mind.

So I walked. I asked two people on my way. On my second try, I got a nice woman who told me it was the red building way down yonder.

I found it, and stood in a one-person line. *Oh, no.* The person taking the pictures was a *man*, not the lady I talked with on the phone. All of a sudden, a woman with a voice that sounded like the funny lady who promised me a Glamour Shot picture walked up and started talking to another employee behind the counter. She saw me eyeballing her. I went up to her and said, "Excuse me, are you the lady I may have talked to last week who can do Glamour Shots?"

She hesitated just a tiny bit... "YES! You called the call number last week about the picture you re-took, but got the old one by mistake?"

"Yup, that was me!"

I slid a Tim Horton's gift card to her with my blog site jotted on a piece of paper. "Please, oh please, can you take my picture?" (Since she wasn't on camera duty, I was pressing my luck.)

She said, "Oh my gosh, I don't need the gift card, just come here, and I'll make you look gorgeous."

I said, "Please, if you can do it, keep the card. And you'll have to read my blog about you."

The other fellow sitting next to her said, "Well, you know, I taught her to do the Glamour Shots."

"Then you two split the gift card. Just do it!"

She told me how to hold my chin, even gave me a mirror, can you believe it? After walking six blocks, I obviously needed it.

Then she showed me the computer pic. I have to say, it was damned good. She even said I looked good, "Except for your lazy eye." I don't have a lazy eye.

Her name is Candy. She's adorable, friendly, and the best. Worth a trip to the DMV at 160 Pearl Street, Buffalo. Visit her. Tell her I sent you.

I'll scan the difference when I get it in the mail.

Ding-Dong, Delivery

A new UPS guy rang my bell today. Actually, it was the same "new" guy as two weeks ago. Marty has this new passion for buying wine online. I'm going to kill him. Not because he buys the wine, but because it requires a signature. However, he buys all red wines. I can't drink red wines, so it ticks me off even more.

This is how I had to sign the damn thing, twice now:

FRESH OUT OF THE SHOWER

Now I ask you, who likes to answer the door looking like this? Do you think he could at least order some nice Sauvignon Blanc for me if I'm going to be seen like this? I think I gave the poor guy the fright of his life. And when I'm not here to answer to door, and I'm back on my crazy schedule, I'm not going to UPS to pick it up. So there.

I clearly have no shame. I printed that picture in here.

Law School Graduation—Done

So *maybe* I got caught up in the promenade of faculty coming down the aisle during Chris's graduation from law school. And I don't mean emotionally caught up, I mean physically caught up—in the middle of it. I was obliviously busy taking pictures of my kid!

So *maybe* I cried, visibly, nose-blowingly, embarrassingly, unstoppably, for fifteen minutes after reading, surprisingly, that our son was to receive a particular award. (Thank you, Sciencegirl, who was laughing at me, for snapping this picture basically from under her armpit toward me.)

MiraLAX® Dissolves in Vodka, Ya Know

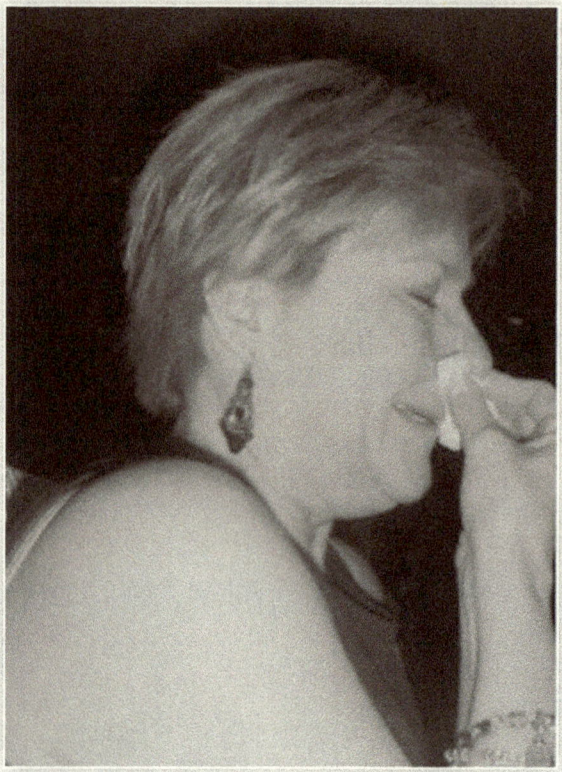

So *maybe* I was the loudest, most obtrusive mother (though I had stiff competition), when my son walked across the stage. I had no shame. This was my kid.

Chris told me afterward that his buddies next to him in line were mocking him: "Hey, so that must be your mother over there?"

"Yup." He expected it of me, which was good for him. He's learned. He actually accepted me and waved at me. This acceptance of me is a new thing.

When Chris walked up the aisle at the end of the ceremony, he apologized to the people sitting in front of me. "I'm sorry you had to sit in front of my mother."

The woman laughed, as she wasn't any different than I was, and I cheered for her daughter *almost* as loudly as I did for my son.

P.S. Poor Sciencegirl. Look what she has to look forward to when she graduates with her PhD. And that'll be in Virginia, where nobody will know me, so I'll have absolutely *no* reason to hold back (not that I would anyway)!

P.P.S. Now the studying for the bar exam begins. When he passes, I will call him Lawyerboy. Wait, I already do.

{ Sarah Berardi }

DMV Revisited

I told you I'd keep you posted on my driver's license picture. Now, granted, my hair seems to be a totally different shade, but so does my face. Plus, I was workin' it. It was worth my while, wasn't it? Freddy Fat Chin is gone. Go see Candy in Buffalo.

Now, how many of you out there are brave enough to put your mug shots up there like this? Lucy eyelid and all.

Steroids and Frenemies

Have you ever been on prednisone? I have to take them for about a week every now and then for my migraines to break. The doctor only resorts to them when we've tried just about everything else short of a lobotomy.

First, let me say that I have a well-meaning friend (wmf). Um…wait, first of all, she's not well-meaning. And now that I think of it, I'm not quite sure she's a friend. This wmf (aka frenemy) thinks that I'm on anabolic steroids when I mention that I'm on prednisone. Prednisone is a corticosteroid used to cut down inflammation, not an anabolic steroid, so you won't be seeing me have "'roid rage" (just my normal Sarah rage). I won't have worse acne than normal, and I won't have he-man muscles, just my regular rolls of Freddy, Betty, and Lucy.

But when I'm on them, I sweat like crazy—as in visibly dripping sweat, non-stop, for the week. The dry-cleaning bill is quite a bit larger during the weeks I'm on these drugs. I cry a lot while on them. But most of all, I'm incredibly hyper. Hyper to the point that the kids and Marty say to me, "You've got to shut up now!"

Once I was up until 5:00 a.m., unable to sleep due to them. I cleaned all my dresser drawers for the first time in three years. My bills got paid, desk cleared. Everything I'd been procrastinating about got done. The same thing happened last time I was on them. So I sort of look forward to taking them three times a year or so.

I have one more day left on them, since you have to taper off. I'm looking forward to not dripping in public. My mother would be mortified at my sweating in front of people.

Logic

While "working" today at THWIV, my new best friend (who is a priest) asked me why I was working past 2:00 p.m.

I said, "Logically speaking, I might as well go home to an empty house at five p.m. instead of two p.m."

He said, "I've seen no evidence of you using logic yet, so why start now?"

Humph. What do you say to that? He's eighty-six, by the way.

JUNE 2010

I'm Sad Today

Today is not a good day. It's a sad day, I'm sorry to admit this to you girlfriends who bought me the "happy" Tiffany charm. Do you think its charm has rubbed off completely already?

It's one of those days when I could cry at any moment, but I hold it together. That is, until I'm standing in the Atlanta airport, alone, and the girl behind the counter looks at me a little funny, gives me my decaf, and then says, "How's your day going, ma'am?"

When this happened, I uncontrollably frowned, an embarrassing tear squirted out, and I haltingly squeaked, "Not very well." She looked so sympathetic, I thought if the counter wasn't between us, she would have come over and hugged me. But after giving me my change, she put her hand on mine and said, "It'll get better, ma'am."

Which only made me cry harder the whole way back to my gate.

I don't care how many people suggest I go on HRT, I'm riding the wave, and they're riding it with me.

P.S. Just went to the ladies' room. Maybe she looked at me funny because I had lipstick on my teeth. So there, I made this blog funny after all.

Mama on the Moped

I rarely back down from a challenge, so I did this one half-assed.

Notice the kickstand is down. But those are kick-ass pumps. Doesn't that remind you of The Great Gazoo from *The Flintstones*?

White-Powder Residue

I have white powder all over my car up front near my gearshift and cup holders. It's a very fine, granular, white powder. I add more to it whenever I go through Tim Horton's for my brewed decaf tea.

It's MiraLAX®. It's a laxative. I carry the travel packets in my car just for these drive-through stops. It's perfect, but it doesn't come out of the packet perfectly, darn it all. So if I ever get stopped by a cop (which happens to be frequently…never mind), the cop will think A) anthrax, or B) cocaine.

I also travel quite a bit. Before they came out with MiraLAX® travel packets, I was hesitant to bring my bottle of laxative powder in my carry-on bag for fear of them taking it out and asking if it was actually cocaine. Why wouldn't they? Why wouldn't someone smuggle cocaine in a MiraLAX® bottle? I've never seen cocaine, but I imagine it might look similar to MiraLAX®.

So I was petrified of putting just two days' worth of laxative powder in a Ziploc bag, not wanting to take the whole bottle. I would have been at the FBI for days, not that Marty would have noticed. Can you see him sunning on the beach, talking to me as if I were there?

I can.

My GPS

I was at dinner the other night with the owner of the place where I bought my new car. I was telling him how stupid I felt with all the new baubles that I can't figure out. He made me feel better, stating that the average person (I'm no average Joe) can only comprehend one-third of what he's told at a time. It actually made me feel better, since I've been in twice already (once to ask how to get the bloody keys out of the ignition).

I asked him why my GPS couldn't understand the voice command "#$% $%^." He said the GPS only understands English and Spanish; it doesn't understand Vulgar.

I Am Athletic Now

I was out to lunch with the gals the other day, and they were impressed that I sneezed without saying, "I just peed my pants." (As was I.)

So when we went out to the parking lot, they asked me, "What other things can you do, now that your leaky bladder is fixed? Can you do jumping jacks?" (They were *taunting* me, thinking I'd never do that in public. Actually, they knew I would, didn't they?) It's crooked, but it's jumping.

❧ MiraLAX® Dissolves in Vodka, Ya Know ❧

Cancer Survivor Day

Today I volunteered at Roswell Cancer Institute for Cancer Survivor Day. I was working at the smoothie stand, taking the required stickers (showing the survivors and family had registered—it was all free), and handing out smoothies to said ticket-holders. Three other women worked with me. One was a stickler for the sticker, I'll tell ya.

One sweet old lady came up with her daughter, granddaughter, and great-granddaughter, and said, "I want a smoothie."

I said, "OK, do you have the purple sticker?"

"I don't know where my stickers are," she said (she was in her eighties, I'd guess). I asked her if she was a cancer survivor. She said she was. In fact, she had just had a mastectomy two weeks prior. I told her she looked great. She told me she felt like crap. I "gave" her a smoothie—without the sticker. Well, the other volunteer who was the "stickler" sort of glared at me. This is what I did back to her:

OK, all for now. Since I told everyone at the smoothie bar that I drink my smoothies with vodka in them, I'm going to make mine now. And remember, MiraLAX® dissolves in vodka, ya know.

Spring Cleaning

OK, for the last two weeks I've been cleaning house. No...you all know me better than that! I'm not physically cleaning house (although I do have my washer running).

I am cleaning my attic—aka my head—of toxicity. I'm trying really hard. I've realized that some people are really not my friends. (You have them, too, don't you?) I need humor in my life. I have enough strife.

Some people believe you just need to "get over" stuff that you grew up with. I always believed that until it became evident that my past was so prevalent in my everyday life—damn, I hate admitting that. I hate admitting that I can't control its influence on my life. "Quick," I said to myself, "get help. Don't do this to your nuclear family the way your parents did it to you!"

You all may have picked up on this when I wrote about my dreams that are violent to the point that I can't have open containers or anything breakable next to my bed while I sleep. I'd been blissfully ignorant for years. Now I know. Poor, poor Marty, on his six inches next to me in bed.

But we, as a nuclear family, laugh at it. With hugs. And that's the best thing, I tell you.

So my psych class taught me a great deal, as well as my friend who happens to be a therapist. Wow. This spring-cleaning was way overdue.

Facebook Schmacebook

I have succumbed to Facebook. Although I strive to be different, I am out to make a name for myself with my blog to prove I am not a "no-good nothing." (This runs in my family.)

I don't like to do things simply because everyone else does—like joining Facebook.

NYC for the Weekend

I'm on my way to New York for a class on "Learning to Write with Humor." A friend of mine said, "Oh, so now you'll come back funny?" I said, "Um…no, now I'll come back funnier, thank you very much."

Nobody was in the line at security—go figure, a Saturday afternoon at four o'clock. So when I pulled out my new, gorgeous ID courtesy of Candy from the City of Buffalo DMV, I said to the fellow:

Me: Check out that DMV pic. Pretty good, huh?

Him: Sure is, ma'am.

Me: I went through a lot for that, you know. The first bitch that took my picture gave me five Freddy Fat Chins. So I had to go to another DMV in the city where they do Glamour Shots.

Him (chuckling, though I'm not sure he's allowed to do so): They probably made you suck your chin in the first time.

Me: Exactly! That's exactly what the bitch did!
Him (still stifling his chuckle): I knew it. You behave now, in NYC.
Me: No way. Misbehavin'.

Upon checking into my favorite hotel, The Benjamin, where you can eat their Benjamin Teddy Bears if you think they're English muffins when you look at them without your glasses on first thing in the morning, I found the most welcoming young man behind the desk who spoke with a little bit of a southern accent.

He needed to see my charge card and ID. Yippee! Again, I go into my spiel about my DMV Glamour Shot. Doesn't he pull out one of his old IDs that was absolutely frightful and show it to me? It was hysterical! He said, "I had helmet hair."

Writing Class in NYC

Yum, I love those vodka-soaked olives. It's 7:10 p.m., and I've just walked the eighteen blocks back to my Grey Goose martini on a Sunday night at my hotel in midtown Manhattan. This place is surprisingly dead, as it was last night. (Sad.)

I know this place is dead because I was a Peeping Tom last night. (A Saturday night!) Through my window, at 11:00 p.m., I saw these things while looking at the high-rise across the street:

1. Very few people on the street.
2. Lots of people under white down comforters.
3. Various activities under those comforters.

But I love New York. I actually found myself giving directions to a group of five people walking ahead of me who had stopped dead in their tracks, which made me go face-first into the sweaty back of the largest guy in the group. I hate those people who stop walking in front of you like that. No warning whatsoever, just—wham—stop—face-plant into someone's (sweaty) back side. Assholes. Anyway, they were questioning among themselves whether they had headed in the wrong direction. I told them they had indeed, and to backtrack two blocks, then turn right for their destination, which I had overheard. Pretty good for someone as daft as me, who has few neurons firing and many misshapen dendrites due to premenopause, right?

❧ MiraLAX® Dissolves in Vodka, Ya Know ☙

I digress (I know, I know, I do it every damned time). I went to my class and loved it. L-O-V-E-D it. It was a very small class, only six of us, with a great teacher who knows her stuff. My favorite guy in the class, "Charlie," was an adorable Asian from New Jersey. English was his second language. Naturally, since English wasn't his native tongue, the article I submitted for critique was pretty damned funny to him. Therefore, he became my fave. On the other hand, there was the mystic, feeling, emotional, ethereal writer "Freespirituoso" (I'll call her that). She was also very complimentary, but in a weird way. Weird, OK? Weird. I actually got great constructive criticism that I hope to implement.

To let you know how huge a step this was for me to submit myself to this critique of my article, I'll tell you this story. When I was in third grade (not that I hold a grudge), my report card from stupid, old, white-haired Mrs. Oldfart had a comment to my parents that said, "Sarah does not take constructive criticism well."

You know what I said to that in third grade? "What the F is constructive criticism? Criticism is criticism!" But, alas, I have matured. (You noticed, right?) And I loved the class's constructive criticism. Kudos must go to the teacher, however, for teaching us ahead of time how to turn criticism into "constructive" criticism. I found everyone's critiques helpful. One of my favorite suggestions came from a younger fellow to whom I confessed that I may have a little bit of an anger issue. He said, "Then let it rip, man!"

JULY 2010

Day Off

Hey, ever hear of a holiday? Give me a break. I can't be funny every damned day. Hope your flag is flying. It's the Fourth.

NYS License Plate

Hey, check this out. I mentioned to Marty that I love seeing the old New York State license plates making a comeback! So when my registration was due, he ordered me a new one. I got it in the mail today:

MiraLAX® Dissolves in Vodka, Ya Know

He does think of me.

Flashbacks

When I was at my New York City Gotham writing course, "How to Write with Humor," the two things that stuck with me the most were these:

1. Tragedy + Distance = Humor; and
2. "Let It Rip"—meaning my tongue, which the class discovered might be pretty funny when I let loose.

I don't know if I can pull it off, though. I have plenty of what some might consider tragedy to write about, and I've got some distance from the so-called tragedy now (I *never* looked at it as tragedy—*never*), but the challenge is, can I actually make it funny to readers? In past writings, I've given little glimpses of some of the stuff I've grown up with (screaming "eat shit" in my sleep blog, for example), but the bottom line is this: *I had crappy parents*! Wouldn't that be a great bumper sticker? Or "I had a dysfunctional family"?

Speaking of the family, the rest of my siblings don't even know I have a blog. As far as I know, anyway. Speaks volumes, doesn't it? We each remember the same events differently. You see, I was the caretaker, so I have the most accurate memories—right?

I have to face it, the only real idea I had of decent parents were Darren and Samantha Stevens from *Bewitched*, Fred and Wilma Flintstone, and Carol and Mike Brady. It would have been nice if my mom and dad had acted their ages and let me act mine!

Mom and Dad have both passed away now. They used drinking as their coping mechanism in those days; they were alcoholics, plain and simple. They didn't have Prozac, or any SSRIs, SRNIs, etc., back then. Lord knows they needed them desperately. As my friend Brian says, some people need a Prozac the size of a grapefruit every day.

And my husband and kids have made me laugh at the most perfect times, showing me just how humorous some of my nightmare memories really are simply from the absurdity of them. Laughter, after all, is the best medicine. So I will be interspersing my normal writings with "flashback" blogs, just so y'all know. I only have a few to post, and not all of them will be about my screwed-up siblings (did I say that out loud?) who are kookadoodledoo victims, spoiled brats, drama queens, or midlife-crisis Pleasure Drivers (not kidding—one sibling has taken up "driving" a horse while dressed in a tux to please someone).

It was tough being the perfect one in the family. And if I'm the sane one, that's pretty scary.

Flashback Jae Ruth

When I was in fourth grade, I remember not having very many friends. Believe it or not, I was really, really shy and incredibly anxiety-ridden (remember, I had crappy parents). Seemed every time I said something, it came out wrong or stupid, so that the other kids would look back at me as if I had three eyes. I always felt it was better that I just kept quiet and alone. I was a dork, plain and simple.

But I always had a soft spot for the other lonely kids—or those I perceived to be lonely. There was this one girl who seemed lonely. Her name was Jae Ruth. She had few friends, for obvious reasons. She grossed people out by picking her nose and eating it in front of everyone. She had greasy hair.

She was terribly overweight. She was always getting yelled at by our teacher, Mrs. Daenhert, for not listening because she would read her own books in the middle of lessons.

At lunchtime at the loser table (where I unfortunately sat), Jae Ruth would finish her lunch…completely. As in licking her pointer finger and dabbing each crumb from the cafeteria table and eating/licking it (even if it wasn't from her lunch). Gross. This might have been when I became a germophobe.

She always stood in line in front of me and sat next to me. Our last names came next to each other alphabetically. Jae Ruth was feisty about her name. Crikey, would she ever get mad when teachers would call out her name for attendance, looking through their bifocals at their attendance sheets and tentatively reading out, "Joe Ruth _____." She'd stand up indignantly and say very matter-of-factly, "It's Jae, J-A-E, not Joe, J-O-E," with the implication that said reader was an idiot. I don't blame her for being feisty about this, in reality.

She was incredibly bright (I didn't know this at the time), which would help explain why she was always getting yelled at for reading her own books while the teacher was teaching a lesson in math or whatever.

One day, I could see over Jae Ruth's shoulder as I sat timidly behind her. She was again reading her beloved, crumpled, paperback book. I could see our teacher, Mrs. Daenhert, giving her the stink eye. I knew Jae Ruth was in for it, again. So out of the goodness of my heart, I whispered over Jae Ruth's shoulder, "Jae, Mrs. Daenhert's going to yell at you any second."

I should have just kept quiet, because she put her book down (loudly), exhaled (loudly), turned around, faced me, picked up my forearm lying across the front of my desk (which had enabled me to lean in and whisper in her ear in the first place), held it like a well-seasoned Thanksgiving turkey drumstick, growled (as in GRRRRRRR, loudly), and bit me. What the *^&%? It scared the crap out of me. What the hell was she doing? This wasn't normal behavior. I was trying to help her out!

Sarah Berardi

I stifled my screech of pain and fright. Next thing I knew, Mrs. Daenhert was throwing the blackboard eraser at Jae Ruth, telling her to pay attention and to turn around, and telling *me* to pay attention. Me? I'm the one who was innocently injured in all this.

So much for looking out for the underdog. I decided right then and there, in fourth grade, that I was the underdog, and that I should look out for myself from now on.

In reality, I wish I had remembered this through all my illustrious years.

And Jae Ruth, if you're reading this, I hold grudges.

My Spray Tan

I love getting a spray tan. I'm not ashamed to admit it. I don't get a really dark color, just sun-kissed. Goose doesn't let me walk next to her when I'm not tanned because she says I look as if I'm ill. Mind you, she's Greek, and therefore has dark skin. Me? I'm albino from the hips down.

⁋ MiraLAX® Dissolves in Vodka, Ya Know ⁋

The spray tan is organic, so I could drink it, I imagine, not that I would want to (well, maybe with a little vodka in it). So I see it as a harmless ego-booster. But the last time I got it, I noticed that I had a white sort of ring around the fronts of my knees and on the backs of my elbows. This hadn't happened to me before. Crikey, I thought, I'll have to mention it the next time I go in.

So today I mentioned it. The sprayer listened kindly to me and nodded. She said I'd have to bend my knees and arms a little when we sprayed this time. I contemplated what she said. I slowly said, "My knees and elbows have rolls of fat, don't they?" She claimed, "No!" But they do.

So as we sprayed, I got a good workout in. Had to do some deep knee bends, lunges, arms lifts. Maybe it's all just extra skin folds. Yup, that's definitely what it is, now that I'm staring at them. Remember reading *The Saggy, Baggy Elephant* to your kids? That's me.

Flashback: B Band

Now you have to remember that I was a painfully anxious, shy, insecure girl in school. It's embarrassing to admit, but I really had few friends. Just Carolyn down the street. She was my safety zone. Unfortunately, she was a grade below me; plus, as we grew older, she grew in confidence, and I didn't.

So with no self-confidence, I found myself in middle school band, seated right next to the band instructor in the *first chair*. Pretty good, huh? I played the flute. I, Sarah Bammel (my maiden name), was first flautist in B Band (we had a huge public school). I had no idea what this meant. I wasn't part of any clique. But if I was part of a clique, I didn't want be to part of the band clique (not that there's anything wrong with it). So I sat there, oblivious, being asked to give the whole band a B-note to tune up at the beginning of every practice, having no idea how "prestigious" this was to be sitting in the first chair.

Apparently I was so damned good, the conductor guy decided it was best to move me up to A Band. I was pretty darned excited. I was a nobody; my older sister was always a somebody (well, in Mom's eyes anyway). Maybe now I would be somebody!

So they rearranged my schedule. On my first day of A Band, I could hardly breathe, not knowing a soul there. I asked the teacher/conductor guy where I was supposed to sit. He pointed to the last chair for the flautists. The dead last.

That's when it dawned on me where I had come from and where I had ended up. I went from the Christmas concert, being all dressed up, sitting right next to the conductor for everyone to see, despite the fact it was B Band, to being moved to the frickin' end of fifteen flute players in A Band where nobody could see me.

Well, I didn't like being a nobody. It was clear to me what I should do. I quit the next week. And I was a damned good flute player. I should have been happy to be promoted to A Band, but I wasn't.

If anyone needs a flute player for any weddings, I'm for hire. Plus, Jethro Tull stinks. They've got nothin' on me. Ian Anderson clearly doesn't purse his lips enough when he blows into the mouthpiece, but I think he's doing that to be cool. Plus, I can hear he's blowing across the mouthpiece instead of into it. Knucklehead.

Flashback: Sunday School

Speaking of being a "flautist," this is another nightmare memory. But, wow, do my kids and husband laugh at this one.

After I made my confirmation in eighth grade (I was raised Catholic), I begged my mother, please oh please, not to make me go to CCD (religion classes) anymore. Those classes were so incredibly anxiety-provoking for me. I still bit my nails to the quick (I had since I was five years old), had no friends, and sat alone. But it was even worse than I can explain in words. The classes were held at a couple's home, so it was typically four loser kids (I was always one of them) discussing religious stuff with the married couple in their living room. Can you imagine how painful that was? Just too much for me.

So I begged my mother: Why couldn't I drop out like my older, spoiled-brat (obvious to everyone she's your favorite child) sister? She said I had a choice. Either I could keep going until I was a friggin' senior in high school, or join my spoiled-brat sister's folk music group, which played and sang at 10:30 Mass.

What a choice! Me? Up in front of everyone? I had an anxiety issue, and she knew it. Mom said I could play the flute and sing! Yippifrigginee. My sister, by the way, *loved* any tiny, itsy bit of attention she could get from any*where*, doing any*thing* (still does). So she was up there playing her guitar, singing her heart out, leading the group, singing the solos, her face full of emotion. She'd belt it out as if she were Grace Slick ("White Rabbit"). I remember being mortified how her hips would sway to the music, *in church*.

So I made the decision that it might be less painful to join the stupid folk Mass. This required me to show up for practice one evening a week and an hour before Mass. I sang. I played my flute. But the best part was this. Ready? *I played the tambourine.* Yup, I was a regular old Laurie from *The Partridge Family* copycat, hair parted in the middle and everything. Stop laughing. Sciencegirl, do you see why I never let you wear your hair like that?

Talk about social anxiety! And this was before Prozac was even around, not that I would have been on it from eighth grade through twelfth grade, though I surely (and don't call me Shirley) needed it from kindergarten on up. Yes, I'm on it now—that's why I don't have the social anxiety anymore. :) (It is not a placebo, Chris!) I would stand stock-still and sing. I would stand stock-still and play the flute. I would stand stock-still while playing the tambourine. I did not sway my hips. I barely whispered my song.

Feelin' sorry for me? You should.

Gift of Love?

Even though this may not look like a gift of love, it is. You see, my friend has been a blessing to me. She makes me laugh. She's a counselor when a mom needs one. She has shared miseries with me about family. She seems to know what I'm about inside and what I'm faking on the outside.

So here's the gift she gave me last time we got together.

Sarah Berardi

I'm Gorgeous

I had to go down to City Hall to get a duplicate copy of an old marriage license for a family member. This type of field trip always proves to be hazardous for me.

I parked where I normally park, but when I walked out the way I came, I found a huge construction site that blocked all the sidewalks I would normally take. This is not good for me. I immediately lose all spatial orientation. Immediately.

After asking several people where the hell I was and finding out where the hell I wanted to be, I went up to the thirteenth floor, filled out my form, showed my ID, and showed my power of attorney. The nice gentleman told me that, since it was such an old license, it would take a while to retrieve it, so I could wait out in the hall in the chairs and they'd call me on the overhead speaker. I said, "You can call me Gorgeous." He burst out laughing, as did the couple next to me. I pulled my sunglasses down a bit on my nose so they all could see my eyes, and I said, "What are you all laughing at? Don't you think I'm gorgeous?"

Ten Things I Love Besides My Family

1. Clean, fresh sheets that somebody else put on my bed.
2. New shoes.
3. Reading in bed all day.
4. Buttered popcorn.
5. Netflix.
6. Clean, fresh sheets that somebody else put on my bed.
7. A no-headache day.
8. A day with no road rage (I'm doing soooo much better). The other day, a lady cut me off. I gave a quick beep and one of those looks like, "Are you serious?" which includes a smile of incredulity. She flipped me the bird. Normally, I would follow her ass as tight to her bumper as I could possibly get. But instead, I just laughed and thought to myself, *Wouldn't it be funny if I could just go up to her and ask her if she wants my therapist's phone number so she can work on her anger management?*
9. (Spray)-tanned legs.
10. Clean, fresh sheets that somebody else put on my bed.

Will I Get Fired from a Volunteer Job?

As I've mentioned, I've been volunteering at our local cancer hospital (THWIV) for about three years now. I handle a lot of data entry, mostly deaths. That's my forte. (Have I found my forte?) Fits right into my persona, actually, being that my favorite type of books are dark, dank, depressing, suicidal stories by Russian male authors who get inside a woman's head.

As I was saying, I deal with death a lot in a data-entry way. But the deaths are nobody to me, just names that I don't even read, foreign names and addresses, sadly. I send out sympathy cards, Mass cards, and a bunch of other things to do with each death. But today I hit a new low. When I'm not paying strict attention (which, unfortunately, is getting more and more frequent due to my migraine prevention drugs), I mess up. My "boss" gave me an envelope with a sympathy card in it marked "return to sender." Humph. Wonder what I did wrong. If I did things correctly, I would have found the correct next-of-kin's address and sent it to them. I chastised myself.

Well, after a quick investigation, I realized I had sent the sympathy card for the poor dead person to the dead person. It's as if I sent a card saying, "Dear Sarah, We are sorry you have passed away."

It's been a fear of mine for two years. I fessed up to the "boss" what I had done and blamed it on my antiseizure drugs, but she didn't buy it. I told her I was using it as my excuse and sticking to it. Thank goodness the poor dead person wasn't there to receive it at her address or I would have been really embarrassed.

I told the "boss" she should fire me. Unfortunately, I'm all she's got right now, so she can't. She assured me that there are specific guidelines they have on just how to go about firing a volunteer. Now I'm a little worried…I just might get fired. But she did buy new rubber stamps, just for me. So that's a good sign.

AUG 2010

Facebook Update

I don't use my Facebook very much. I really only joined so I could post my blog site on it for more of my friends to read (there, confessed). Though I have to admit, I have been up until the wee hours in the morning Facebook stalking. I love that part of it.

So remember how my kids wouldn't "allow" me to join? My daughter relented, my son never has. I never told them I had joined, just did it. Soon after my joining, I saw Sciencegirl had "friended" me. I ignored the invitation for a while, not knowing how I should handle it. But I should have known that she would have already set her restrictions with me so that I couldn't see most of her stuff. I soon "friended" her back.

I loved seeing the new photos she posted, her updates, etc. I was even having a blast bantering with one of her undergrad friends, when one day I logged on and her "wall" was gone. She had blocked me from her wall.

Humph. I guess I learned a lesson. You can't hit return after each thought, and then add another. No worries, though. In my vast maturity, I blocked you back, Sciencegirl, sweetheart. xoIloveyou. And Chris is sitting there reading this, saying, "I told you so," isn't he? That's the worst part. They were right, I can't handle it. I'm obnoxious with it.

I still don't get the lure of Facebook. Other than the pics and stalking.

Lilydale

This Sunday, two of my gal pals and I are zipping down to Lilydale. It's a(n) (in)famous place where spiritualists can "help you" by seeing dead people, basically. The last time I saw a spiritualist, it was just for blog fodder.

I left fuming, spitting nails, as the reader told me I was a spoiled brat. I found myself having to defend myself for having gotten a little self-confidence recently. She told me that my life growing up wasn't so bad. Hers had been *far* worse. Her father would beat her, kick her out, blah, blah, blah, and nobody had a worse life than she did, so I could basically stick it in my ear. Alrighty then. You win.

Here's what started her off. When I sat down, she said right away, "Oh, you're going to be a tough little one, aren't you?" You see, it was suggested to me not to give her my personal info but to let her "read" me. But she said, "Honey, if you don't show me the junk in your trunk, how am I going to read you?" Huh? Isn't that what I'm paying sixty dollars for?

So, my gal pals are a little frightened that when I see her in Lilydale, I may go at her. *Because I will.* They have vowed not to walk *with* me, but either ten feet *ahead* of me or ten feet *behind* me. Humph, some friends they are.

Plus, they're embarrassed by the shoes I'm going to wear. They look particularly manly, and I'm trying to throw the psychic off. I'm going as a devil's advocate, you see, and my gal pals are not. Aren't I naughty? (It's all way too ambiguous for me—I'm way too black-and-white for this.)

I'll blog just what happens—if the gal pals even let me ride home with them, that is.

Karma, Baby

Ring, ring.

    Me: Hello?

    High School Alumni Person (AP) Hired to Get Info: Is this Sarah Berardi?

    Me: I don't know, why do you ask?

    AP explains herself. She's making up the directory for Orchard Park High School alumni.

    Me (laughing): "I hated high school, and all the people in it. I had an anxiety disorder, which means I had no self-confidence and was really shy. I didn't know it then, but I know it now. And people were mean to me. I had no friends. So I don't know what info you're going to get from me." I laughed again.

AP: OK. (She laughed—thank goodness, or I would have seemed like a freak.) Would you like me to list your name in the alumni directory?

Me: Sure, let them know I survived.

AP: And your address as well?

Me: No.

AP: Your phone number?

Me: No.

AP: Your e-mail?

Me: No.

We are giggling. OK, she's giggling, I'm hysterical. I give her little sidebars.

Me: They were all nasty to me. Mean girls. And the guys thought I was a piece of dog poo. I wasn't. I was just a Nervous Nellie, shy.

AP: OK. (We are still giggling.) This is a little fun.

Me: For me, too. My husband isn't home, so you're all I've got.

AP: Would you like to list your career?

Me: I don't have one. I raised my kids. Not a career, apparently, but I did it damned well. I'm perfect.

AP: So, would you like to list your career?

Me: Sorry, I digress a lot. No.

AP: (Laughter. Nice laughter. As if she's on my side.) Sure I can't list your e-mail?

Me: No.

We talked after the questions. I found out about her. She seemed adorable. I told her I hoped she was getting paid for this phone call instead of volunteering for it. She said she enjoyed "meeting" new people. I said, "Well, haven't I just made your night?"

I told her how I went to my ten-year reunion, so proud of my husband, his position, my kids, blah, blah, blah. And I was voted bloody *"Least Changed."* Did they not notice I sat under the pay phone after calling my mother every day during lunch while in high school? Do they *not* think I've *changed*? I didn't look at it as a compliment. They based it on looks, apparently. But I *had* changed so much. They never knew me then, how could they know me ten years later?

I told AP it was almost worth buying the alumni book she was selling just so I could get everyone's e-mails to tell them they were poopy to me.

But I am counting on karma, baby. Karma.

❧ MiraLAX® Dissolves in Vodka, Ya Know ☙

I'm a Class Act

On my way out to the doctor today, Marty kindly said, "Hold on, let me fix you."

This is the third time since blogging that this has happened to me. Do I get up too fast from the potty? What's my problem? And my legs used to be much thinner. Darn it all.

I'm a Little Stressed

I don't know what's wrong with me lately. Well, I'll say "lately," but some of you might say this is normal for me. I keep screwing up on so many details, big and small.
1. I have, more than once (OK, lots of times), paid the same bill twice, giving me credit but leaving me with nothing in my checking account (online banking).
2. I have, more than once (OK, lots of times), paid the balance due on Credit Card A to Credit Card B (online banking). Then I get a late bill

from Credit Card A. This consequently also leaves me with nothing in my checking account.
3. I have, more than once, neglected to pay the umbrella insurance, therefore having to frantically pay over the phone via credit card to get reinstated. No, this is not insurance for my umbrella, but insurance for our cars, homeowners, and something else I can't remember. And do not tell Marty this.
4. I have made incorrect plane reservations, in many ways. For example: I've booked for the incorrect days or I've booked prop jobs for myself. I don't fly prop jobs. (I'm usually so darned careful not to book those darned little prop planes). Let me repeat, I don't fly prop jobs. Marty says I now have to fly the prop job since it's too much money to change it. I will have to put on my big-girl panties and deal with it, take extra Xanax, and fly. If it goes down, that'll show him, won't it? Humph.
5. I have lost a wedding invitation. It's here somewhere. Probably with that plane reservation I screwed up.
6. I've sent sympathy cards to dead people (a previous blog).
7. I've stared at red lights and driven right through them with horns blaring at me and tires screeching.
8. I've stared at my hair appointment time of 1:45 p.m., but mentally registered it as 3:15 p.m., so arrived at 3:05 p.m.

It's just getting worse and worse. So, I was wondering if I shouldn't get an assistant or secretary. Wouldn't it be so neat to be one of those wealthy women who live in New York and have an assistant who comes early in the morning and leaves after dinner each night? They lay out your clothes for you in the morning, tell you where you're going for the day, have the car brought around, make all your reservations, etc.

H-e-a-v-e-n. I would read all day in bed. Every day. I would sip my decaf with MiraLAX® while snacking on fresh, organic cherries.

But I'd better just keep on doing what I'm doing, since I think having someone help me would make me look like a spoiled brat, and I wouldn't want that Lilydale lady to be right, the bitch.

SEP 2010

Flashback: Dad's Stupid Socks

Parts where you should giggle shall be in CAPITAL LETTERS. You may not know that these things are funny to me. Therefore, I feel compelled to point them out to you.

This is a weird post. Especially as it's a flashback. These are particularly difficult to make funny to everyone else. You all may think they are horrible and miserable and OMGs, but in reality, where I am now, my husband, kids, Goose, and her boys all laugh at these types of things. We have to. It's Darwinian.

After typing the blog from yesterday, I was thinking of Elaine from a *Seinfeld* episode where she is in a dead-end job having to purchase tube socks for her boss that were "just the right height." It triggered a flashback. Back in the earlier days of my marriage, this would have been a nightmarish trigger; now, it's ridiculously funny to me.

One day, Dad came home, had his four or so martinis (to start), and picked me for the LUCKY one to argue with. The five of us (Mom and four kids) would usually duck and cover and hope it wasn't us, but at the same time, we'd feel sorry for the person who was picked.

This particular argument of his with me has to be the most absurd, therefore funny to us all. I hope you can see the humor in it. He came home, drank, and

❦ MiraLAX® Dissolves in Vodka, Ya Know ❧

confronted me in my bedroom where I was studying (A LOT O F GOOD THAT STUDYING DID, I WAS A SOLID C STUDENT IN SCHOOL). He BARGED (STUMBLED) into my room. I turned around, frightened by the intrusion. He said, "WHAT DID YOU DO FOR ME TODAY?"

I was stunned. "Huh?" I was sixteen or so. I thought to myself, *CRAP, I didn't do anything for Dad today. Was I supposed to? I went to school, went to gymnastics practice, went to work for three hours, came home, and now I'm studying. What do I say?*

So I said, "NUTHIN'. I was busy at school and work."

BZZZZZZZTTT...WRONG ANSWER. I knew it was. (You see, nobody sassed me then, nor do they now. I was baiting him, wasn't I?)

Dad: DID YOU AT LEAST PRAY FOR ME?

Me: Um, no. (PRAY FOR YOU? I DON'T EVEN LIKE YOU. YOU'RE MEAN.) But I didn't pray for anyone.

Dad: Did you do anything for anyone but yourself today?

Me: No, I don't think so.

Dad: Well, then I have a chore for YOU. Get your butt up and go MEASURE MY SOCKS. You should be doing something for me each and every day. You should be thankful there's a roof over your head.

Me: Measure your socks? (Remember, I'm sixteen and sober; he's a lot older and drunk.)

Dad: YES.

Me: How?

Dad: Go get the GD yardstick and measure my GD socks. (This is not said in the pleasant conversation decibel level, THIS IS SAID AT ROCK-CONCERT DECIBEL LEVEL.)

Me: Measure them for what? (Eyes are now leaking. I'm scared. I'm quivering, AS I'VE NEVER QUITE LEARNED HOW TO MEASURE SOCKS.)

Dad: I DON'T WANT ANY SOCKS THAT ARE TOO GD SHORT (s-h-r-i-l-l).

Off I went to the kitchen closet where we kept the yardstick. I measured each and every pair of his stupid socks, hating him as I did so. Can you believe it? WHO WOULD MAKE THEIR KID MEASURE THEIR SOCKS? I don't remember what his exact requirement was, but they had to be "not too short." That's ambiguous for me, you know. You all remember I don't "DO" ambiguous, right?

But, the funny part is, *I know* how stupid it was. And I knew it then. AND STILL, TO THIS DAY, WHEN I SEE A MAN CROSS HIS LEGS, AND I SEE HIS BARE CALF, I KNOW THIS POOR MAN DID NOT HAVE A DAUGHTER

{ Sarah Berardi }

WHO MEASURED HIS GD SOCKS FOR HIM. And I have to laugh. I laugh at my father's absurd, drunken request that I measure his stupid socks.

So the next time you see a bare calf on a man who crosses his legs, will you at least giggle for me?

Prop Jobs and Applesauce

I know that title makes no sense. It just rolled off my tongue from *The Brady Bunch*, the episode where Peter keeps saying, "pork chops…and applesauce." Does anyone remember that besides Marty and me?

So I got up this morning, the day of my prop-job flight. I had this great idea. I thought, *Why don't I go early to the airport and try to catch a proper jet on standby, then it won't cost me any extra. I can* be brilliant at times. So I went to my computer to check all the flights on Continental, which goes straight to Newark, and see that *all* their flights are prop jobs. On one hand, it made me feel better that I didn't make a mistake in booking it, seeing as I had no choice but to fly the prop job. On the other hand, I still had to fly the gol-darn prop job.

I jumped in the shower with my mind racing about packing, stopping at the doctor to get my tranquilizer prescription, getting it filled at the pharmacy, eating, MiraLAX®ing, etc. My lack of concentration was so great that as I mechanically started to squeegee the glass shower walls, I realized it wasn't working well, probably because I still had the *shower on and running*. I was so glad Marty was out of town so as not to see me doing that.

Then, when I went to the pharmacy to pick up my tranquilizers, I told the nice lady behind the counter (they all know me) that I was off to New Jersey to say good-bye to my nieces, as their mother was moving them to the middle of nowhere in a faraway state, away from their father (my brother). The lady quickly said, "Oh, how horrible. What a horrible person she is to take those children away from their father. I think you should beat her up."

I cracked up laughing and told her I needed *no one* to instigate the issue with me. I had been on the edge for about two years, holding back. I told her I couldn't blow my top on my now ex-sister-in-law as Marty, Chris, and Sciencegirl have all told me they would not come get me if I ended up in jail. The pharmacy lady said she would bake me cookies and bring me Swedish Fish, however.

Then I ran into my neighbor from way, way up the street who I haven't seen in years. She said she didn't recognize me. She said, "Wow, you look like a

{ MiraLAX® Dissolves in Vodka, Ya Know }

Hollywood movie star, cha-cha-cha!" That made my day. (Or was it those tranquilizers I had already taken?)

So, here's the plane we all have to furiously pedal after the pilot hand-starts those propellers:

PROPS—YIKES.

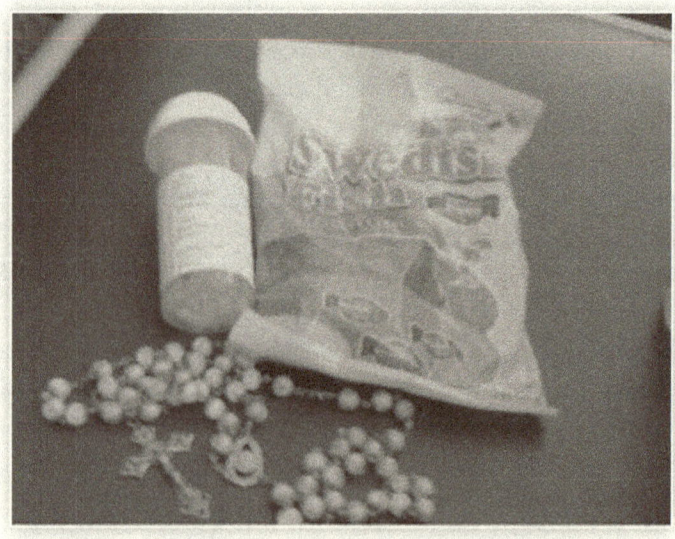

THIS IS MY FLIGHT PACKAGE. I DON'T PRAY, BUT IT'S MY NONNIE'S ROSARY, WHICH IS GOOD ENOUGH FOR ME.

Sarah Berardi

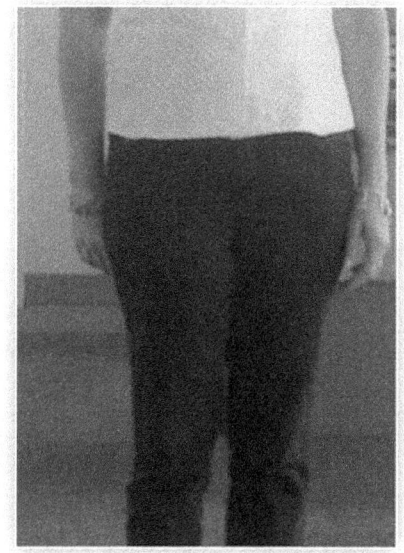

AND BEHIND THESE BLOBBY THIGHS ARE MY BIG-GIRL PANTIES.

bitsy Back Fat

I'm feeling better about my back fat today.

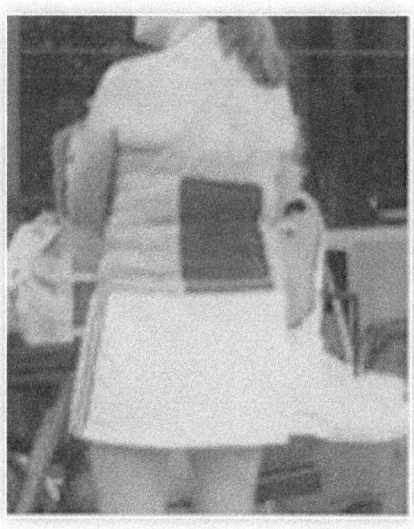

❦ MiraLAX® Dissolves in Vodka, Ya Know ❧

I may look like this, but I wouldn't let y'all *know* I look like this. My kids or husband would have kindly said, "Um, Mom, you've got back cleavage."
Cheers,
Skinnyback

Huh, Pardon Me, What?

I took a phone message for my "boss." (Technically I don't have a boss, as I'm a volunteer.) When she came back from lunch, I gave her the message that her brother, Bob, had called, and that he'd call her back later.

She: I don't have a brother Bob.
Me: Really? Darn it all, that's what I thought he said!
She: I don't have a brother Bob.
Me: Well, Bob's gonna call ya later.

This happens pretty much on a daily basis. I end up writing down the wrong phone number or the wrong name on the message sheets I give to people. I've taken to repeating the number to the person on the phone. This helps when I remember to do it. I'm always so overwhelmed and doing so many things at once, that I feel I can't waste the time to ask them if I have their bloody number or name correct. Guess I should swallow my pride and do it.

So I'm getting my hearing tested. But I really don't think it's a hearing issue. I think it's a concentration issue. I've already been tested for ADHD or ADD, whatever it was, and passed with incredibly flying colors. So what gives? Like I've said before, my medications make me dumber, but I hate to think I can't overcome it. (I don't have a prayer.)

So in order to avoid having a migraine every day, I have to look like a dummy?

OCT 2010

Irritable Bowel Syndrome

Mortified would be a good word. Or humiliated. Of course, it couldn't happen when the air conditioning was blowing loudly, the music was playing, the small group of people was singing, the video was playing, or any of the clapping was going on. Nope.

My stomach did its flip-flop and gurgle digestion oh so loudly when it was deathly quiet. But it didn't sound like my stomach, though I swear it was. It sounded as if I had passed gas.

This is where the mortification and humiliation comes in. I was in a church, but I did not pass gas in a pew. (I'm so funny.) As soon as it happened, I didn't move. I pretended it didn't happen. This sound was so loud it could have been heard clearly four pews up and back. I couldn't really shout, "I didn't pass gas, I have an irritable bowel." Or, "I didn't take my MiraLAX® today." Really embarrassing.

The Didgeridoo

I was introduced to one of the artists-in-residence at THWIV. He was adorable. The instrument he carried was obvious; I just couldn't pronounce its name. I had learned about this instrument previously in detail when an Australian teacher at the kids' primary school brought one in for class. So here's the conversation I had with this artist-in-residence:

Me: Oh, I know what that is in there! (It was in a case.) It's a jijijieroodoo.

Him (laughing): Yup, a didgeridoo.

Me: Yeah, that's what I said. Not many people know how to play that. You must be pretty talented. And it's so cool that you bring it here for the patients.

Him: Actually, not only do the patients like its sound, but it's been scientifically proven to build muscle strength in the back of the mouth, where some people have had surgery for esophageal cancer and such.

Me: You mean the palate that goes soft and causes sleep apnea? (Can you see where this is going?)

Him: Yes! I've even been teaching one of the doctor's wives how to play the didgeridoo to improve her sleep apnea to build her palate muscles up.

Me: No way!

I told him about the sleep apnea test Marty and I have coming up. (Mine is for migraines. I don't even know if I snore.) So we decided that when Marty and I check into our king-sized suite with room service and martinis for our test, we should also have a didgeridoo at our bedside.

I Am Not Out of Shape

After quitting my comeback to tennis this past summer due to two issues, I set out to learn just what was at the root of the two issues.

Issue 1: My coordination and eyesight were a little off. OK, maybe a bit more than "a little" off. As my degree from the U of Google leaves me with so many sources of information, I've come to the conclusion that my constant dizziness was exacerbated by the heat on the court while having to take my migraine pills. Plus, my progressive lenses make it a little difficult to find just which area of the stupid glasses I'm supposed to be looking out of exactly in order to focus on that *little* yellow ball. Know what I mean, progressive-lens wearers?

Sarah Berardi

Issue 2: I couldn't breathe. If Steve, the head tennis instructor I've had for years, didn't hit that *little* yellow ball straight to me, and I had to run to get it, we had to stop for a few minutes so I could catch my breath. This cut our hour-long lesson down to about twenty minutes of actual playing time.

So off I went to my beloved internist to find out why I couldn't play tennis or even get up the freakin' stairs without having to sit at the top to catch my breath. (At this point in our relationship, my doctor is well aware of my anxiety condition.) We acknowledged my asthma, but agreed this was different. He ordered a simple chest X-ray, then called and said they found a spot in the lung they wanted to check further with a CT scan. I wasn't worried at that point, thinking it was a dust bunny on the screen, on the film, or on something, but not on my lung.

I went for the CT scan. It came back with the same dust bunny. They decided it was possibly a piece of scar tissue left over from my spontaneously collapsed lung twenty years ago, which turned into pneumonia and an eleven-day stay in the hospital. Hmmm. They'd like to follow up with another CT in six months. Meanwhile, the internist sent me for a pulmonary function test and a cardio stress test. My pulmonary function came out on the low end of normal—but *normal*. The cardio stress test came out great! The fifty-year-old cardiologist (it was his birthday) said to me, "Well, your problem is not your heart. I think you're just out of shape." I turned my head with my bare boobs standing out all stuck with probes, and said straight to his face, "You should never, ever, tell a fifty-year-old woman who weighs under a hundred and thirty pounds that she is out of shape, got it?" He looked stunned and scared. He said meekly, "OK." Then I said, "Thank you, and happy birthday." I covered my boobs and left.

But they never told me why I can't breathe when I walk to the cafeteria from my office at THWIV. Or when I load the washer. Or walk up the stairs. Or when I laugh for more than ten seconds. I was convinced it was the calcium channel blocker I take every day for migraine prevention. I was also convinced it had nothing to do with how in- or out-of-shape I was.

So I started to worry about this damned dust bunny. Off I went to a pulmonologist. I told him what my cardiologist told me, and then I told him what I told the cardiologist. He laughed. After explaining everything on the CT so patiently to me, and *not* finding any dust bunnies that the radiologist had found, and examining me, he said, "Now, as for why you're having this persistent shortness of breath, please don't take offense…but you are just out of shape."

I burst out laughing and said, "You are a very brave man!" He laughed, and I said, "Do I *look* out of shape?" But before he could utter an answer, I quickly put up my pointer finger and said, "Wait, don't answer that, stop while you're behind." We got a good giggle about the whole thing. I thanked him for his time and his patience with my anxiety.

But here's the worst part. When all this started to happen with my shortness of breath, Chris and Marty kept telling me it was because I was out of shape. I told them if they *ever* told me that again I'd...I don't remember what it was, but it was scary enough to make them stop. Damn it, I hate it when Chris and Marty are right. Don't tell them. They won't read this.

I used to play tennis three or four times a week. Then I blew my shoulder out. So I swam every other day. Shoulder got worse. So I walked on an indoor track every other day. Then I got my shoulder fixed. Migraines set in. Surgeries, a few bouts of staying in bed for long periods of time, more surgeries, and voilà, I'm out of shape.

Damn, I hate it when Marty and Chris are right.

Flashback: No Whistling or Tickling, Please

There are quite a few triggers that immediately bring bile, fury, exasperation, etc., to me. Tickling and whistling are both triggers for me. Isn't that a bummer?

While most families enjoy a bit of good old-fashioned fun with a little sly tickling here and there, it's nightmarish to me. My father used to think he was oh so funny by tickling me to the point where I was laughing so hard that I couldn't catch my breath. His face betrayed his enjoyment of control. I would try to kick and writhe my way out of his grip, but to no avail.

So for something as simple as tickling, it's a shame it's never, ever been allowed in my house. Our kids have missed out on it. Or have they?

Whistling is another no-no in our house. When my father would start whistling, the rest of us (four kids and Mom) would look at each other with knowing, eyes wide, and run like the wind for cover. "Time for bed," we'd all say. "Lights out!" Because this meant he was on the warpath. He'd always whistle some song, "Living on Jacks and Queens." Marty tells me it was the theme song to *Maverick*. This meant he was in a good mood. But this good, drunken mood would change so fast, which was why we'd run for bed, even if it was just 7:00 p.m.

So you can imagine when I'm in a bookstore, the grocery store, THWIV, or the airport, and somebody starts whistling—I cringe. I think it's rude, actually. It's sort of like smoking in my space. Don't whistle in my space, man. You might even go so far as to say I flip out a little. If Chris, Sciencegirl, or Marty forget and give a little whistle, I scream, "WHAT ARE YOU DOING?" Then they feel awful. It's like fingernails on a chalkboard to me. You should pay attention while you're out and about. You'd be surprised how many people freakin' whistle. I think I actually hear it almost every day somewhere.

So while my warped father left me these things to remember him by, these freaky triggers, I have oh so many fun things for my kids to remember *me* by, right? I'm hoping the word *blog* will be a trigger for them. I have made them promise to read some funny ones at my eulogy (along with other specific directions, such as to bury me upside down so the world can kiss my ass).

I hope I haven't left them with any fingernails-on-the-chalkboard triggers. Hmmm. Scary thought. I think stromboli will haunt Chris forever. Or rolls of hockey tape. (I've been known to throw them at him in fits of anger.) Maybe my cupcake-with-a-bite-out-of-it hairdo (late '80s, early '90s that her friends mocked) will haunt Sciencegirl forever. Who knows?

But it won't be tickling, and it won't be whistling!

P.S. I was once so angry at a mouthy little Chris that I picked up the nearest thing to throw at him. It happened to be a well-done piece of homemade stromboli I had just pulled out of the oven.

Anointing

In THWIV, one of the priests (I call him "Priestieboy") was getting ready to go on his rounds, and asked me if I wanted to be anointed for the medicated migraine I've had for four or five days now (it's called "Anointing of the Sick"). FYI: Traditionally referred to as Extreme Unction of Last Rights, the sacrament of the Anointing of the Sick was previously most commonly administered to the dying for the remission of sins and the provision of spiritual strength and health. In modern times, however, its use has been expanded to all who are gravely ill or about to undergo a serious operation, and the church stresses a secondary effect of the sacrament: to help a person recover his health.

❧ MiraLAX® Dissolves in Vodka, Ya Know ❧

PHOTO COURTESY GETTY IMAGES

I said, "Sure, go for it." So he anointed me, and I felt pretty special for a bit, waiting for some sort of peace to come to my aching head—so special that I texted my girlfriend to tell her that Father had just anointed me. Knowing me as she does, she knew just how mind-blowing this whole thing was. I'd tried everything else to date, so why not this? What could it hurt, right?

But Father and I got the biggest laugh out her text back that said, "Are you sure it wasn't an exorcism?"

FYI, I double-checked with him. He promised me it was not. So I still have a little devil in me, thank goodness. Otherwise, what fun would life be?

Go Away

I was in one of my deep, dark-blue funks for about a week when one of my friends made me go out to dinner. I was already sitting outside the restaurant sipping my wine when I saw her walk up the sidewalk toward me with an awkwardly shaped bag.

She was laughing to herself all the way until she sat down and gave it to me. This was my gift:

She knows me well. She told me to use my imagination. I could use it anywhere—inside, outside, perhaps in front of my bedroom door, the front door, the back door, my office, hang it from my front bay window, duct-tape it to my rear window in the car—the possibilities are endless.

Valet Parking

I walked out yesterday afternoon from "work" and waved to the valet guys. This was the conversation that followed:

Me: Have a good night.
Valet guys: Hey, how come you not valetin' the car no more?
Me: The doctor says I'm out of shape. I'm walking until the snow flies.
Valet guys: No way, you's beautiful.
Me: Well, he's telling me to take the stairs and park my own car, because I can't breathe.
Valet guys: He crazy, man. Crazy.
Me: Don't think I didn't tell him that!

I walked over to the parking lot, walked up the stairs to the second floor of the ramp (OK, I rested a bit on the landing in between), walked to my car, and wheezed in. Blaaaaaaah. Apparently I *am* out of shape, as two doctors now say. Damn. I'm trying, but I miss my bed. I miss my bed. I miss my bed. I swear those dumb doctors are missing something. This isn't normal. Even one of my friends says I sound horrible when I try to breathe. She's heard me laugh and seen me walk like a five-hundred-pound lop arse gasping for air. Ask her. Mark my words. (And bury me upside down so those doctors can kiss my ass.)

Prepping for Sleep Study

So tonight Marty and I go to our sleep study test. We have separate rooms, despite my request for a king suite with room service that includes an extra-dry martini with an extra olive for my husband.

We are to come prepared, washed (with no products in our hair), comfortably attired, and ready to sleep. I've been told I'm not supposed to take my prescribed Xanax for my insomnia. Won't this be fun for them to watch on video? I'll be talking to them all night long on their video feed:

Me: I'm not asleep, nor have I any desire to sleep. Just so you know.
Them: Try to relax.
Me: R-I-G-H-T. That's my middle name.

I'll let you know the results upon hearing them. Mark my words, Marty has apnea, and I'm *perfect*.

{ Sarah Berardi }

Sleep Apnea Test

Sleep test night. When I checked us in, we all had a good laugh at my request for the king suite and room service. Marty was chivalrous and paid my co-pay. We trundled down the hall with our clipboards filled with eight pages of questions and accompanied by six other people. We were the only married couple there.

The paperwork we received in the mail for preparation said we could bring our own pillows if we wanted, and to bring comfy sleeping clothes and our regular nighttime medications.

We signed up for this test because I was convinced Marty had sleep apnea and wanted to rule out apnea for me as a source of my migraines. I had just recently read that some NFL football player whose name Chris and Marty can roll off their tongues was sidelined a good deal by debilitating migraines. They discovered that the source of his migraines was sleep apnea. So since I've been hounding Marty (snoreboy) forever to take the test, I decided we'd do it together. True love. Barf.

We started by filling out the questionnaire. Marty laughed at most of the questions, knowing how I would answer them. His answers were the exact opposite of mine in most instances. And his caffeine intake was the equivalent of my alcohol intake. So what? We each get through our day and relax a little differently, right?

Some of the questions included: Are you tired most of the day? Do you fall asleep when trying to read a book? Do you fall asleep when trying to watch TV? Do you struggle to stay awake after driving for short periods of time? Do you find yourself making odd mistakes, such as mixing chocolate with gravy? (Does putting the Windex in the fridge count?) Marty answered no to all of these. I had to answer yes to all of them.

The rooms were incredibly large and spotless. Each room included a bathroom with a shower and toiletries. Just like the Hilton. The nurse hooked Marty up first, so I sat cross-legged on his bed, watching (and maybe bouncing a little). I sent a picture to the kids of him all hooked up, and Sciencegirl replied, "I don't like it." Even I said it made him seem so vulnerable somehow. He just looked so pathetic, like one of those sad, droopy-eyed dogs with the long ears.

{ MiraLAX® Dissolves in Vodka, Ya Know }

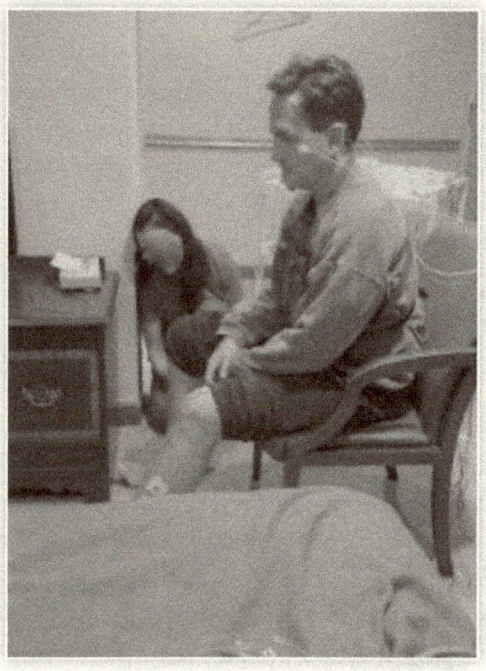

The nurse said it was my turn, Marty said good night to me (actually he said, "Get out"), and off I went for my hookup.

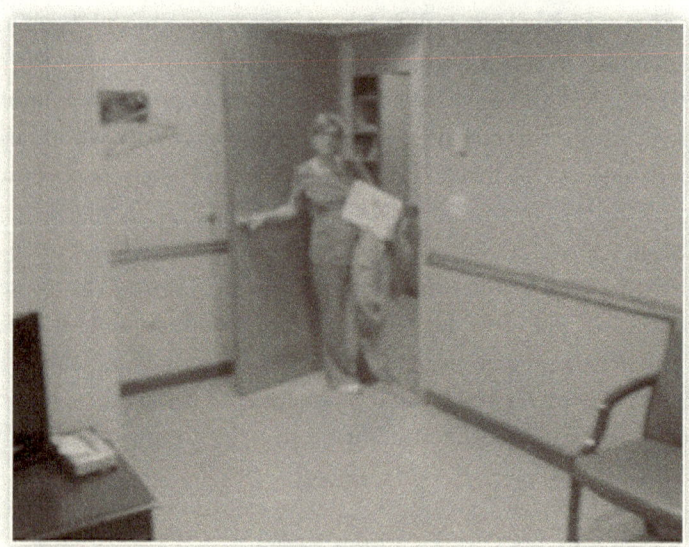

MARTY: "GET OUT."

ME: "WHAT, NO KISS?"

I talked to the nurse while she applied my things, and I warned her of my nocturnal outrages. She asked me a few more questions about how I beat my pillow or Marty, or stand up and appear to be air-boxing in my sleep (dreaming it's some dummkopf family member). She said, "Oh, that's RBD." I said I had heard of it, didn't feel like going into it with anyone at depth, and the doctors know about it. (That's a whole different blog.)

There was a TV and reading material in my room, but it was "lights out" after I read just three pages of my own book. They did a little testing through the monitor (they can see you and hear you the whole time).

There were no clocks in the room. When I asked why, the nurse said because the LED on the clocks actually has the same effect as a TV being on, and can wake you up. (Chris complained of this constantly growing up, and I never believed him. Don't tell him he was right. Since he doesn't read this blog often enough, it's his loss.)

She told us both that if someone clearly had apnea, they would be in during the night to apply the mask. I was sure Marty would have the mask applied in his room next door. She said it's normal for people to stop breathing a few times during the night, but insurance sets the limit at fifteen times—that's what determines that you officially and clearly have apnea and require a mask. Good old health insurance people. Sometimes you come up borderline, and it's up to your doctor to interpret the results to see if you need a do-over.

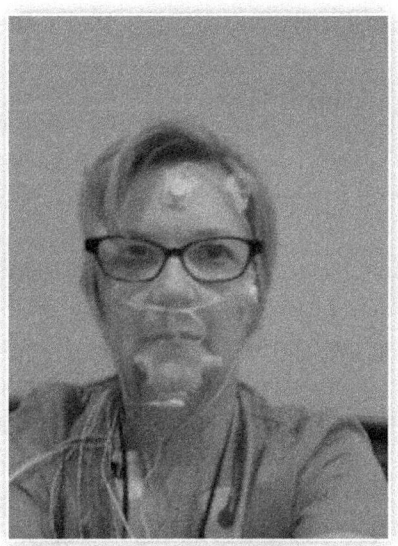

I AM BEAUTIFUL, NO MATTER WHAT THEY SAY

❦ MiraLAX® Dissolves in Vodka, Ya Know ❦

(Those are lyrics from Christina Aguilera that are up on my fridge.)

Part of the test requires you to sleep for a bit on your back. I'm not a back-sleeper, but I decided to try to start out that way. All of a sudden I woke myself up *snoring*. I said out loud, "Crap, you caught me! Don't tell my husband!" She didn't say anything back, not wanting to wake me up fully, I suspect. I quickly rolled over. Then my next wake-up, I had to visit the ladies' room. I simply said, "Laurie, I have to use the loo now, sorry." She came in and unhooked me, I went, and she hooked me back up. Marty said he heard me closing my bathroom door through the wall, knowing it was my once-per-night wee time. See how he loves me?

Upon wake-up time for me, I quickly said, "Did Marty need the mask during the night?" She said he didn't. I was flabbergasted. But she added that it was a close call. The doctor would have to interpret the results, and he'd probably have to come back for another study. I said, "YES, I knew I was (almost) right."

Then she said, "Same with you." *What?* She laughed and said she might be seeing us both again, depending on what the doctor said. I'm actually excited. If they could find anything else to help my migraines, I'll do anything. She then said that Marty asked her if I woke up before him. She replied that I did not. He then forewarned her that I could be pretty scary in the morning. Humph. He's right, though.

Nightmare on (an) Elm(a) Street

Last night I pulled a "Jae Ruth" on Marty. I don't know how or why he stays with me. You'll have to go back and find one of my "Flashback" entries to refresh your memory.

My family and friends, and most of my blog followers (who are the same, in most cases, though I know I have others, thank you! I'm still around fifty-eight people reading. This is why my kids can't stand me telling a story. I digress all the time.) know that I have nightmares. Well, they're more than nightmares, as I told you in my "sleep apnea" blog as well. I act out my dreams sometimes, scarily so.

The last few days, these nightmares have come back with a vengeance, and I can't figure out why. As usual, I'm trying to find the trigger: particular stress (Who, me? Anxiety for no reason?), medication change, migraine, didn't like my waiter for the evening, whatever. I can't pinpoint it.

❧ Sarah Berardi ❧

A few nights ago, I stood up, jumped out of bed (this is the first time I've gotten out of bed to fight; I usually stay in bed) and punched the air with all my might. It just so happened I was punching toward the window, which was a short ten or twelve inches away, when I woke up with Marty saying, "What's going on?" The poor guy. He comes home jet-lagged, not knowing what the hell country he's in, and I'm in the middle of combat.

Then last night, I was dreaming of another dumb family member—she might be a putz—and Marty said I was violently punching the pillow, up on one elbow pummeling it. When Marty tried to grip both my arms to stop me, I felt a human arm, his forearm, and bit down on it like a well-seasoned turkey drumstick. Good old Jae Ruth.

Halfway through my bite, I woke up, realizing I was biting Marty's forearm. I realized this because he was saying, "Owww! You're biting me!"

Like Sciencegirl says, "We are a family of genetic freaks, Mom." Don't you feel sorry for my husband? I do.

So I called up Libbylicious, who I'm rooming with in New York City next week, and told her to bring her body armor. She said she'd bring her boxing gloves as well. She felt confident she could take me. She said one punch to my head, and I wouldn't wake up till morning. God love her. She is brave.

❡ MiraLAX® Dissolves in Vodka, Ya Know ❡

http://abcnews.go.com/Technology/Sleep/violent-dreams-precede-brain-disease/story?id=11326759

GREAT. JUST GREAT.

Sleep Apnea Test Results

We don't have it! But we were both borderline. The doctor said I usually stopped breathing five times per hour; Marty sometimes went to seven times per hour. He also said that we were both better when sleeping on our sides, which is normal.

But Marty is only a little better on his side, I know this from experience. He needs to lie on his stomach. And don't think I don't poke him in that direction every time he shifts out of it.

So, we have at least ruled out apnea as a migraine trigger. So the conclusion stands that I have migraines because of barometric pressure sensitivities, some food triggers, and alas, premenopause. (Who doesn't fit this category?) Lord, help us all ride this wave, because it has whitecaps, baby.

At the last minute, the doctor said, "Oh, they did have one recommendation."

"Oh, great, what was that?" I was eager to find out.

"They suggested you lose some weight."

My chin dropped. He started to laugh at my dropped chin. I asked him if he was pulling my leg. He said he was not, and quickly explained through his laughter that it's pretty much their standard answer. Now, I don't like putting this out there to the general public, but I just fit into my size four pantsuit (so what if I couldn't sit well or breathe, that's not important), and I'm supposed to lose weight? I've been accused of being underweight my whole life up until two years ago, now I have to lose it? You know what I say: eat shit.

I was flabbergasted at the recommendation. My neurologist knows how sensitive I am about my weight. (One time I had to go see him, as my forehead had caved in above my eyebrow due to a nerve block for my migraines, and he jokingly said, "I could always fill it in with some fat from your belly.") And I've also asked him *every* time he gives me a new scrip if it will make me gain weight. So he knew I'd blow a gasket at this, and was sort of enjoying my flip-out.

I already eat about five calories a day. It's that stupid exercise/out-of-shape thing they're all hung up about. Buttheads.

Cheers in snoring. It was worth the blog fodder. And Marty is happily sleeping soundly next to me (snoring), on his stomach. AARRRGGGH. That's what my earplugs are for! Actually, I'm headed for Sciencegirl's empty room.

I'm Seeing Letterman, Finally

I'm going to *Letterman* tonight, finally! After years of me and Libbylicious (yes, that's the correct grammar) trying to get in for free, and getting oh so close, oh so many times, we are finally going, but at a price.

Marty got them at an auction for me, since he said he was tired of hearing me piss and moan about not getting to see the *Letterman* show. He ended up paying *way* too much for them, but I was happy, and nothing but the best for me, right?

We will be in the first row of the balcony, VIP seats. If you ask me, VIP seats should be right up front, in the first row, as in I-can-see-them-spit-when-they-talk close, *not* in the flippin' balcony. I think I got ripped off, man.

Then we're off to see Al Pacino in *The Merchant of Venice* on Broadway.

What could be better? Well, a martini in the middle of the two, of course.

Apparently, Will Farrell is going to be Letterman's guest. Love him. Especially his *SNL* skit in his undies.

So I've been conceptualizing ("thinking up," Goose) ways to get on national TV. One of our deacons at THWIV suggested that I tell the people who let us into the VIP area how much I paid for these *free* tickets, and Letterman may just say, "Hey, say hello to the idiots up there who paid three thousand dollars for these free tickets." Where does this eighty-three-year-old deacon get his sense of humor? (I love him.) Besides, I said I wasn't the idiot who bought them; my dear husband bought them for me, because he *loves* me.

Chris suggested I tell them I have a stupid pet trick and start practicing (as being the stupid pet). Funny guy, huh? Chris also suggested I buff up on my cuts of meat.

My nephew, Andrew, said I don't have to be *on* TV for him to see; he will be able to hear me laugh.

Broadway Shows

Okeydokey, now for the Broadway blog. We saw two shows. We saw Al Pacino in *The Merchant of Venice* and then we saw *Next to Normal*, where I didn't recognize any of the actors.

The Merchant of Venice didn't start out so great. Libby couldn't find the tickets she had purchased. "No biggie, just go downstairs to the lobby and reprint them while I open us a bottle of wine," I calmly suggested. We had both just showered and were lounging in our fancy bathrobes supplied by the hotel. So she pulled on her jeans and a top and went downstairs. It was 6:00 p.m.

She burst back into our room to find me and the housekeeper desperately trying to get the damned cork out of the bottle of wine. She screamed, "Holy crap, the show starts at seven p.m., not eight like all the other million Broadway shows I've been to!"

The first thing out of my mouth to the housekeeper was, "We'll still need the wine!" She popped the cork (that was the weirdest corkscrew I've ever seen). I slipped her a nice tip, gave her a hug, and shoved her out the door. We were all laughing. Libby and I knew we'd never have time to dry our hair, put on makeup, dress properly, blah, blah, blah. So I said, "Just give your hair a quick blow-dry, throw on a dress and shoes, throw your makeup in your purse, and we'll get a cab or limo. We won't have time to walk."

We breathlessly arrived in front of our doorman, spitting out, "We're trying to make a seven o'clock show. What can you get us? *Now.*" He pointed at a limo sitting in front of us. I said we'd take it, and in we went. We were so busy laughing with the limo driver about our hustle to get out the door, we forgot to put on the makeup that we'd hastily thrown into our purses.

We arrived while others were still being seated. Phew. With five minutes to spare, actually. So we settled into our seats, took a picture of ourselves to remember the moment without our hair done properly and no makeup, and went through our purses to turn off our cell phones and get tissues, cough drops, etc. (All things you never do during a show—we're not ignorant of the rules.)

All of sudden I felt a tap on my shoulder. I exhaustedly turned around and politely said, "Yes?" The biatch said, "Could you please be quiet?" WTF? The show hadn't even started yet. I wasn't being loud. Libby would have told me to shut up if I was.

{ Sarah Berardi }

SEE THE BIATCH BEHIND US? THAT'S HER. BUT DOESN'T MY SKIN LOOK GREAT? YEAH, SO DOES LIBBYLICIOUS'S, I GUESS. REMEMBER—NO MAKEUP OR HAIR STYLING.

I replied, "Oh, I'm so sorry!" So, all through the whole show, every time someone coughed, looked through her purse (a huge no-no), talked with someone, made any noise whatsoever, I childishly turned around and kindly said to the biatch, "Could you please tell them to quiet down?"

I am the mother of all grudge holders.

Al Pacino was just OK. It was a little difficult to hear the actors sometimes. Maybe they were speaking in that one tone that's at the lowest end of normal on my hearing test. After the show, I stood outside like a moron and snapped a pic of the back of Al Pacino's head as he got into his limo.

I wish Libby and I had been wearing these shirts when that woman tapped me on the shoulder.

❦ MiraLAX® Dissolves in Vodka, Ya Know ❧

KIND OF SAYS IT ALL. THE SHIRTS SAY: I'M BUSY, YOU'RE UGLY, HAVE A NICE DAY, AND I HATE YOU.

The other show we saw was *Next to Normal*. It's about a dysfunctional family. I love, love, love dark, depressive, moody, sad things. I cried, OK? Big heaving sobs, all through the play. So did the unknown lady next to me. Libbylicious had seen it before, so she had done most of her crying then, I assume. The lady next to me never looked at me, but handed me a tissue while we both cried. Then later, I did the same for her and Lib. At the end of the show, I hugged her. She was a stranger, but now a kindred soul.

NOV 2010

Go Vote?

I learned a lot from Supreme Court Justice Roberts the other night when he was at Canisius College. He shared with us that during his recent trip to Australia, he learned that citizens who did not vote are fined! (Sounds like when we lived in Germany, where you were taxed for being Catholic, having a TV, etc.)

While I'm quite happy I won't be fined if I don't go vote, I still find myself in a conundrum about the race for governor of New York State. I do not want to vote for either of the candidates.

I know people have fought for my right to vote. But as Marty pointed out, they fought for my right to decide whether or not I want to vote. I want to vote. So, when presented with this problem, as I was during the last presidential race, the only clear-cut answer to me is this: I should be the governor of New York State. I think I'll have to write my name on the ballot.

Change Your Damn Clocks

I've had how many days now—five? six?—to adjust my clock in the new car to the time change. So far all I've managed to do is set some type of alarm that goes off whenever I go over the whopping speed of...wait for it...one mile per hour. Therefore, it goes off at every stop sign, red light, start up, you name it. No idea how I did that. It goes, "bleep, bleep, bleep, bleep, bleep, bleep, bleep, bleep." Yay, me.

I managed to find the cruise control I've been looking for, though.

I just don't have time to get the book out and interpret the misinterpretation of the German into English. I would probably understand the regular old German better.

Now it's become a challenge to me, to figure out how to do it without reading the book. Damn.

I Passed That Damn NY State Bar Exam

Oh, wait, Chris (now to be known as Lawyerboy) did! I have to say that Marty and I have never, *ever* seen him work as hard as he worked in the last three years. Especially during the six weeks of prep for the damn bar. He studied at our house every day for about fifteen hours a day for two weeks straight after his four-week course of prep, when he continued to study at his house after the class each day. That seems like a run-on sentence, but it's not—it just shows how many hours he put in. He needed more room to spread out than he had at his house. And spread out he did.

I SAW THIS IDEA ON SEASON THREE OF *THE BACHELORETTE*—USING THE POSTER PAPER.
(THIS IS IN HIS HOUSE, STUDY PLACE #1)

{ Sarah Berardi }

HIS HOUSE

❧ MiraLAX® Dissolves in Vodka, Ya Know ☙

IN MY BASEMENT, STUDY PLACE #2

THEY WERE ALL OVER THE BASEMENT WALLS

Sarah Berardi

"my brain is fried"

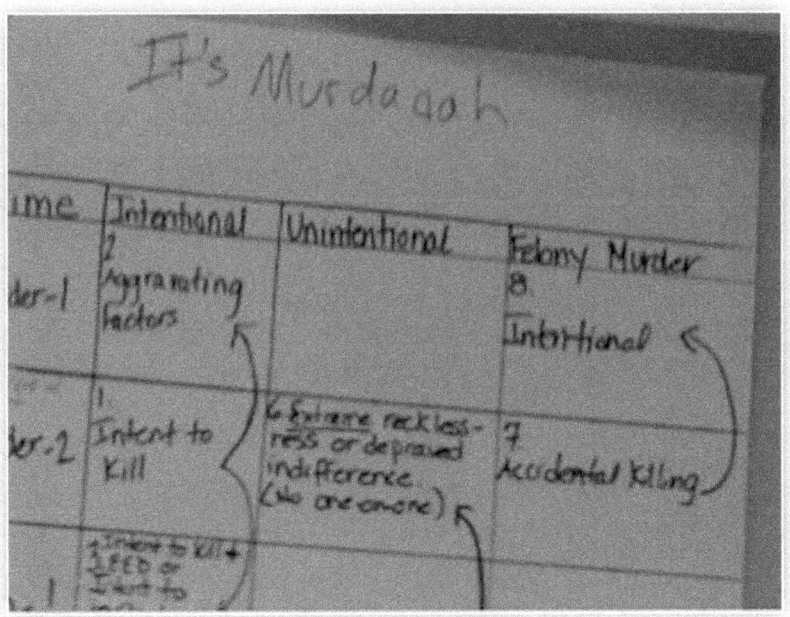

STRATEGICALLY PLACED NOTES

❧ MiraLAX® Dissolves in Vodka, Ya Know ❧

CHANGE OF SCENERY AND SOME CAFFEINE

Sarah Berardi

I FED HIM, DO YOU HEAR ME? I FED HIM.
LOOK AT THAT FRIDGE! MARTY LOVED HAVING CHRIS STUDYING
AT OUR HOUSE SO HE HAD FOOD IN THE HOUSE.

I hugged my boy good luck on the day before the exam. I told him I loved him and that I didn't care if he passed or failed, since I saw with my own eyes that he couldn't have worked any harder. I knew he had done his best already. (For cripes sake, he even went to bed each night with tapes of his lessons playing in his earbuds.) I loaded him up with groceries for the next two days. (Just light snacks, no heavy meals. I researched what one should eat, since I'm perfect.) He was staying in a local hotel where the bar exam was being administered to avoid any stressful drives, car accidents, etc. (It's highly recommended one does this.) When I got home from THWIV that day, I saw this in our usual spot on the kitchen floor where we leave notes for each other:

❧ MiraLAX® Dissolves in Vodka, Ya Know ❧

I shall frame that.

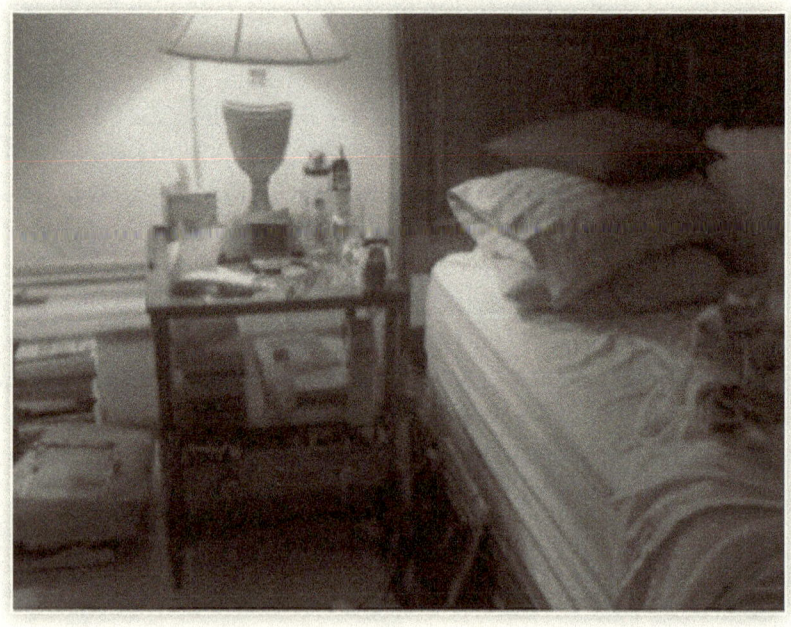

WE WAIT, WAIT, AND WAIT FOR FIVE LONG MONTHS FOR RESULTS
(YOU KNOW WHAT A PATIENT PERSON I AM. EVERY SINGLE GIRLFRIEND WORRIED WITH ME.)

❧ Sarah Berardi ❧

THIS IS THE LOOK OF RELIEF

I rest my case.

DEC 2010

December in General

I am Scrooge. I do not care for Christmas. I will take a break. I am grumpy. I get a little depressed now and then.

Friends Can Warm Your Heart

No, I'm not "back." Just had sort of a good day.

Good days always have something to do with friends, right? I met up with friends from my kids' old school, which they attended from grades five through twelve. It was the holiday concert, which I've loved and attended for fourteen years now, I think. And there was my Mr. Max, with all his Russian ethnicity pouring out that I love. You keep laughing, Lawyerboy and Sciencegirl. I'm hiring him to play at your weddings, if/when those ever happen. (Lawyerboy, remember, you are not allowed to spawn.)

Soon after I gave a few hugs to some parents and teachers I haven't seen in a while, I settled into my seat next to my friends to ready for the concert. A tap on my shoulder from behind took my attention from the program to the

MiraLAX® Dissolves in Vodka, Ya Know

mop-headed fifth-grader behind me. "Could you move over because I can't see, Big Head Elaine?"

Actually, my "lunch friend" said he didn't say that last part—"Big Head" or "Elaine." But I swear I heard it (for you *Seinfeld* fans). Thank goodness there were no pigeons flying loose in the room.

I replied, "Oh, I'm so sorry, are you telling me I have a big head?"

He said, "Maybe."

As far as this adorable kid being disrespectful, he really wasn't. I needed the little grin he had on his face. He was bantering with me. So I just went with it, stuck my tongue out at him, and said, "Fine." I moved over a seat, now sitting alone, not next to my friends anymore.

Every now and then, I turned back to mop-head boy and asked if he could see OK, to which he always replied, "Yup."

Then it came time for him to go up for his performance with the middle-school group to sing. I knew he was going up to stand on those high risers because I heard him complaining to his friend. I, therefore, mocked him a bit (boys rarely like chorus), and he complained that he was even in the front row. I told him I'd be watching him. And so I did. I caught my newfound friend's eye from afar, waved at him, and got the cutest embarrassed smile out of him during his singing that made my day. Never got his name, but loved him for warming my heart for the first time in two months or so.

It was downhill after that, unfortunately. I went to pick up my leather purse from the shoe repair and proudly slapped down my repair ticket on the counter (I rarely still have any ticket for pickup when required). The woman behind the counter said, "That's not our ticket stub, this is a parking stub for Pearl Street in the city."

Need a drink. Still riding this wave. The premenopausal wave.

Someone please come help me pick up my house, put away my dry cleaning, do my overflowing laundry, vacuum the rug where I wrapped, pick up my catering, buy me more vodka (for our very little party tomorrow), go through a week's worth of mail, read three weeks of beloved magazines, fix my incorrect insurance bills, and get four hours of sleep a night for me? It would help a little. If you were my real friends, you would, you know. How did I get so far behind? I used to be called "Patty Perfect." I'm out of control.

Family Can Suck

Dysfunctional. That should have been my maiden name. Sarah Dysfunctional. I don't choose to hang out with or befriend certain types of people, so it makes it extra hard when those same type of people are related to me.

A family member actually stood in my den and "whispered" into her cell phone about me, in *front* of me. No, she wasn't sixteen at the time, she was pretty close to my own age. Then she proceeded to have a temper tantrum since I called her out on it.

Another family member, he called the local sheriff. He asked the local sheriff to give me a "warning call." I told the clay-brained sheriff during that phone call that if he couldn't see right from wrong I wondered how he slept at night, and he could feel free to come arrest me. I would bring a big, thick Dickens book to read while sitting in my jail cell. The world is black and white to me, there is no gray.

Family can suck.

Meet My Dog Spot

I thought I should introduce you to my dog. Spot is the best; he doesn't bark, chew, jump, shed, pee, poop, or bite. You just have to dust him now and then.

Just about every year since the kids were born, we've had one of those photo Christmas cards. Spot's been in almost all of them. In the event we didn't have Spot with us, I would make sixty copies of him, cut him out, and tape him onto each picture card. I would sit at the kitchen table and laugh out loud (all by myself) while doing this. (Again, I crack myself up.) I also sign these cards, "Love, The Griswolds," instead of, "Love, The Berardis."

One year someone asked us, "How do you get Spot to always be in the same position every year?" We do try to get creative with him. We put hats on him, necklaces, pose him lovingly between us.

Spot never gets carsick. He's a very good traveler and loves sticking his head out the window in the wind, like most dogs.

So here's a pic of Spot, who is patiently sitting here next to me as I type, waiting for a few pats on the head.

{ MiraLAX® Dissolves in Vodka, Ya Know }

My Dog Spot At Christmas

Christmastime and all its chores always put me in a deep, dark-blue funk. One of the things I look forward to the least is choosing the type of picture I'd like for our Christmas card. I usually put a great deal of thought into them. This year was no different. Since we have all gone our separate ways—I'm empty nested, remember—I thought I'd be the only one on the card again this year, along with Spot, of course. (I've done this before instead of fighting to get the family all in town at the same time—it was funny. Plus, the kids aren't so keen on still appearing in the family Christmas card.)

So I called Goose after two days of brainstorming. She was game to come with me and fulfill my Christmas card caper. I rolled out of bed, splashed some water on my face, put on some "Endora-type" makeup, jewels, and gown, strapped Spot into the car, and off we went to the nearest mall to see Santa. Goose met us at the mall. Spot was so thrilled for his car ride. He *loves* car rides. But he does *not* like to get his feet wet, therefore:

{ Sarah Berardi }

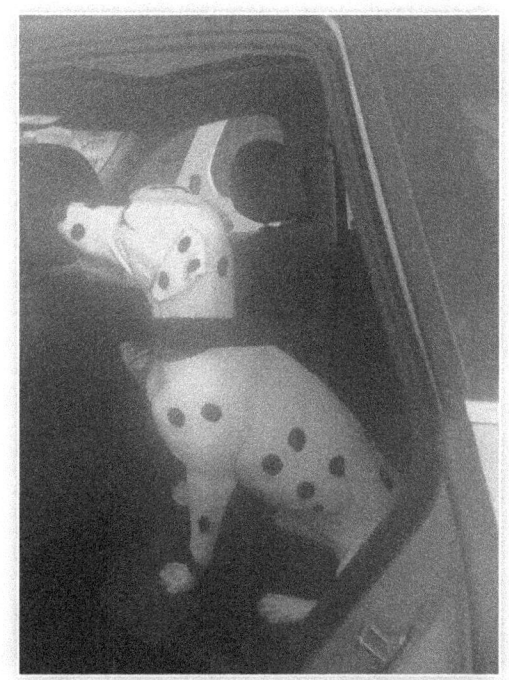

MiraLAX® Dissolves in Vodka, Ya Know

Our first stop in the mall was Tuxedo Junction to get him fitted for a nice Christmassy-themed bow tie. Then off we went to stand in line to sit with Santa for our picture. As I changed from my boots to silver pumps, the family after us asked if there was a story involved in what I was doing. (This question was based simply on my ball gown, I surmise, since Goose was busy fixing Spot's bow tie so that they hadn't seen him yet.) I explained that it was tradition to have our annual Christmas card sent out with our dog, Spot, in it, and despite the fact that the kids had flown the coop, I refused to give up the tradition. They thought it was a great idea and pitched in to help. Here are the results of one of the tartiest holiday scrooges you'll ever see on a Christmas card.

OUR CHRISTMAS CARD THIS YEAR

Just me and Spot. Lawyerboy said I look tarty here. No, I don't, but Spot does, a little.

Disclaimer: My attorney and others have asked us how we get Spot to be in the same position every single time. Please tell me you *know* Spot is a statue? If you don't know, does it make the story funnier, now?

Christmas Is Almost Over

In a short three days or so, Scroogie McScrooge (me), can put another year away, thankfully. Usually my tree is down by now (it's almost midnight Christmas Day), along with all decorations. We put so few out this year—Marty put them out—that it will be simple to put them back.

As I ponder why Christmas is so horrible for me (that's a whole different book), I realize one of the biggest things has always been the returns I've had to make to keep everyone bloody well happy. But I think I've got the sizes down now, as well as the likes and dislikes. Or maybe I just have the, "Screw you, it's the thought that counts," down now.

Recognition

I've heard it twice now, so I know it's true. Lawyerboy said to me not long ago:

Lawyerboy: I just figured out that you always tricked Sciencegirl and me when we were young with those fun toys that were actually educational.

Me: Yup.

And today LB said:

Lawyerboy: Hey, Nick and I were just talking. Remember those books we published when we were in primary school?

Me: Yeah?

Lawyerboy: Didn't you have some part in that whole project?

Me: Yeah, I typed up a bunch of them, and I even had to go to the Poconos for some New York State school conference. I presented our little book publishing caper to New York State people with the other moms at our school to show how we put the books together after the kids wrote their stories. I remember it clearly, as I had panic attacks about it daily until the day I got back home.

❦   MiraLAX® Dissolves in Vodka, Ya Know   ❧

Lawyerboy: Nick and I just figured out that that was a great idea you moms had, making us learn to write and want to publish our own book. What a caper that was. You tricked us way back then.

Me: Yup.

Ta-da! Moms' jobs well done. Mission accomplished. I just love it when a kid realizes that his mom might have a clue.

JAN 2011

What Do You Do?

Marty came into THWIV today to meet my office mates. He got into a discussion with one guy about my messy desk at home. After they talked a bit, the guy asked Marty, "What does she do at home to warrant a messy desk? She hires out for *everything*."

This made me think. Yes, I can think. Screw you all, I can, indeed, think. It's just a little slow (due to medications, of course). I wasn't always this way. (No, I was not, Lawyerboy.)

So in essence, I don't know what the hell I do. I keep track of the four travelers in our family, whose trips are actually numerous. I take care of health insurance for three of us, which is always wrong and which needs constant—need I repeat, constant—correction (meaning I have to fax over a receipt showing I paid for something they are trying to bill me for). I do the stupid old mail (once a week). I get a gazillion bits of mail that I have to sift through for my husband who's on lots of mailing lists that I have to screen. Then, of course, I screen the mail I get for the kids. I pay our bills, I keep our social calendar—HA! Mind you, this is what you all do at your desks.

I have the following projects on my desk:

Order a new vacuum filter thingy.

MiraLAX® Dissolves in Vodka, Ya Know

Find in my pile the paint chips Joanne the Decorator ordered for me.

Find in my pile my Lady Gaga tickets.

Track down those free certificates from American Express points promised to me last week for my free rental car.

Get a guest membership from our insurance for my twenty-four-year-old. Pain in the ass. Should be simple, but it's not.

Find a place to file away my new scrapbooking hobby. Stop laughing! I made the best scrapbook for Lib from our New York City trips. I giggled and got teary-eyed making it—maybe it was the wine? The "place" will probably be the trash. It wasn't that good.

Collect all my blogs/articles/published stuff into one file for my class in New York City.

File away my THWIV stuff.

Keep a dedicated file on apartments for rent in the next town over for a friend. Y'all know I'm a little obsessive, so this is a bit time-consuming. I have lots of clippings.

Make sense of my "planning small" dinner party in February. In other words, start planning.

Find someone to come fix Marty's wine fridge.

Arrange two maintenance things to be done in Virginia while I'm there for Sciencegirl. That's what a mother is for when her kid is a busy student.

Keep our personal medical files up-to-date. Never-ending. Sorry, I'm a genetic freak. Therefore...well, genetic freakdom manifests genetic freakdom. It's a little overwhelming.

My blog. When the funny bone ain't broken.

Peruse my many magazine subscriptions to read later: *New York, Psychology Today, Spree, The New Yorker, Time, Newsweek*, as well as the numerous catalogs I get to keep up on the latest fashions. I'd never go out without the latest fashions. Unless I'm migrained.

Look up and research things I've ripped out of my magazines that I'm curious about. This can take me hours. I am a virtual wealth of half-assed information.

Type up a new Christmas card address list, as I've been using bits of paper as a list for about five years now.

Collect the tax info and get everything ready for our accountant.

Sync calendars.

E-mail, obviously. This takes up an enormous amount of time.

Shop online. Just about all my shopping is done online, even my groceries. Therefore, I sit here, at my desk.

{ Sarah Berardi }

So those are the things I do at my bloody desk, damn it. And as I re-read this list, I do nothing to warrant a messy desk. I think it's just that I'm not home very much to do anything with the papers that get piled up. (I am at THWIV forty hours a week, so *there*.) So I guess, in essence, that is my answer, after all that justifying. And I'm sure as I head off to bed now, I'll come up with a few more things that I forgot to put on my list.

But now I'm clearly exhausted and must go change my grody sheets and pick up my latest book for a continued read. I feel better, though—a bit more justified for having a messy desk.

What Does My Sciencegirl Do?

Since you've seen Lawyerboy pass the bar, you have to read about Andrea, my Sciencegirl. She's getting her PhD in biology, studying evolutionary ecology (I think), which puts her in places that are not glamorous but where she needs hats with bug netting, lots of bug repellant, and lots of antihistamines on hot days. I think. I'm not really all that clear on *exactly* what she does (but I try to get it; with my PhD from U of Google I should be getting it.) She's my little lovey. She also does not want to be in this book.

Accessorizing Is Important

My friend, Geraldine, and I chat every day at THWIV. Today she noticed my earrings, necklace, and belt that matched. She said, "I like your accessorizing. You are *one jazzy white girl!*"

Made my day.

Nurse Mommy

I flew to Sciencegirl's on my broomstick Sunday night for some surgery she's having. This is how Nurse Mommy arrived:

Sarah Berardi

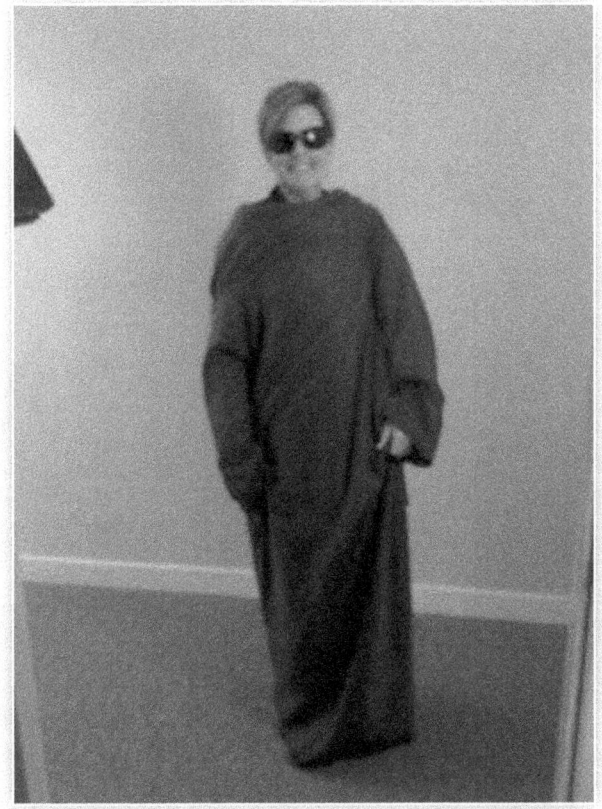

WRAPPED IN A BRAND-NEW SNUGGIE® FOR THE PATIENT

Today I thought of a quote I read somewhere about how when you travel and forget your magnifying mirror to apply makeup, you end up walking around all day looking like Catwoman. That's what I have a feeling I look like today. Apparently, Hilton Honors Points won't get me a magnifying mirror like they get me a *USA Today* waiting for me at the door each morning.

Watch Your Step

While Marty was in the airport, he went to the men's room and did his duty. After washing his hands, he wadded up the paper towel he used to dry his hands, and from about ten feet away, threw it toward the garbage can.

❦ MiraLAX® Dissolves in Vodka, Ya Know ❧

As it was in midair, a Buddhist in full orange garb came around the corner, and the wet, wadded paper towel smacked him right in the face. He stood there, startled, and just started moving forward again toward the urinals. Marty apologized profusely, but the monk seemed pretty stunned. So Marty just picked up the paper towel (it was going to go in, he swears), and left.

He laughed the whole way down to his gate. Out loud.

Just Call Me "Zippy"

Flew home today. Marty was waiting for me at the airport. He insisted on dropping me off and picking me up. That's new—kind of nice, huh? While I was in Virginia, I rented a Ford Focus. I *loved* it! I was zippin' here, zippin' there. My car at home now seems so damned big. No zippin' in my current monster. But of course, I worried about my safety in the Focus, as I need airbags in every orifice, and every safety system ever invented built into whatever car I have. But I sure felt zippy in that Focus. As a matter of fact, as I zipped out of Sciencegirl's driveway, this is what was staring at me:

The infamous sneakers on the telephone wires! (They were boat shoes, actually. It's a preppy university town.) Crikey. My kids *cannot* get away from them. Though I suppose you'll find these in every university town, right? Jeez, Louise. (Remember my past post about when Lawyerboy was living in New York in a drug-ridden area where he needed to carry a hand cannon? There were the infamous sneakers hanging out there as well.)

Then, while boarding one of my planes today, a woman called out, "Ma'am. Ma'am? Ma'am!" I turned around to look for the stupid woman who was not hearing the other woman call out to her. The stupid woman was me. She held out the magazine I had dropped. I apologized by explaining I wasn't used to being called "ma'am" yet, and that I preferred "miss." She said, "How about 'Hey, lady'?" Everyone in the line laughed. I said, *"Fine."*

As Seen on TV

Libbylicious and I usually send each other gag gifts for birthdays and Christmas, something to make us laugh. We don't set out to find something, we just know when we see it that it has to be purchased and gifted. We wait with bated breath to call each other and laugh hysterically about the gifts we've just received. (Yes, *bated* is correct, versus *baited*.)

This year, Sciencegirl, her boyfriend, and I were sitting at the kitchen table when I said, "Oh, this is from Libby. Sit here with me, it should be good." Well, that flat-bellied, no-whiskered, non-Freddy Fat Chinned girlfriend of mine sent these things:

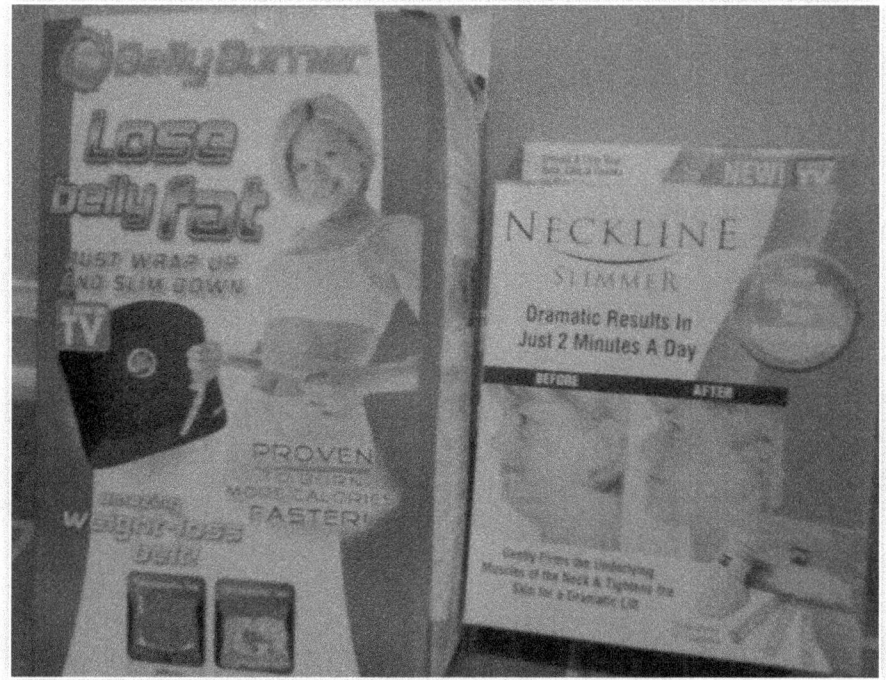

We all burst out laughing. (In fact, I'm wearing the Belly Burner now while watching TV in bed. We all tried the Neckline Slimmer. It hurt Sciencegirl's TMJ for about four days—*thanks*, Libby. Maybe I could get Lawyerboy to sue for that. They should have a warning label on it, don't you think? "Could damage TMJ further." Hey, I'm just watching out for y'all.

She gave me a few other things, which I already had and are a little too naughty to post. Humph. Let's just say there were some "holder uppers" and "cover uppers."

He Thought "Manual Labor" Was a Taco Chain

On a recent Sunday morning after about eight inches of snow, neither Marty nor I had bothered to shovel the walk. His back is touchy, and I'm...um...lazy. There's no need for anyone to use it. I have a large delivery box out by the garage, so people can use that if needed. We just hadn't given it a second thought.

Marty was up reading his paper early Sunday morning. I still dozed half-heartedly in bed around 9:30 a.m. We were expecting Lawyerboy to come over

MiraLAX® Dissolves in Vodka, Ya Know

some time in the morning, but weren't sure when. Suddenly we started hearing a very loud, screechy, fingernails-on-a-chalkboard noise every five seconds or so. I got out of bed and asked Marty, "What the hell is that noise?"

"I don't know," he said. We opened the front door, peered out into the bright snow, and saw this:

We were stunned! We looked at each other, then back at him, and Marty said, "What the hell are you doing? For years we cajoled you, bribed you, paid you, threatened you, grounded you, you name it, to shovel that damned sidewalk. Now you're doing it?"

Lawyerboy yelled back, "Well, I know it's a liability now. You could be sued."

Sarah Berardi

Great to have a Lawyerboy in the family. He shovels your sidewalk for you. Didn't cost us a dime, just seven years of college and grad school.

But at the end of the day, the exertion ended up being a bit too much for him, and someone had surreptitiously borrowed my Snuggie.

I Am an Office Problem

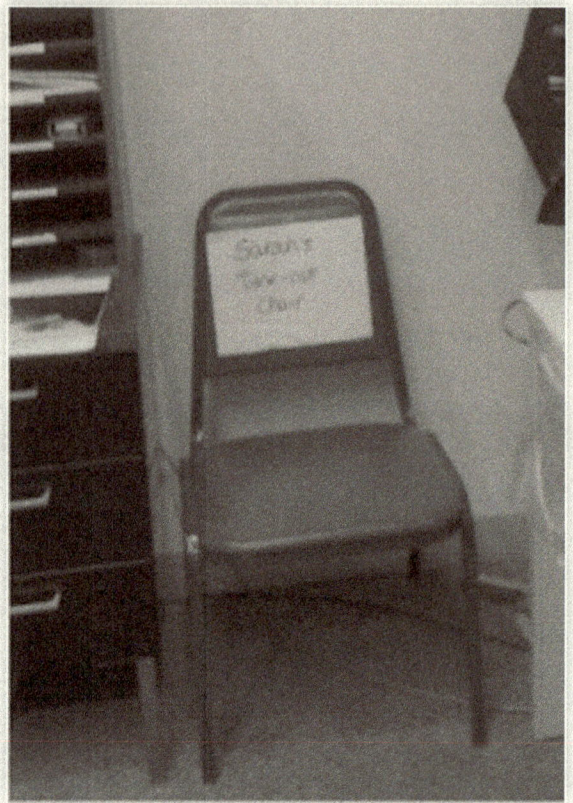

THIS SIGN SAYS: SARAH'S TIME-OUT CHAIR

I think I bring a little laughter into the office where I volunteer. I have a feeling my "boss" just hasn't figured out how to fire a volunteer yet. Sometimes I get a little too sassy and have too much fun. We are, after all, a professional office. When we recently rearranged the office furniture, I found a chair with this label on it. Humph. I know, it's true, I can get a little carried away. I can't help it. I crack myself up.

When I was in the mailroom last week, the workers there kindly pointed out that I forgot to put my division/department under the preprinted return address on my envelopes in case they came back as undeliverable (many of mine do, due to the nature of my work—sending sympathy cards). I had only remembered to put "SB."

Sarah Berardi

"What does 'SB' mean?" they asked.

I said, "Sarah Berardi. What did you think it meant? Shit for Brains?"

They laughed. "Well, if the shoe fits…"

Guess what—if I ever forget to put my division/department on the return address again and they just see "SB," they're going to remember who it is now, won't they?

Today I left a note for one of our chaplains. The "boss" came down (thankfully) and saw the note before the chaplain. She said I couldn't work in her office if I couldn't learn to spell *chaplain* correctly. I had spelled it "chaplin."

Hey, a mistake is just a different way of doing things, *remember*? I swear I didn't used to be this dumb. *I did not.* Menopause + migraines + verapamil + Zonegran = lower cognitive functioning. Meh. (Those are my preventative drugs. I'll explain later.)

I ASKED MARTY TO GIVE ME A GOOD "D'OH!" PICTURE FOR THIS SPOT

http://migraine.com/blog/when-meds-make-you-lose-your-mind/

Bustin' Out

I went to an off-site meeting in Florida for a board Marty sits on. Wives were included on this trip, and since I'm new to this group, I was just a little apprehensive/nervous. To get properly attired for the trip, however, I purchased a new girdle-type undergarment, the type that has bra coverage all the way down to thigh coverage in one piece. (I still needed an extra girdle in the middle for Betty Big Belly.) But that's not my point. There's a huge "point" to this. About one hour through dinner, I glimpsed down to my cleavage and saw this: BOING.

I thought (quickly) to myself, *What the hell is that bent piece of plastic-coated wire, and get it the hell out of here!* I decided to push it back down and under versus out, because what would I do with it otherwise? Lay it on the table? Put it in my napkin? Put it in my purse (didn't fit)? Therefore, the quick answer was to push it back where it came from. But where the hell did it come from? I'd never seen such a thing. What could be growing from my cleavage? Surely it was something to do with my new undergarment versus my new vitamins for my migraines, right?

After smooshing it in, I decided to fess up to the wives at the bar after dinner. I got their undivided attention and said, "Check this out, where do you think it came from?" One of my new friends, Suzie, said, "It's clearly an underwire. Which side did it come out of?"

I had no idea. But wait, I thought, didn't I just pay a hundred dollars for this undergarment? So you *should* be able to tell which boob it came out of. And not only that, but a hundred bucks should buy you a "Pass 'go' and collect two hundred dollars because you look so fab and your underwire won't keep popping out" card. So the three women studied my boobs, to no avail (thanks to Ralph Lauren, my dress covered it nicely).

Suzie said, "If you're going to blog about his, you *have* to get the facts straight." So she dug into my cleavage, but could not determine on which side my misplaced underwire should go. Off to the ladies' room she sent me. Voilà. Right boob much lower than the left.

Question: How does a well-known, brand-name undergarment allow its underwire to creep up, up, up, up, and OUT of its bodice? Is this something I could sue for? I have many witnesses at my dinner table. I have a lawyer. It caused me distress—major distress, clearly. OK, there. I have to stop. I did not have distress. I had flabberghastedness. I knew straightaway I would blog about this conundrum. I wouldn't sue anyone, but I would laugh about it.

So this undergarment company had better get its act together. No woman in her right mind would wear one of these knowing the underwire might pop out of her cleavage between the appetizer and the salad courses during a board meeting dinner with the wives.

Humph

This is for all the ignoramuses who've never had a migraine but say to me, "Oh, I have bad headaches, too." Or, "Why are you wearing sunglasses? Because you have a headache?" (Said to me a few times, even though I've told this person a thousand times why.) Actually, she found me out. I *love* wearing huge sunglasses to make people look at me. I love the attention I get—puleeze. *I look like a bloody fool walking around indoors with them on.*

❧ MiraLAX® Dissolves in Vodka, Ya Know ☙

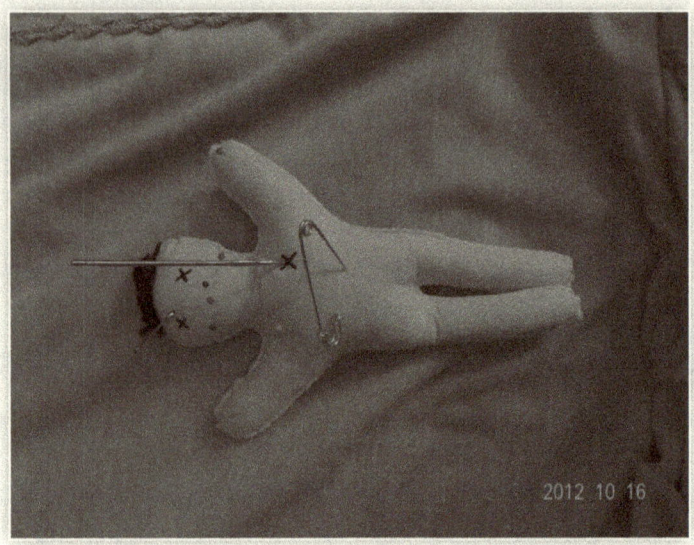

See the pin right in the eye? That's called an ocular migraine. Hope this works right now, because I'm thinking of the people who've said those things to me. Thinking…thinking…thinking… What goes around, comes around. As my nephews say, "You don't #%& with my Aunt Sarah." Just a quick and *kind* reminder for y'all. 'Cause I just ordered myself one of these dolls.

Additionally, Lawyerboy sent me this from a sports article:

After a hands-on review at league headquarters in Manhattan Thursday afternoon, the league has rejected the shaded goggles Wade planned to wear against the Knicks. Officials determined there was too much tinting and it would have given him a competitive advantage because opponents would not be able to see his eyes.

Wade, who has been suffering some light sensitivity after a bout with a migraine last weekend, practiced with the glasses over the past several days and was going to use them out of precaution at Madison Square Garden.

(http://sports.espn.go.com/nba/truehoop/miamiheat/news/story?id=6065190)

Now I agree that it would be an unfair advantage to play with the sunglasses on, but boy, do I know light sensitivity, don't I, Sciencegirl? Andrea just calls me "Paris" (as in Hilton) when I wear them. They're huge.

Sarah Berardi

PARIS, OR HUNCHBACK OF NOTRE DAME? I SLOUCH.

FEB 2011

Mommy Dearest

I could never appreciate the "no more wire hangers" part of Faye Dunaway's portrayal of Joan Crawford (find it on YouTube) until I would incessantly find Lawyerboy's closet full of wire hangers hanging perpendicular to the floor. Which means he would pull the shirts off the hangers, then the hangers would fling into the ceiling, dent the ceiling, then remain at that perpendicular angle. All thirty or so of them.

It drove me crazy. Absolutely nuts. I don't know why. It must have been BP (Before Prozac). Lawyerboy *claims* that one morning I woke him up for school by throwing said perpendicular wire hangers *at* him. For the life of me, I don't remember this, nor would I be proud of this if I could remember it. He also said that he had been fairly forewarned by me, had disobeyed, and so had it coming. But did I *really* throw them at him? (Did he *really* see the Easter Bunny's tail bouncing out of his bedroom door on Easter morn?)

Much to my chagrin, I walked into my closet last week, and this is what I saw—horror of horrors:

❦ MiraLAX® Dissolves in Vodka, Ya Know ❦

MY CLOSET!

I had been committing the same crime. I fessed up to Lawyerboy. *I am Mommy Dearest*, in more ways than one.

Not only that, but I've clearly scarred the kid for life:

CLOSET CLEANING DAY—SHAME

{ Sarah Berardi }

How Not to Tick Me Off (Today)

1. Don't walk too slowly in front of me.
2. Learn the zipper feed while driving. Merging is not an option, it's a bloody necessity. Always has been, always will be. Get used to it.
3. Accept responsibility for your errors or get out of my life, thank you very much. (This is *my* list, right?)
4. Don't talk to me ever, ever, ever, ever about steroid use, UC, celiac disease, diabetes, endometriosis, migraines, OTC drugs, tinnitus, gallbladder disease, breast cancer, bunions, diets, cysts, adhesions, bladder leakage, colon cancer, thyroid problems, anxiety disorders, depression, therapists, menopause, hormones, acid-reducing medications, alcoholism, kidney stones, or delusions of grandeur. Okeydokey? (It's *my* list, right?) Thanks. 'Cause I already know more than you do, unless you have "MD" after your name or you've suffered *properly* from these things yourself and have actually researched them as well, and perhaps have been *properly* diagnosed with them. Don't tell me steroids are bad for me after I've had a migraine for ten days, OK, *sweetheart*?
5. Please oh please, be inquisitive in life. Look things up. Read! My seventh-grade social studies teacher asked me to answer a question during class. I had no clue of the answer, despite the fact that I had paid attention, done my homework, etc. I just didn't *get it*. So I hesitantly and shyly (yes, remember I was shy then) gave an answer with a questioning lilt at the end of my words. You know what he said to me in front of all thirty-some classmates? "Don't show your ignorance." I have never forgiven him. Saw his obit in the paper about six months ago. Still mad at him for humiliating me. But I read and research stuff now so that I can understand things. I just didn't get that whole political scene he was painting back then. (Still don't, 'cause I don't give a fiddler's fart, I think.)

So how many friends have I made today? Doesn't matter. *My* blog, *my* list—and *my* shoulders are slowly dropping away from my earlobes.

P.S. The receptionist at the dentist told me that when she had her worst migraine, she took off her belt and put it around her head as tightly as it would go (the pressure feels good on migraine pain). She was driving in a car. Can you picture what she looked like?

❦ MiraLAX® Dissolves in Vodka, Ya Know ❦

OF COURSE, I'D HAVE MATCHING RED PUMPS ON SINCE THAT'S A RED BELT

i'm a Little Daft

I was just talking with Sciencegirl today about how embarrassing it is when somebody tells me I said something or e-mailed something to them the night before, and I have *no* memory of it whatsoever. If I had been drunk as a skunk I wouldn't think twice about it. Sometimes I am, so that's understandable. But most of the time, I am not. I'm telling you, it's the darned Zonegran, the antiseizure medicine. It's known for making you daft. (I take it for the migraines. Many migraineurs take some type of antiseizure med.)

So Sciencegirl suggested that I not communicate with anyone if A) I've taken a "rescue" drug for a migraine, or B) I've taken my nighttime medications, which include the antiseizure.

I retorted, "Wow, how boring. That's when I do my bills and e-mailing." Hmm...therein lies the problem. Multiple problems, come to think of it.

About three hours later, Sciencegirl texted me: Did you put a pen in my freezer?

I replied back: Aw crap, I hope not.

I did have one migraine while there, and therefore took one "rescue drug." And I was cleaning like mad. It's entirely possible I did.

And we *all* know that the proper place for Windex is the fridge, right?

My Beloved Picture Replaced

The picture of Lawyerboy (then Chris) and Sciencegirl (then Andrea) over my TV has been replaced. Bummed. I LOVE that picture. I love it because of the story behind it, not so much because of the picture itself.

Lawyerboy proclaimed he did not want a senior picture. No ifs, ands, or buts. OK. So I reached a compromise with him that I could have a large portrait of both Lawyerboy and Sciencegirl (they are only eighteen months apart) for the family room. This way I would kill two birds with one stone. But if Sciencegirl decided she wanted a senior pic, she could have one. Agreed.

We went to this very nice photography studio where I sat inside while the photographer and the kids went outside to her backyard for the photos (it was summer). When it was over, we got in the car, and they both burst out laughing. They spurted out how the photographer had them doing some normal poses, which were fine. But then there were some…well…dorky ones. At one point, she couldn't remember Sciencegirl's name, so she said to Andrea, "Sissy, put your head on your brother's shoulder." Oh, dear. This is not what my kids are like—they are not lovey-dovey touchy-feely. So Andrea clunked her head as hard as she could on Chris's shoulder while they laughed through their smiles for the camera. We belly-laughed all the way home.

Unfortunately, when I walked into the studio and saw that picture, I *loved* it. I'm pretty sure the story behind it made me just love it; seeing them laughing at the photographer through their smiles, knowing what was going through their heads and that they were sharing that laughter surreptitiously.

I ended up getting the picture so large that one of Lawyerboy's friends said I probably sit it at the kitchen table when they're away at college and have dinner with them. So?

❡ MiraLAX® Dissolves in Vodka, Ya Know ❡

SO THE PICTURE HAS BEEN REPLACED, BUT NO WORRIES. IT'S NOW OVER THE MANTEL IN MY BOUDOIR.

Always Put Your Glasses On

Simple lesson in life:

When you have two nights in a row where you've only had three to four hours of sleep, make sure you put your glasses on before you take some ibuprofen for your groggy-foggy head or this is the surprise you will realize about six hours later:

❦ Sarah Berardi ❧

AMAZING HOW MUCH THEY LOOK ALIKE WITHOUT GLASSES ON

MAR 2011

Yes, I Have Friends Despite My Anxiety, Depression, Formidableness, and Grudge Holding

You know, despite my horrible moods, I still have friends. Tried and true, they are. I think they know I'm in there somewhere. My friends are the type that can tell me my hair looks like shit today. Or they can tell me to "grow a pair." Sometimes I get the old "whaaaa whaaaa" from one friend, which means, "Put your big-girl panties on and deal with it."

Perhaps all my friends are "viper tongues," though that name must be reserved just for Heather, as she's got a special talent for it.

My friends make me laugh, more importantly. Especially at the most inappropriate times, which is great. It brings me back down out of the tree from where I'm about to jump.

We talk about what horrible mothers we are and how we've clearly scarred our children for life in so many ways. We talk about how men just don't get us. We must band together and stay a united front. That's what girlfriends are for. Though I'll never forgive Jen, who never told me about the boogie I had in my nose all day.

I, Sarah Berardi, Am Amazing

Today I went to the Mac store to get my huge twenty-four-inch computer fixed. The first time I carried it in for service about two years ago, I pulled a muscle in my neck. It's pretty darned heavy. I also looked like an idiot carrying it with two hands gripped onto the one handle while it banged on my knees in front of me. The next time I took it in, I scheduled an appointment with my husband to carry it in for me. This time…

I had just had a manicure and massage, and I was not about to ruin either of them. So I pulled up to valet parking, took out my pre-loaded dolly from home (one of my all-time favorite purchases), stuck my computer on it, and away I went.

I sat down at the Genius Bar for my appointment. When I told the nice guy, Aaron, what was happening, he looked a little puzzled, but he was so cool and smart—and mostly *patient*—that he figured it out. I am writing a letter to his supervisor to tell him that Aaron deserves a raise as soon as I post this blog.

The first complaint I had about my Mac was that I would occasionally see colored rectangles on the screen that would build from the left to right and continue down, then the screen would freeze. Then, I would get the "pinwheel of death." He burst out laughing and asked me if I would begrudge him if he didn't type in "pinwheel of death." I said yes. I told him that Liz had coined that phrase, and it was appropriate. I don't know what he typed in, but he was laughing as he did so. I also told him to put in his computer log that I was not on hallucinogens.

Long story short, his perseverance prevailed. When he told me he would like to wipe out all my stuff and start over, as he found numerous software glitches, I winced. He asked me when I last backed up. I told him I tried on three different devices last night, but they all seemed to fail. He looked them up. Sure enough, they each said, "application failed." He discovered I had been backing up to my own hard drive. Apparently this is almost impossible. He said it was "amazing" how I could have done that.

I told him that I am amazing in every which way, including backup procedures on Macs. Where there is a will, there is a way. He said he'd never, ever seen it done. I have no idea how I did that. I also told him that if the proper window had popped up in the first place, I would clearly have chosen the correct one. (Right?)

❦ Sarah Berardi ❦

So I am sitting here at home now, on my MacBook Air, watching my huge Mac computer backup properly. He said it may take three to six hours. Then he taught me how to delete things from my desktop properly. He said having all those things on my desktop (which I love for handiness) slows the boot-up quite a bit on any computer. Poo. He also taught me that photos and videos are "deleted" differently than documents when dragged to the trash.

So kudos to Aaron, who has just met the most amazing woman on earth.

⁋ MiraLAX® Dissolves in Vodka, Ya Know ⁋

Dear Mr. Manager

Apple Store Walden Galleria
G116 Walden Galleria
Buffalo, NY 14225

Dear Manager of Apple Store Walden Galleria:
 I was in today for a fix on my desktop. The poor unsuspecting fellow at the Genius Bar who got me as his customer was great. Aaron. He was funny, persistent, incredibly knowledgeable, and most of all, *patient with me* in finding the problem. Being patient with me, a fifty-one-year-old, premenopausal woman who has brain cells leaking out of her head faster than a speeding bullet is difficult, so I quite think he should be rewarded, really.
 Sincerely,
 Sarah Berardi

My Laugh-Out-Loud "Free Makeover"

As I politely said, "No, thank you," to the lonely girl doing Shiseido makeovers in the middle of the Ralph Lauren section at Lord & Taylor, I thought how bored she must be. She had a very quiet voice, obviously not comfortable asking passersby if they'd like a free makeover. "Free" meaning you'll be cussed out behind your back if you don't end up purchasing at least some of the products they use on you.
 After I had completed perusing all seven floors of the store, I found myself back in front of the same girl, with her chair still empty. So I went up to her and said, "If you can make my eyelids look less puffy, then game on." Of course she said she could do that with her new product—the night serum that you massage around your eyes every night. Now, do you really think I would take the time to massage lotion around my eyes every night? Nope. Never have, never will. Nor do I believe any serum would do the trick. Nor do I really care because I think it's part of my genetic makeup. But I felt sorry for the poor girl. I figured I'd purchase some little thing at the end to give her the commission she worked for, and sat down for the holycrap makeover.
 She took *forever*. I told her I typically wear hardly any makeup, just a little powder, eyeliner, and mascara, and occasionally some blush. Only if I'm black-tieing it do I put on eye shadow. (Who can see it with those damn eyelids?)

❦ Sarah Berardi ❧

I could tell she was laying the makeup on heavy, but I wasn't worried because A) nobody knows me here in New York, and B) I wear my sunglasses all the time. But when she got to my lips, she said, "You have very tiny lips." She then proceeded to take a lip pencil and outline bigger lips for me, I kid you not. I couldn't wait to see them just for this blog.

Then she penciled in my brows for what seemed an eternity. I thought, *I'm going to look like Bert from Sesame Street by the time she's done!*

Here's the outcome. It's hysterical. Check out the eyebrows and lips:

BERT WITH BIG LIPS—MAKEOVER IN NYC

❦ MiraLAX® Dissolves in Vodka, Ya Know ❧

I purchased a few things from her. She was so excited (she was young). I have every intention of taking them back to my Lord & Taylor in Buffalo, because she made me look like a frickin' clown. I'm now wondering if she thought I looked good or if she *knew* she was making me look clownish.

APR 2011

Eeyore at Home

❧ MiraLAX® Dissolves in Vodka, Ya Know ❧

"When stuck in the river, it is best to dive and swim to the bank yourself before someone drops a large stone on your chest in an attempt to hoosh you there." (Eeyore from *Eeyore's Gloomy Little Instruction Book*.)

I'm back in Buffalo—boo. I much preferred pretending to live the life of the rich and famous in New York. Alas, I am home, with a suitcase full of clothes to launder, groceries to purchase (maybe I'll just eat those stale crackers in the pantry versus grocery shop), a week's worth of mail to go through and act on, etc.

Things I Do When Driving That I Shouldn't Even Admit To

Things I do when driving that I shouldn't do:
1. Floss my teeth. I carry floss in my purse and in my car. I love to floss. This must only be done at stoplights, as it requires two hands.
2. Go through my feed-bag of a purse for miscellaneous items that I should have looked for before I started driving.
3. Tie or zipper my shoes or boots.
4. Take my Spanx® off. I usually don't even make it three miles down the road before it gives me acid reflux and I have to shimmy it off.
5. Eat anything at any time. Hence the Betty.
6. Clean my dashboard with car wipes at stoplights.
7. Put my jewelry on.
8. Put on my Crest teeth-whitener strips.
9. Laugh out loud to the Laugh USA channel on Sirius, or whatever it's called.
10. Drink my decaf and fill it with MiraLAX®, which makes my gearshift look like it's filled with cocaine in its leather crevices. Hence the dashboard wipe-downs.

The Seven Dwarves

I have a really cool collectible set of the Seven Dwarves. I've researched them, even took them to one of those *Antiques Roadshow* things here locally. When I brought them out, everyone went "ohh, woooow, ahh," etc. Yeah, for a collector, they're pretty amazing. There's even a picture of them in one of my antique doll books. They aren't worth near as much as they could be, they told me, as I need Snow White to go with them. I've searched high and low, to no avail. I can find a bunch of random Snow Whites, but not the proper one to go with my set of dwarves. (I purchased one of those random Snow Whites until I can find the proper one. Have you got one?)

I grew up with them on a shelf above my bed. I loved them. I would stand on my tippy-toes and study each one. I was not allowed to touch them. They were even covered in custom-made plastic. My aunt remembers also growing up with them, so we figure they are from around 1935, give or take five years, when they were purchased by my grandmother, Nonnie.

When I inherited them, I took their plastic covers off and put them in a glass cabinet for all the world to see. But there was a slight problem. As Lawyerboy would lie on the couch watching TV, he would claim Dopey was giving him the evil eye. Dopey was freaking him out.

"Mom, get this freaking scary Dopey out of here! He's creepy. Downright creepy!"

"I absolutely will *not* take Dopey down. He is adorable. Leave him alone."

The next day I was in the room and noticed this:

So for the past fifteen years, depending on who's been in that room last, my poor little Dopey is either facing forward or facing backward. Sciencegirl quickly agreed, and joined Lawyerboy in turning Dopey around. Even Emily from across the street, who Sciencegirl grew up with, does it. In fact, just the other day she came over, walked into the kitchen, did a double take, stopped dead in her tracks, looked at the dwarves, and said to me, "What's Dopey doing facing forward? Just because Lawyerboy and Sciencegirl aren't here doesn't mean he should be facing forward. He's still creepy."

Poor little Dopey. I love him. I always stand up for the underdog.

Ah, Good Old Online Dating Services

A friend of mine decided to try Match.com. This is after she tried eHarmony and some other site I don't remember. The matches on the last two sites I mentioned weren't even good enough to contact during her trial period. Match.com, however, has been giving us quite a few laughs.

We are flabbergasted at the goofballs, or should I say *liars*, who are on there. One fellow she actually dated for about four months turned out to have quite a bit of hidden baggage. Slowly but surely (and don't call me Shirley) little suitcases (aka baggage) began to drop from the sky during conversations. As usual, the "fix it" person she is started to help with all this baggage. It became a full-time job.

In his bio, he stated he loved to cook, go for nature walks, and camp. Never once did he ever offer to cook for her or get off his barstool to even think about going for a nature walk. It was usually too hot/cold out.

I finally mentioned to her that perhaps this baggage was something a therapist or doctor should be working on, not her. It was pretty deep, I thought. In the end, it was indeed too deep, and it all came to an end.

Then came an e-mail with a picture of good old General Petraeus—yup, from the US government—saying he was interested in her. He had "winked" at her (that's how Match.com lets you know somebody is interested in you). We all read the e-mail he sent to her and found numerous discrepancies in what he said versus what we knew to be true. Though his e-mail was pretty darned close. This was, again, another *liar*—actually, a FRAUD. What was his point in doing this?

One man took her out to the same chain restaurant twice and told jokes to her the entire night—both nights. (Actually, it's an admirable trait. I can't tell a joke to save my soul.)

Then there was the "man" whose name was "Barb." I kid you not. So when I started doing my usual background search on this "Barb," I found him/her on Facebook. The picture was of a woman. And her name was Barb. So my friend wrote back (as my friend's bio clearly says she's only interested in men) and said she was confused whether "he" was a man or woman. He/she never properly answered her question. He/she was indignant with his/her reply: "I have never, ever lied to anyone about anything with such serious implications."

We thought that would be the end of it. Nope. Eight days later, Barb wrote: "How are you? Was thinking about you. Hope to hear back from you ASAP."

Annual Health Assessment

Time for my annual health assessment at THWIV. The most important thing they need to check is our TB status. I filled out the checklist, and it made me look like a freak. Or as Sciencegirl says, a "genetic freak."

Allergies (latex, medications, etc.): I'm allergic to six antibiotics as well as certain types of stitches. I noted them all.

Night Sweats: Are you kidding me? I've had them since I was thirty (twenty-one years, thank you).

Blurry Vision: Hell yes, I have progressive lenses that only work if I don't have a migraine.

Hearing Loss: Yes, but only in my husband's and my "boss's" frequencies.

Asthma: Yup—exercise-, allergy-, and cold-air-induced.

Nervous System: Headaches: Hell yes, queen of them.

Psychiatry/Emotional: Anxiety/depression. (Do I tell them?)

Respiratory Section: See asthma question above, buttheads.

Weight Loss or Gain of Twenty Pounds: I plead the fifth.

Change in shape of face (scars, surgery, new or removed beard): I remove my beard once a week.

Breathing Problems: Yes, can't go up the stairs or walk farther than the mailbox without needing an inhaler or a good five-minute rest on my laurels. Doc says I'm out of shape. I say he can go to hell.

Hospitalizations/Surgeries: How much time do you have, because there isn't enough room on this sheet?

Medications: How much time do you have, because there isn't enough room on this sheet?

I might be the first volunteer to get fired—well, besides Kramer, of course.

Last Will and Testament

...being of sound and disposing mind and memory and over the age of eighteen (18) years, and not being actuated by any duress, menace, fraud, mistake, or undue influence, do hereby make, publish, and declare the following to be my Last Will and Testament, revoking all previous wills and codicils made by...

OK, what does "disposing mind and memory" mean?

OK, *every day* I'm actuated by duress, menace, fraud, mistake, and undue influence. So, how will I ever make my proper last will and testament?

On a previous living will, I may have instructed, "Yank that plug after ten days." Lawyerboy says it's not proper legal language, but it should fly. Not only that, but I've asked my friend, Priestieboy, to come in and give me Anointing of the Sick on my deathbed. He said, "Are you sure you don't mean an exorcism?"

Hey, I can pull a Linda Blair on him, no problem. Even on my deathbed. I asked him if he'd pray for me. He said, "Of course, because I know where you're going." Did I hear "heathen" under his breath? *No.* He did remind me what sulfur is rumored to do to your hair, though.

He promised me this:

He'd be there with my family. He'd say, "It's time to yank the plug. I'm sorry, those are her wishes."

But Marty might pipe up and say, "No, let her suffer...um...just another few hours."

"If that's the case," he said, "we'll have a martini, extra olives for you at your bedside. Then, when all is quiet after the official yank and our heads are bowed in sorrow, I will press your fart machine app on your iPhone."

Great. Thanks a lot.

A Day in the Office (Remember, I'm a Volunteer)

The "boss" asked me to make a bunch of large (8½" x 11") labels for the plastic bins in the basement of THWIV. In the middle of the packet of about twenty or so, I slipped in one that said, "Sarah is very pretty," hoping she'd get a little laugh while she was down in that creepy place by herself.

The next thing I knew, it was taped up on the wall in the office.

Someone said: Who put that up there?

I said: I typed it, the boss put it there.

He said: Why?

I said: Because nobody at home tells me I'm pretty. I like to pretend I am, so I have them hung up all over the house to remind people in my family to tell me I'm pretty. I don't see the harm in it. It wouldn't kill anyone to tell me I'm pretty.

He said: You are sick.

I said: So what?

Within a week or so, the little sign began to take on a life of its own. Others started adding their own two cents on there. My name is written in Japanese on it now. The other Sara without an *h* added her name, stating that she is pretty as well (she is).

But when I went in today, *someone* (I like *this* someone) had crossed out "may" and added "w/martinis, will." I have *no* idea what they are talking about.

I added in another area, "Mistakes are just another way of doing things," which comes from Winnie the Pooh. My therapist says I have to allow myself three mistakes a day.

So now I allow myself to make three mistakes a day before beating myself up. New rule. It's tough for Patty Perfect to do this, you know. Very.

That's What Friends Are For (I Think)

When I wasn't feeling too funny and wasn't posting, I had two friends send me messages that said:

1) Hang in there; and 2) It'll get better this week.

Then there's my friend, Bonnie, who said, 3) Fix it; I need a laugh to prevent me from sticking my head in the oven. (I'm paraphrasing and was a bit worried, but I asked if there was room for two.) Ah, *The Bell Jar* (one of my faves).

And then there's Viper Tongue, who said: 4) Knock it off. Don't you realize how you affect other people's days (when you don't have a blog for the day)?

We moved on to another discussion about how I already knew what I was giving her for Christmas since I am full of good ideas. She said, "Really, then why don't you @#$@#$$ write about them?"

I hate it when they make me laugh when I don't want to.

Migraine Update, Not That Anyone Cares

But if you're a migraineur, you devour the net for these things.

After a fourteen-day streak with no break in sight, I went to my neurologist. I said blatantly, "It's clearly not working anymore." The rescue drugs work, but I have to take them every day, which I know is a no-no, as it can cause rebound migraines, not to mention strokes. But it's the only way I can get out of bed and function each day, and most days I prefer to function, now that I'm out of my deep, dark-blue funk. I asked him, "What do you think if I weaned off the preventative, noxious, toxic drugs that don't seem to be working, and switch over to some of that bioidentical hormone stuff I've read about to try to fix it?" (Not to be confused with regular old estrogen HRT to help me ride the menopausal wave. We're all still here with inner-tubes around our bellies and swimmies jammed up our arms riding this menopausal tidal wave.)

He readily agreed. But I don't have much hope. Cross your fingers, toes, boobs, whatever you can. And if you can cross your boobs, I'm jealous.

This migraine journey has been going on since May 2008. I just need the reprieve, you know? On the downside, when I asked the doctor who gave me the scrip for the magic hormones if I would gain weight with this treatment, she said, "Sarah, let's not worry about that right now. Let's see if it helps your migraines." You know what that means, right?

Freddy and Betty are gettin' bigger and bigger as I write.

Typos, Mistakes, and Throwing Your Free Help Under the Bus

I'm a volunteer. I do the best I can. And remember, I take those nasty drugs with the side effects of "confusion, and difficulty in thinking and concentrating." (Yes, I'm weaning off them, but it will take *weeks*, I tell you, *weeks*.) Imagine that you find out the secretary you are helping (as a volunteer, which means giving freely from your soul) highlights your typos and shows them to the boss while saying, "There are a lot of mistakes on this." Mind you, I see and correct her boo-boos on a daily basis without childishly pointing them out to anyone—because I am mature.

Humph. Today I was going through some of the files she left for me and found this sticky note she had stuck to some papers:

1. EXTA'S should clearly have an "R" in it.
2. EXTRAS does not require an apostrophe, as it is not a contraction nor is it possessive.
3. It's not even a typo. It's a printo. That is worso.

⁂ MiraLAX® Dissolves in Vodka, Ya Know ⁂

Lesson for the day: People in glass houses should not throw stones. Too bad she's clearly not aware of my list.

And I need not worry that she might see this, as she doesn't know what a blog is.

Who Drinks Too Much?

Uh-oh. Last night I went to my University at Buffalo MiniMed School. I met up with my friend and her sister. Her sister is a nurse, and my friend has previously worked for a doctor for a long time, so let's face it, we're all pretty much doctors.

One of the discussion topics focused on how our region here in Erie County is particularly unhealthy, due to factors such as radon, socioeconomic climate, physical development, etc. The one part that caught my attention was the "personal behaviors" section. Uh-oh.

Alcohol Consumption, 2006–2008:

Percent of Erie County adults who binge drink: 24.1 (vs. New York State: 18.1).

Percent of Erie County adults who heavily drink: 7.1 (vs. New York State: 5.0).

Now, the definition of binge drinking is five or more drinks in a sitting for men and four or more for women. The definition of heavy drinking is more than two per day for a man and one per day for a woman.

Methinks (this is Shakespearean-speak, not pirate-speak) these percentages are skewed. My friend, her sister, and I all looked down the row at each other and shrugged our shoulders. We're obviously in trouble *deep*.

MAY 2011

Should My Feelings Be Hurt?

In reality, no. I'm the first to admit I've gained weight. You hear me say it in this here blog almost daily. I'm a little obsessed with it, right? I hardly eat a thing, but I also never exercise anymore.

So Marty came home, and I wanted to show him the two dresses I bought for a black-tie event. One was fun and Audrey Hepburnish, my favorite. It has crinoline under the skirt! The other was very conservative, and I figured he'd like that one better. He usually doesn't go for fun. He usually goes for proper and conservative. (Can you hear me say "boring"?) I was determined to have him approve of the fun one.

As I tried my fun dress on, I mentioned that they only had the one size at Lord & Taylor, which I purchased, and it was pretty darned tight around my ribs. I didn't have time to go online and order a larger size before our party. So I needed to take at least four ribs out to, A) eat for the evening; B) sit at any time during the evening; or C) pass down any liquids besides my own saliva during the evening.

Despite the fact I had already said all this, I didn't think it was particularly appropriate or nice that, as he struggled to get the zipper up (the girl in the dressing room next to me at Lord & Taylor didn't have this problem), he mentioned it would be easier if he had a pair of pliers. *Pliers.*

I think I'll find another date for the evening and keep the dress.

Who's Vain?

Wow, when making myself the butt of a joke, I pointed out what I thought was obvious—that I wasn't vain, since I had just confessed to my friends something stupid I had done. One of those "friends" laughed and said, "Right." She thinks I'm vain?

I like to look nice. In other words, my socks match, my shoes match (though not every time), my lipstick is on my lips versus my teeth, and I think my hair is combed nicely (OK, Snookied). I happily admit to spray tans for formals so my legs don't scare people—ask any of friends, they will tell you my legs warrant the spray tan. But am I really a picture of vanity? I hope not. Is it perhaps my sign in the office that says, "Sarah is very pretty," which is clearly a joke made by someone really insecure?

After all those pictures I've posted of myself with sticks up my nose during migraine treatments, no makeup on, belts wrapped tightly around my head, goggles on, my Betty Big Belly out, my Freddy Fat Chin out, my dress tucked up into my panties, toilet paper stuck to my shoe or underwear…I don't know, I was just plain stunned at this "friend" throwing vanity at my face. Stunned right back into…questioning myself.

If there's anything I dislike equal to a liar, it's someone who is not humble. Perhaps I should start wearing different clothes? Find those sneakers? Get out my old painter pants that I loved in high school (as if they'd fit)? I could wear mismatched earrings, not wash my hair. I could sit quiet as a mouse so nothing I say can be misconstrued as me being uppity or vain. Hmm.

After all my years of stupid ol' therapy, I think I know what it *really* is about. But I prefer to wallow in this a bit. And at the same time, you can bet your sweet bippie (*Laugh In*), that person is on my list. Whether it was constructive criticism or just plain criticism (remember, they are the same in my book), they go straight to the list. Plus, she'll probably be in hell, where the sulfur will do horrible things to her hair.

P.S. People keep asking me, "Just how long is that list, by the way?" It is miles long, and it's in my head. I am the vainest grudge holder you'll ever know.

Sarah Berardi

Yeah, she's right, I'm vain. You can tell by that beautiful pic I just posted with that Freddy Fat Chin hangin' there.

Sarah Means "Princess," Look It Up

The other day, Marty was asked, along with another fellow, to give a little presentation in front a group of businessmen. He does this a lot, so it's easy peasy for him to say things off the cuff and be funny during his presentations.

The fellow who spoke before him introduced himself to the group by saying what he did for a living, what his wife did, and that he had five children. He said the oldest was in grad school, described the next three…and said that right now the youngest (four years old) wants to be a princess. This got quite a few laughs.

When Marty's turn came, he introduced himself to the group by saying what he did for a living, that his son is a new attorney, that his daughter is pursuing her PhD, and that his wife…well, she *is* a princess.

He claims he got a roar of laughter.

The Grass Is Definitely Greener

...when the septic overflows.

Ew. For twenty-two years I've lived in this house we built with a septic system. We've never had the need for it to be pumped ASAP. Not until today.

I can remember standing on an empty, muddy lot holding Lawyerboy's hand, holding Sciencegirl in my arms. Marty was explaining the whole layout of the house we were going to build. He could envision this whole thing, and I have a feeling four-year-old Lawyerboy could, too. Marty also mentioned that we would, of course, need a septic system. I asked him what the heck that was. I'd never heard of it, having grown up with proper sewers.

For twenty-two years I've managed just fine with my Scott toilet paper, which is see-through thin (I always try to remember to switch it to a thicker ply when I have a dinner party). I schedule my poop truck to come whenever they recommend I schedule the poop truck to come. I'm very obedient, because who in the world would *not* be compliant or want to take a chance of having that volatile thing back up?

Imagine my surprise this morning when I found a sticky note left from our houseguest that I might perhaps want to have the poop truck come. Oh, dear. So I called the poop truck and made an appointment for Friday (today is Tuesday). About an hour later, while I was working at THWIV, I received a call from my cleaning lady, who was cringing on the other end of the line, explaining that I needed the poop truck *now*.

Fast-forward.

I raced home to meet Mr. Poop and his truck.

Mr. Poop lumbered out of his huge, stinky truck in his overalls that couldn't be buttoned up all the way because his large Santa belly was in the way. He wore a baseball cap that covered the top of his head, but let his shoulder-length gray hair hang straight down. He had a funky-looking mole on the tip of one of his nostrils and a large smile.

He bellowed to me: I hear y'all got a problem!

Me (standing in the doorway in my new Circa Joan & David pink heels): I sure do. The lid isn't off. Do you want me to help shovel?

Mr. Poop: Yeah.

Me: Really? OK. (I kicked off my heels and put my muck boots on.)

Mr. Poop: No! (Hardy-har-har.) I don't want y'all to help me. Betcha didn't expect me to say yes, did ya?

Me: Nope. Now I'm warnin' ya, I'm gonna follow you the whole time, 'cause I want to learn the whole system this time.

Mr. Poop: Whatever you want, ma'am.

I followed him around just like I follow the electrician and the plumber. I just wanted to see the "waterworks" under there. I wanted to see it gummed up, then I wanted to see it run clear and free! He said the only other woman customer he had who was fascinated with all the workings was a heart surgeon. I told him I was a heart surgeon, too.

When he was done, he told me to run into the house and flush a toilet. So I lumbered up the hill to the house, kicked off the muck boots, and flushed. I poked my head out the door. He told me to come look. I re-booted, went down the hill, and saw it was still plugged.

Me: What the heck?

Mr. Poop: Need to unplug this pipe, too.

So he worked on unplugging that there old pipe. He told me to go flush again. I repeated my flush maneuvers. I came back outside and down the hill. Looked a bit better, but needed more work.

Mr. Poop: OK, now go in and turn on all the faucets and flush all the toilets.

Me (halfway up the hill): Hey—you don't really need me to flush and faucet the house, do you? You just like watching me bust a gut trying to run up this hill huffing and puffing!

Mr. Poop: That's *not* true (laughing), I do need you to flush and faucet. Now hurry on up in there.

I was amazed at how clear that water ran after unplugging all that crap, literally. Septic systems are so gross.

Mr. Poop cleaned up his long vacuum hose, wrote out my bill, and told me he'd be waiting for an invitation to our annual Christmas party. (I make fast friends with everyone I meet.)

P.S. I don't have an annual Christmas party, so don't wait for an invitation, 'K?

Ich Bin Müde

I am so, so tired. Three nights of not enough sleep will give you a migraine. Have you ever been so tired that you pull into the garage at 7:30 p.m., throw your purse down on the bedroom floor, climb into bed, pop your bedtime pills, and call it a night?

I have, and tonight is that night. I have *never* slept in my clothes. It's gross. Tonight just might be the first. Too tired to even move. And so what if after I got up from my pedicure the back of my skirt was tucked into my bum and everyone in the salon could see my undies?

Good night.

Migraine Update #572

Whoa. Thought I was cured. Today is one of those days when I think I just can't do this pain roller coaster for another day without a cure right around the corner. For three and a half weeks or so I had the most blissful days of the last three long years, all due to trying hormone pills as a preventative. The neurologist and I decided we needed to get a handle on the hormones since Mother Nature was being negligent. So estrogen and progestin to the rescue. Bliss.

Until those blasted migraines came back with a vengeance.

I have to admit that I've never considered myself to be someone with "a." But when I was on Cafepress.com today to make my own t-shirt that said, "Back off, I have a migraine," or, "It would behoove you to stay away, I have a migraine," I saw there was already a whole migraine section. The section included chronic pain funnies. Not that Cafepress.com is a medical site, but I gave it some thought (difficult as that was) and realized I pretty much *do* have chronic pain. How miserable I must be to be around! (Not to mention how miserable I feel.) Y'all shut up who hang with me.

I *may* have purchased two things, just for kicks and giggles. A T-shirt and this:

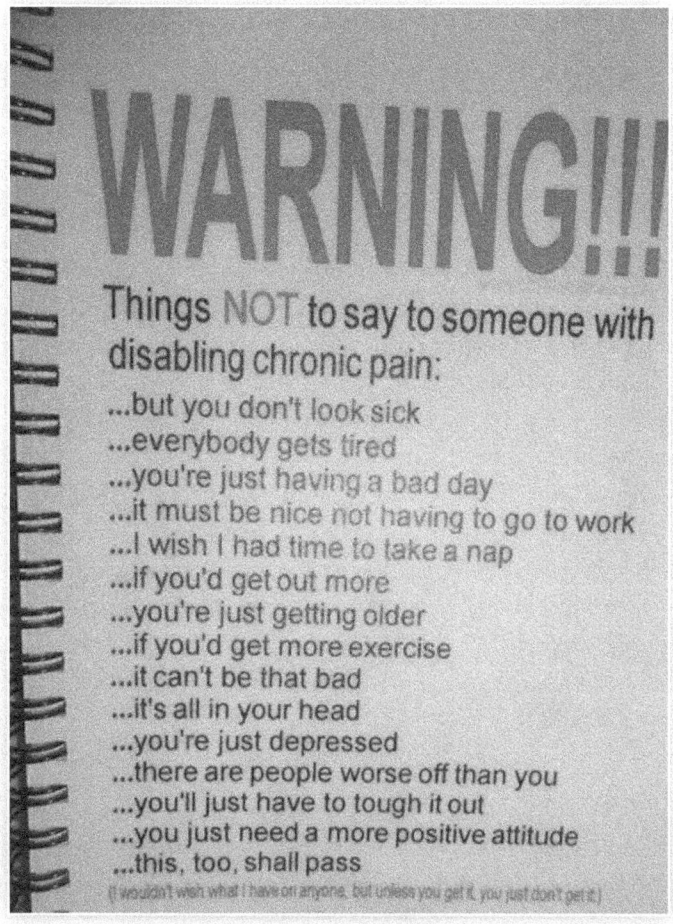

CAFEPRESS.COM

If I had a nickel for every time a "loved one" said one of these things to me, I'd be in my gorgeous townhouse in New York City near Central Park right now. (I don't have one in reality, just in my pretty little head.)

I shall persevere, however. I refuse to give up, nor will I let my neurologist give up. I'm still trying to convince him to come live in my finished basement "suite." Though if he reads my blog about the septic, he will never come, will he?

Bah.

Mom

Speaking of Mom (I wasn't), today is her birthday! Good old Friday the thirteenth! Which has always been Lawyerboy's favorite number, and still is. I like to believe it's his fave because my mother was actually born on a Friday the thirteenth. I'm pretty sure that's why. I don't dare ask him why in case the answer is otherwise.

Mom passed away in 1996. She was only sixty-eight. She was a victim of living in our house, as we all were in that darned dysfunctional family. I really believe many people of her generation were alcoholics due to their generational ignorance about alcoholism. Plus, living with my psychologically impaired father, she probably figured, "If you can't beat him, join him!" Don't know at this point if I blame her for that or not.

So as I dig through therapy, which often involves just plain learning *not* to let people take advantage of my wide scope of talents that I give them on a silver platter (please insert laugh here), I see so many similarities between me and Mom. She was a very giving person to people in need—in need of health support, emotional support, etc. Yet she was no stable person herself, though she never knew she revealed this fact. I fancy myself a little more stable than she (please insert laugh here).

One huge thing I learned from her was perseverance. Right? Have I ever *not* persevered?

I'm So Confused

I wrote out a check to pay a bill, put a stamp on the envelope, and stared at it. It looked funny to me, but I couldn't figure out why. I stood there, staring at it. Finally—aha!—the stamp was in the wrong place. This is actually the second time I've done this. Duh. Just starting a new trend for the US Postal Service that I know they'll appreciate.

I have no idea what's brought this state of extra confusion on or how to end it. I even had Marty sit with me last week to monitor me as I filled my little pill carrier for morning and night again. So I don't think it's my drugs.

My doctor swears I am normal in comparison with other women my age. She claims not one woman comes in to see her without the same complaints/issues I have about being confused. Not to mention the fact that I have the migraines. She said pre/menopause will do it to you. She suggested telling the rest of the family that they may have to pick up the slack for a bit. R.I.G.H.T.

Could you write me a prescription out for that? Does it work? I bet I already know the side effects, and I bet it only works in 20 percent of the people.

How to Hold a Grudge

Forever. Expect nothing less from me. That is all.

JUNE 2011

On Vacay

While on vacation last week with my nephew, Andrew, his girlfriend, and Goose, I took a trek with Goose into Subway to bring lunch back for the gang. I don't cook, remember? I don't even like slapping sandwiches together, obviously. (Go ahead and judge me. I was a perfect mother for nineteen years. It was too exhausting, and it broke me—broke me, you hear?)

I said to Goose, "I don't think I can handle Subway. We'd have to spell out too many choices for too many people. I'd rather go pick up some ready-made sandwiches in Winn-Dixie." But alas, *somebody* likes to give everyone their own little choice so it's perfect, and it's not me. So off we went to Subway. You know, where you have to pick out the bread, the exact filling each person on your list wants, then the sandwich spread they want. This, on six subs. The line was out the door when we walked up. My anxiety kicked into overdrive.

After making those anxiety-driven decisions for each sub, I went over to fill my drinks. I came back to the checkout counter to pay. I thought to myself, *Phew, I made it. No loss of limbs, just additional grays*. I moved my soda over to pay when I discovered I had not fastened the lid on that damned soda securely. My soda went all over the checkout counter, my Betty, my feet, and some of my food, wrapped and ready to go.

¶ MiraLAX® Dissolves in Vodka, Ya Know ⁋

The poor, harried lady at checkout, who was about sixty years old, looked up at me and said, "Wow, during rush hour—why don't you just slap me, too?" We both burst out laughing as we mopped up. I apologized profusely, and I told her how I was so pleased with myself that I had made it through the stress-provoking *Seinfeld*-esque, Soup-Nazi line unscathed, then went and topped it off with spilling all over our order and her counter.

Thank goodness for that lady's sense of humor.

P.S. When people in the south say, "Bye," it sounds like, "Baaaa."

I Told You I Lack Pigment in My Legs

I think if you look somewhere in the introduction, you'll find "lack pigment in legs" in my description of myself. Here is proof. Goose is on the right. Granted, I stay in the shade, am "the queen of sunscreen," and she is half-Greek, but this is pretty wild:

{ Sarah Berardi }

Valet Parking Conundrum, Again

I'm having another conundrum (when am I *not* having a conundrum). At THWIV, volunteers get complimentary valet parking. I always find it puzzling that when my car is brought around for me at the end of the day, Howard Stern is blasting out of my radio. I do not listen to Howard Stern. The ride from the parking garage to where I am waiting is hardly enough time for them to change the Sirius station I had been listening to before I handed my keys over to them. "Them." They are my friends. Or so I thought. Since I cannot tip them as per the rules, I bring them treats once a week. I think I would rate as a "good" friend. After the radio debacle started happening continually, I decided they were turning tricks in my car (think *Seinfeld* episode) during my eight hours in the hospital.

My family told me I was crazy.

Then get a glimpse of what I found between my console and seat today whilst vacuuming the car:

Just want you to know, I don't own an afro comb since I do not sport an afro. What do you think? A little bungle in the jungle goin' on in my car while listenin' to Howard Stern?

Call Me "Sarah Curie," 'K?

Wow, today I raced from one appointment to the next. First I had X-rays of my spine, looking for any elusive reason for my migraines (a never-ending quest) in the occipital nerve area. Then I raced over to the foot doctor, where I again had more X-rays of my foot, which has been *throbbing*. I glowed bright green by the time I got home from all the radioactivity. I am usually glowing, but not in that particular color of green.

The results, interestingly, were both the same: degenerative arthritis. I hate to tell y'all this, but most of you reading this have DA, too. This I know from my classes at University at Buffalo's MiniMed School. Though degenerative arthritis is very common, sometimes you can live with it, sometimes you can't. Depends upon how much it degenerates and where it degenerates. (If you end up rubbing bone on bone or pinching a nerve because of it, for instance. Pinch a nerve *root*—surgery.) I am an MD, remember, so I know these things. (See inserted pic.)

DR. BERARDI

The foot doctor recommended (admonishingly so) that I give up the offending pair of heels that I confessed started this new round of pain. (They are *gorgeous,* I tell you, and this was big of me to admit.) What he doesn't know is that there are many offending shoes in my closet. This was a no-brainer, though. He then recommended some physical therapy. If that doesn't work, we'll try one—and only one—shot of cortisone into the offending joint. Bah. Then, if there's no progress, I'll have surgery to put in a new joint. He's very conservative, which I love. He also said I should always wear something on my feet at home, such as Crocs! I told him I will not wear Crocs, aka birth control shoes. He became exasperated with me, but I made him agree I was right. (I wore Crocs after the first surgery he did on my other foot, the one where I slipped on the shower step one week after surgery and broke my just-fixed toe. FYI, months later the pin he put in on the *other* side of said fixed foot came out and had to be surgically removed. *I love the drugs.*)

Glowingly,

S. Curie

P.S. Tomorrow I'm off to a TMJ "manipulator" to see if she thinks TMJ triggers the migraines. I'm leaving no stone unturned. See how desperate I've become?

P.P.S. Interestingly, I read in the X-ray report that the degenerative arthritis might also actually be *herniation* of three discs, possibly narrowing an artery or something in my neck somewhere, therefore decreasing blood flow to brain! Ha! (Stop nodding. I can see you.)

Migraining Again

After losing it in the neurologist's office—as in crying like a big ol' baby saying I just can't do the headaches anymore (not that I have a choice)—I managed to calm myself down to a halting cry versus the full-fledged, can't-breathe cry (I hate it when I let myself break down like that). The neurologist's PA started the Botox injections that go into my scalp.

She said, "Hold on, hold on here."

I said, "Now what?"

She said, "You have a huge, black, mole-type thing in your ear, here." (She sounded a little alarmed.)

I chokingly said back to her, "Oh, that's just probably a clump of mascara."

❧ MiraLAX® Dissolves in Vodka, Ya Know ☙

She said, "*You wear mascara in your ears?*"

I explained that the type of mascara I wear has silicone in it and comes off in sticky clumps when I cry. Therefore, the mole was probably just a clump of mascara. Indeed, it was.

She thought she had discovered the root of my migraine problem, that I had been shoving things in the wrong places, like mascara in my ears, or whatever...

JULY 2011

My Sheets

I think I've mentioned before that one of my all-time favorite things is to have someone other than me put clean sheets on my bed. Every birthday and Mother's Day, that's what I ask for. Doesn't happen much, but I keep asking.

Last month, I saw a great deal on Overstock.com for eight-hundred-thread-count sheets. I've never owned eight-hundred-thread-count. I bought two sets. One for here and one set for our place in Georgia. They are, indeed, heaven. So when my gal pal and I got into our place in Georgia (on our long drive from the airport), I kept saying to Jen, "The cleaning lady better have put those new sheets I sent down on *my* bed, not yours." It was clear I was going to be sooo upset if I didn't have those sheets on my bed, that she calmly said, "If they are not, Sarah, we will just take them off my bed and put them on yours." I think I heard her say, "What a pain in my ASS," under her breath.

When I climbed into bed, I texted her downstairs. "I HAVE THE SHEETS!" But she was apparently already asleep.

In the morning, she said she thought the text read, "I HAVE THE SHITS." I told her a million times she should just get glasses and wear them all the time instead of those dollar-store ones she only wears every now and then.

Honk

I was minding my own business driving to meet another gal pal for our usual "cheap fish fry." I pulled up to the corner to turn right on red when the pickup truck next to me beeped. I thought to myself, *Crikey, just leave me alone! I have a headache, and I didn't do anything wrong!*

I looked over and rolled down my window. I asked the two fellows, "Why are y'all beepin' at me?"

They said, "Just being friendly."

I said, "Really? It's not because I cut you off by accident, or I'm super ugly and you're making fun of me, or I have a booger in my nose?"

They laughed and said, "Nope!"

"OK, then, peace out."

Off I went for my ninety-nine-dollar cheap fish fry. How does that happen in Elma, New York? A whopping ninety-nine dollars for dinner for two? Ridiculous. We have a miraculous propensity for starting out cheap and ending up eye-poppingly expensive. Only two drinks (total), by the way.

Off to Boston Doctor

So I've officially been accepted as a patient with Dr. Carolyn Bernstein at Beth Israel Deaconess, the teaching hospital for Harvard Medical School. She wrote *The Migraine Brain*. Apparently she doesn't take just any kookadoodle-doo who calls up and says, "I have a headache." I had to send all my records from the Diamond Headache Center in Chicago where I started out, as well as my records from here. My doctor here is happy to work with her, which is great.

This doctor specializes in female migraines—YAY, since last time I checked, I was still female and I have migraines. I couldn't get in until August 8, six weeks away. I'm already planning my shopping on Mulberry Street the weekend of my appointment, if I'm not migraining.

One of my latest blood test results came back, saying, "Your body cannot properly make the enzyme responsible for breaking down folate or folic acid into a usable form for your brain. It can result in problems with your motivation, initiative, *alertness, concentration,* mood, and sociability."

For cripes sake, migraines themselves cause confusion and trouble concentrating. On top of all that, the antiseizure medication I take for the prevention of my migraines can cause... *confusion* and *trouble concentrating* (among other things).

And here I volunteer at least forty hours a week at a hospital where the secretary highlights my mistakes. Yup.

What goes around comes around. That's all I'm saying. Remember, I'm a grudge holder.

Beg Your Pardon, Dumbass?

I was at the dinner table when "she" (I'm just going to call her "she" to protect myself) said, "Yeah, but you don't know what marriage is really like, Sarah."

My fork desperately wanted to stop midway into my mouth, but I knew better. She might blow her stack if I didn't just calmly listen to her BS (blow worse than me—yup, worse). It would be the normal scene where she turns into a childish, self-righteous prig. She's always been a self-righteous prig, but she can turn into an unusually self-righteous one once when she's ticked off. Take my word for it, you just don't want be around her then. Nobody does. She turns into a five-year-old having a temper tantrum. Nice.

Interestingly enough, her new little sad-eyed husband (she's had a few husbands) who seems afraid of her said, "Yeah, Sarah, you don't know what it's like."

Okeydokey. Just how was I going to deal with this? I simply asked, "Why do you say that?" knowing full well where she was going with this—that Marty traveled so much of the time during our marriage, how could I possibly know what marriage is really like? Indeed, that's what the biatch said. Believe it or not, because I've experienced her psychoness, I just said, "Humph, I guess that's one way to look at it."

I excused myself ASAP after dishes were done, went upstairs to call Marty, and cried with anger at this ignorant remark. Ignorant on so many counts. My definition of marriage has something to do with commitment, fidelity, and devotion of my life to someone. This is how I've made my marriage work for twenty-eight years now.

Meanwhile, I was aware of the affairs she had while she was married. This last affairee she ended up marrying after her divorce became final. As for *moi*, I think I *made* my marriage work. Actually, I worked really, really hard at it. I had the kids call Daddy if they hit a home run that day in baseball/softball; were voted in as president of the class; got a compliment from the dance teacher; or maybe got third place in the science fair or some other thing that I thought was necessary to keep Daddy connected to the kids and to me. I'd call him if I had a bad day, if I had a good day (yes, I had them back then), or if I just plain missed him. We'd talk all the time to see how our days went. It's part of marriage. When he lived in Germany six months before the kids and I got there, I wrote a letter to him (handwritten) every single day, even though we talked on the phone twice a day. We still talk at least once a day when he travels now. (We talk once a day on the phone when he's in town!) All this happens no matter what time zone he's in. So you see, I *do* know what it's like to be married. I just worked harder at it than she ever did. Marriage isn't just about "I am not happy." That's for babies—selfish babies.

Part of her misconception is that she thinks I feel "entitled," the definition of which is: to furnish with a right or claim to something. I couldn't think of what she thought I felt entitled to. (Is that a dangling participle?) The only thing I claim in life is my dignity, my kids, and my husband. I think the kaleidoscope she's been looking through all her life is pointing backward, don't you?

I Am in Love

I am in love. I am in love with Sir Paul McCartney. Marty has been a huge Beatles fan since he was about seven. I, however, was always a Monkees fan—as in Davy Jones. Yum. But no more. Paul's my man, right behind Marty, of course.

All our family road trips always included little snippets (provided by Marty) of info for each Beatles song Marty played (and sang) on the CD player. Even when the kids were still young enough to be strapped into their car seats, he would quiz them by shouting back to them, "Who's the lead singer in this song?" Jeez. I think they've been scarred for life from this because I've actually seen one of them in a public setting, when a Beatles song came on the sound system as background music, blurt out (in the middle of a conversation), "George Harrison!"

So Marty said to me that if I *really* loved him, I'd arrange for us to go see Paul McCartney on his concert tour and not whine about it as an early birthday present (both the nonwhining and the tickets being his birthday present) for him.

Sarah Berardi

Great. I sent him the concert tour link so he could pick out where he wanted to see him in concert. He picked Wrigley Field in Chicago, historic in itself.

Three weeks later, off we went. Never mind that I had just spent the last thirty-six hours in bed with my doggone usual migraine, I was saving up my rescue drugs for the concert. No way was I going to ruin this for him.

We checked into The Drake, which I love due to its history. Google it, I'm too lazy to tell you about it and it's off subject. I've stayed there before whilst going back and forth to the Diamond Headache Center. They recently converted to a Hilton, making much-needed renovations. It's beautiful and grand.

The gates were supposed to open at Wrigley at 6:00 p.m. We stood in line for forty-five minutes in ninety-three-degree heat until they opened the gates at six thirty. Marty didn't drip. He's a freak. How does he do that? I dripped enough for the two of us. We had floor tickets, center stage, twelve rows back. Sooooooo worth it. The show was supposed to start at seven. It was ticking me off that everyone was sitting around the bar/snack areas instead of sitting in their seats. Was that why Paul McCartney wasn't coming out yet?

He finally came out at eight thirty. He played until eleven thirty—a solid three hours with no breaks and three encores. How did he do that? I think he's sixty-nine years old! Where does he get that energy? He was so personable; not vulgar, not a goober, just a normal Joe.

There were no drunks there (well, maybe the woman behind me who laid on top of my head for a bit for a quick rest). The audience was mature and so well-behaved. Quite different from my Lady Gaga concert! He sprinkled his performance with little bits of commentary.

1) "I try to remind myself not to read the signs when I'm performing because then I can't remember the words to the song or the cords I'm in the middle of playing." He then read a few signs (I'm paraphrasing):

Please hug my wife so she shuts up.

I'm a priest. I want to do your next wedding.

2) "We were brought up in school thinking of the USSR as BAD, then suddenly I'm over there in Russia meeting their defense minister, and he's telling me the first record he bought was 'Love Me Do.' I also met some other big-deal fellow (among lots more) who said he learned English by listening to our Beatles lyrics. Then he shook my hand and said, 'HelloGood-bye' all in one word."

❧   MiraLAX® Dissolves in Vodka, Ya Know   ☙

THIS IS AS HAPPY AS MARTY GETS

Taxi Drivers

I know taxi drivers in general drive fast so they can get from point A to point B in order to pick up more customers to make more money. I also know when Sciencegirl, her friend, Liz, and I were in New York City, I was really, really bamboozled by some slimeball, which still makes me mad since I didn't call the cops right then and there, as he would have hightailed it out of there without any payment at all. Instead, like a wimp, I paid him, but not what he claimed we owed him, since between the three of us we didn't even have that much. He claimed because we went into another borough, it was three times the cost… this was obviously a few years back. He's on my list.

Fast-forward to last Saturday night. We flew into Chicago, got into a taxi, and Marty so kindly asked the driver if he'd take it easy, as I was a little sick to my stomach due to flying and my headache. The driver said, "Oh sure, sure." It didn't slow him down one darned bit. Poophead. Those corners are sharp at fifty-five miles per hour. Then, way too early Monday morning, we hopped back into a taxi to get back to the airport. Again, Marty asked the same thing. The driver wasn't very interested in his tip, apparently. I poked my head up through the open plastic divider and mentioned to him that there was no need to go fast as we were plenty early for our flight. He acknowledged me. Then Marty did the same a few wheelies after that, to no avail.

So I copied down the "complaint" phone number (hee hee), the driver's number, and his name in my phone. As we stopped to purchase our morning coffee on the way to our gate, I put my big-girl panties on and called the number to tattle on the fellow—he disobeyed me, after all. So I reported him. I felt a bit guilty in doing so. After answering all the pertinent questions, the man on the other end of the phone thanked me for calling in, but then explained that he needed my phone number, just to make sure I wasn't an angry ex-wife or something like that.

I said I understood, and gave him the name and number of one of my "frenemies." Ha! Cross one of those @#$%& s off my list! Killed two birds with one stone. I am so efficient.

Still Working on a Fix

❦ MiraLAX® Dissolves in Vodka, Ya Know ❧

AUG 2011
SEP 2011
OCT 2011

Whoa, I had a few issues for a few months. I think it was a little depression—a mini-funk, 'K?

It's Just Too Hard to Be Beautiful

Last night we took Lawyerboy out to dinner to celebrate his birthday. He's old, I'm not. Being I didn't sleep well the night before (hormones), I was a bit teary-eyed, exhausted, and just feeling like crap getting dressed for the evening. I felt fat in my dress, my dark circles couldn't be hidden, my right ear was not cooperating with putting that one earring through...

Then came the designer panty hose. I spent a lot on those darned hose. I actually had researched the best hose with people's reviews before I purchased them because they were so expensive. They were gorgeous. They had sheer, black, vertical ribbon-striping running down them.

I put the first leg on no problem. It was the second that brought me to tears. After struggling for a good ten minutes on that right leg, I gave up. They just kept going on twisted. You can't have twisted vertical striping up your leg! I hobbled downstairs in tears (menopause) with them twisted around my ankles, and tearfully cried to Marty, "I can't get my panty hose on."

The poor guy is trying so hard, he deserves something; I'm just not sure what yet. He softly (and I think a little fearfully) said, "What do you want me to do? Take them off for you or help you put them on?"

"ON," I pathetically blurted through mucus (my makeup dripping like Alice Cooper in concert). He looked at them from afar and said, "Sarah, those are not right, there is no possible way they can be made straight. They are just plain made wrong."

I said, "Oh," with great relief that it wasn't because of my medications or premenopause that I was stupid and couldn't get my panty hose on—something a lady learns to do when she is twelve. I ripped them off, threw them on the ground, and found a different pair that was so tenuous that if the small, small run that had already started in it continued, I would look just like Britney Spears. And off we went.

Doctor's Office Staff: Bring It On, Baby

Some of you guys who thought I had no cojones obviously don't know my Italian family. Should I just get a tattoo on my forehead, "I have cojones"?

Today I arrived early for my much-prepared-for doctor appointment to see about getting a spinal epidural (or something like that) injected between my herniated cervical discs (slight chance it might have something to do with the migraines). My "physical medicine and rehab" doctor recommended it. It took weeks, I tell you—weeks—to get the appointment, so I was Johnny-on-the-Spot in filling out all my records beforehand per their explicit instructions and faxing them to their office within the required amount of time. This was a totally new Freudian-annalistic predocumentation procedure to me. All my fax transmittals came back with the sheet confirming transmittal was A-OK. A-OK. A-OK. It's not rocket science to follow their instructions, just a general pain in the ass.

I made my first mistake when the office girl called out what I thought was the name "Sarah." I went up to the counter, and she started yelling and accusing me of not having the forms filled out properly. *Whoa.* Upon further discussion, she told me I was not a new patient. I said I was. She told me the primary doctor I had written down was wrong. After being told I was wrong so many times, I finally said, "Did you call Sarah Berardi?"

"No, Sharon." So sorry, must have been because *I've had a migraine for three years now*, and Fox News is blaring in my ears in your waiting room. Keep in mind, this is a chronic-pain doctor we're all waiting to see. Everyone must have been on narcotics but me to be able to tolerate the decibel level of the TV.

Fifteen minutes later, she called me back up as, "SARAH"—as if I had a hearing problem and was three years old. Not to be outdone and ever so officious, I already had my co-pay, ID, and insurance card out—oh, and an attitude.

The bitch then (accusingly) said loud enough for the waiting room and the office next door to hear, "You don't have your doctor's recommendation/referral here." I told her I had already faxed them.

"Well, we only have this part."

"Well, you should have both parts, as I have proof both went through with my fax transmittal form here, plus the MRI results speak for themselves—I have a funny feeling the doctor can figure them out."

All of a sudden, another office girl chirped in, "Plus we don't have your current medications listed." (Please insert another accusatory, inflammatory tone in that statement.)

I said, "Are you talking to *me*?"

My medications were clear as a bell on the form in her hand I had faxed already—I could see it from where I was standing.

End of rope for me. I quietly said, "I'll take my ID, co-pay, and insurance card back right now, please," and I left. I drove down the street and made an appointment with a different doctor who was also on my list of doctors who could perform the same damn thing.

Bring it on, baby. Angie's List, here I come. "Rate Your Doctor and Rate Your Physician," here I come.

P.S. I am mailing a copy of this blog to the doctor so he can see how his office staff is so friendly. You know I will.

I'm in Salt Lake City

I decided I would tag along on Marty's trip out to Salt Lake City while he's visiting the office here. I might as well lie in bed here versus at home, right? It's a city, after all. It's still so beautiful from the Olympics, even though statues of what's his name, Brigham Young, are all around. Boy, he sure does have quite a compound here. http://www.utah.com/mormon/temple_square.htm. So I thought

❦ MiraLAX® Dissolves in Vodka, Ya Know ❧

while I was here I'd find myself a few sister-wives. You know, one to clean, one to cook, and perhaps one to do whatever I fancy whenever—as in, go fill my car with gas. You can tell all the fellows who work at the compound, all dressed in dark with white shirts and tags hanging off their belts. Women look…well, let's face it, dowdy.

I've been here before when Marty lived here for bursts of time. I've done the tours. I found it amazing how little the "sisters" who gave me the tour of Brigham Young's house really knew about the outside world. Very sad, indeed. And every story they told me, I said, "Holy cow, that's the same as in the Bible, and all those other religious books, ya know?" I also talked to them (just making idle conversation—I was the only one there) about things that were happening in everyday life that were similar to things they were "teaching" me from *The Book of Mormon*. They were clueless as to what was going on on CNN! Last I knew, they, too, were allowed to watch TV. Maybe not.

I don't go for that whole "sister" thing. It's pretty disgusting. Any man who is narcissistic enough to think he could keep more than one wife happy deserves to go ahead and try, though. He gets exactly what's coming to him. Man whores.

Today I was able to prove to Libbylicious why I need to stay close to our destination in New York City when we visit and take taxis versus subways. I took the free city bus/tram thing down the Ute Mile. Well, I don't think anyone else calls it that, but I do. I needed to get to the Mac store at the mall. It would have been an easy walk for someone with a toe that didn't have a cortisone shot in it and that didn't do diddly-squat. (More surgery, drugs.) But it was freezing out! I didn't bring my woolies, nor my hat and gloves. But I looked sharp, I'll tell ya. I had my *Mad Men* suit coat on from Banana Republic, straight-legged jeans holding in that twenty-pound gut, and my black ankle booties. Yeah, well, I got lost. I don't know how, it's a straight line.

Maybe it's because I bumped my head whilst doing the backstroke in an unfamiliar pool this morning. Nah, I'm always like this.

Do you know about the Utah liquor laws: *Metered Dispensing—Utah law requires restaurants, private clubs, and airport lounges to use a metered dispensing system that is calibrated to dispense no more than one ounce of primary liquor in a mixed drink. Secondary alcoholic flavorings may then be added to a mixed drink as the recipe requires, not to exceed a total of 2.75 ounces of spirituous liquor.*

This makes my cosmos a little light. Just sayin'. Plus, you are never allowed to have another ordered drink delivered to your table until your first one is gulped down. So "gulp" is my middle name here.

Love,

Sarah Gulp Berardi

Me, Move?

Since I've been empty nested, migraining, and menopausing, I've had this new love of cities. Whenever Marty's going on a cool business trip, I yank out my charge card (well, his—I don't earn a lot lying in bed writing this blog) and threaten to book a flight alongside him. He usually lets me come. Sometimes I'd be a pain on his trip, other times I'd be tolerable, apparently. (Hence my Salt Lake City blog.)

Recently, we've been talking about selling our beloved house, which we built some twenty-four years ago. It's just a ten-minute drive to Marty's office. It's also in the middle of just about *nowhere*. I have never minded that nowhere up until now. Same with Marty. I used to drive our kids twenty-two miles each way (uphill, barefoot) to school. This obviously would include drives to all sorts of sporting events and so forth that they participated in that were nowhere near where we lived. Even the grocery store is a twenty-minute drive. I put my blinders on for twenty-four years without a problem. Now they are off.

Now I want to walk on sunshiny sidewalks (we currently have no sidewalks). I want to walk to dinner/lunch/breakfast. The closest place to go eat would be about a forty-five-minute walk on pea gravel on the side of the road. I want to order food delivery—as in groceries. I want to order dinner in if I want (we have a pizza place that delivers; I can't eat pizza). I want the availability of maid service, valet parking, and a doorman. Taxi drivers who can't speak English. Limos I can flag down to take me to a show. A driver. You name it, I want it now. What a spoiled brat.

Oy vey, life has changed. So what's holding me back? This is my home. I love it for weird reasons, apparently. I raised my kids here—in other words, I had control of things then. I can smell the manure fertilizer from the farms behind the creek. It's so quiet and peaceful. I have a nice lawn. I don't need any of that anymore, but the simple thought of taking down the posters from the now

❦ MiraLAX® Dissolves in Vodka, Ya Know ❧

twenty-five- and twenty-seven-year-old kids' bedrooms breaks my heart. (Yes, I have a heart, and no, they haven't lived at home for eight years now.) I want my grandkids to sled down that hill in my backyard with their grandma (me). Though since I've told Lawyerboy he's not allowed to spawn, I don't know if that will happen. Don't know about Sciencegirl.

But we've got an appointment with a realtor to see a condo unit in the city of Buffalo. Hey, Marty's still got to work. It's not New York, it's not Boston, and it's not Chicago by any means. When I complain about that fact, Lawyerboy points out, loudly, "You won't be walking any sidewalks in Buffalo, New York, Boston, or Chicago from December to March. Who are you fooling?" But on the other hand, the place in Buffalo has #$%-&#$% room service—my dream!

So every time I let myself think too much about taking down those posters, I cry (still waiting on that new prescription change—I think Marty's waiting more so than I). I know I can put those posters in their new bedrooms. Sciencegirl's poster is one that says, "Strive to be Different," and Lawyerboy's are of Kramer and Star Wars. Says it all, doesn't it?

Black-Tie Affairs Make Me Feel Fat

Trying to find a gown doesn't even rate compared to trying to find a bathing suit or a pair of jeans. But when you've put as much weight on as I have in the short amount of time that I have, that size on the gown label is quite a shocker. The "weight gain" listed on my Sibelium as a possible side effect proved true very quickly. And it's not showing any sign of stopping, #$%&. So I came home with two gowns to show Marty so he could help with this weighty decision (I'm funny). He couldn't get the zipper up on one—not because of my fat (he said), just because it would not go. Indeed, I couldn't get it up even when the dress was off. The other was a tight, uncomfortable fit, but doable. In fact, if it weren't for the Betty, I would have looked a little bit downright regal.

A few days earlier, I had ordered one (OK, maybe two) more dress(es) online for overnight delivery. Neither fit. Blah. I had one last standby from about a half dozen old gowns in the closet. It was the only one I could get by with if I wore a damn corset. Yeah, that's going to be comfy. And yes, they do make corset girdles (I am beyond the help of Spanx).

So the clock was ticking as I arrived back in town with just hours to spare, raced out to Lord & Taylor, tried on six more gowns in ten minutes, came home with one, and Marty said, oh so very cautiously, "Find anything?" I grumbled something in his direction that would suffice for an answer. Then I said I couldn't even *think* about what bag and shoes I would wear/use to go with the gown. He was incredulous. "You have about sixty pairs of shoes out there. How could you not find a pair?"

"It's just not that easy, Butthead." No more black-tie affairs for me. From the "filling the table" part to the "filling the gown" part, I'm O.U.T.

Tai Chi and Repulsing the Monkey

I repulsed the monkey today when all I really wanted to do was rock the casbah. My yin and yang did not go back into their fundamental, natural harmony.

I don't know what got into me, but something got my arse out of bed today. I decided to try out that cortisone shot in my toe and see if I could walk the indoor track like I used to at the Y. As I did, other people walked three abreast and broke the rules; particularly the rule about slower people staying on the outer ring while faster people use the inner ring. There are only three darned rings. Not rocket science. But nooooooo. The three-abreast ladies have to chitchat. Tell me, what's the quality of that chitchat, anyway, if you're walking fast enough to call it exercise? Move it.

Then there was this little gray-hair putting me to shame with her fast walking. Her hair was perfectly coiffed—washed, curled under a dryer hood, teased out, and combed into place. She twitched her little bum in front of me and passed with her fast walking, all five-foot-three of her. I wanted to—oops—trip the old lady, which is really not like me, but she had this smirk on her face. She circled me three times in thirty minutes.

So on I went to an hour-long tai chi class. I don't know what moved me to do that for the first time, either. There was one other lady there, who was also new to the class. Then who walked in but the three-abreast ladies? Great.

Apparently tai chi is sort of really slow self-defense. I've seen guys in yoga shorts on the beach out on a sandbar doing it. Sorry, after I found out I was repulsing a monkey, slaying a dragon, and then letting a butterfly go down my waterfall, I was out. Plus, we had to go around the room and take turns counting to ten with each move. That in itself made me really nervous, awaiting my turn to count so I didn't mess it up. Sciencegirl knows what I mean, I bet; that social anxiety crap.

When is that doctor appointment that's supposed to give me that friggin' happy pill? My cocoon is so much better, here in bed, than that big anxious world out there. So bottom line, tai chi is not for me. And the next person who gets in my way at the indoor track by not following the rules is going to get a sharp elbow in the solar plexus.

Irish Coffee to Start the Day (Just a Wee Bit)

Holidays are not my bag. Those fond childhood memories of cherished, beloved holidays most people have aren't in my shrunken-dendrite brain. Except last year, of course, where I planted that remote-controlled fart machine under Lawyerboy's chair.

This year, Sciencegirl is sciencing in Germany, still, which means she and her boyfriend won't be here. My nephews won't be here where they belong. Sad but true, it's just me, Mart, Goose, and Lawyerboy. Sounds pathetic, but Marty is determined to make this a proper festive holiday (he's such a sport).

At ten thirty this morning he came up and asked me if I was alive (I was sleeping, of course). I just gave him the "Andrea grunt."

You see, the dank, dismal-dreaming thought of Thanksgiving means Christmas is right around the corner. Christmas is oh so much worse. Worse since *someone*—a boil-brained boar pig in my growing-up family) became Mr. Midlife Crisis. But mostly it's just so overwhelming. But then again, showering is overwhelming to me, so how is a holiday not going to overwhelm me? (That doctor appointment isn't for another few weeks. Sorry, folks.)

So as I sit here writing in bed, I hear my thoughtful husband (through sickness and in health), prepping the turkey I bought and defrosted. He is the turkey-meister. We smoked our turkey last year, but this year he wanted his good old-fashioned turkey in the oven. He takes great pride in his bird, yelling at anyone who peeks by opening the oven.

I did go downstairs to get a cup of coffee, and added my MiraLAX® with a little Irish whiskey (it's a holiday). I shall eventually make the bed today (unusual), shower, pick up my bedroom, and await the arrival of Lawyerboy and Goose's dog Scampainintheass—I mean Maddie—the most spoiled dog I've ever seen. If she pees on my rug, she's going to be roasted and basted, too. And never fear, I will love having Marty, Goose, Lawyerboy, and the life-size picture of Sciencegirl at my table.

But hey, happy Thanksgiving.
Little Miss Sunshine

Sarah Berardi

I Love My Honest Friends

I was explaining to my honest friend how I thought Audrey Hepburn was such a classy lady, and how I admired her look, especially her short bangs. It was such a bold look. And then I explained how Katy Perry has those same type of short bangs (well, sometimes). My friend kindly said, "Yeah…but Sarah…that haircut's not for…you know, *everyone*."

When I showed my friend that I was wearing my manly Oxford shoes today, knowing full well she hates them, I apologized for their filth, explaining they needed a good shine. She said, "You actually wear them that often that they need a shining?"

When I rhetorically ask the kids if I used to be this stupid (as stupid as I am now), they say yes. (It's a loving type of yes.)

When I ask Goose if my dress makes me look fat, she simply says, "Yes, Cruella."

I warned a friend of my latest caper at the office in THWIV, explaining that when he saw the capered picture of me it would have a few extra pounds on it compared to when he last saw me. He texted me the next day, saying, "Nice picture, Porkie!"

Another friend, tired of hearing me blather about my weight gain, said, "Nice to hear you're bulking up for the winter."

But these are my friends, and these things make me laugh. They know they make me laugh with these types of comments. They're snarky. I love the snark. It's all good, it's how we float.

DEC 2011

Pre-Surgery Testing Requires an Education

When I was getting dressed this morning, I decided I might put on something nice instead of my usual "pretend I'm a doctor" scrubs, as I was headed out for my pre-surgery testing. My first encounter with a human was the blood-taker lady at a pre-surgery screening. She was being nice and making conversation, and said, "You look so nice. Are you headed back to work?" I was a little embarrassed to say, "No, back to bed."

She took my EKG and blood, and sent me to the nurse for questions. The new nurse filled out the form as I answered her questions. Around the seventh question she asked, "What is the highest level of your education?" I took a second to think (shut up, I *can* do it). I said, "I mean no disrespect, but I don't answer that question." She looked up from the paper she was so arduously filling out and just looked puzzled. I said I didn't generally answer that question, unless she wanted to put "enough" as my answer. I asked her if she knew why it was asked. She said, "Just for general information so we know how well the patient will understand what's going on."

I felt insulted. I told her I had three PhDs from the University of Google. She looked even more puzzled. And she wasn't laughing.

It puzzles me why this question is so commonly asked. I know, I know, it's her job to fill out that form. But the question she had asked previous to that was, "In your own words can you tell me what surgery you're having done?"

I said, "Partial turbinectomies and septoplasty."

She said, "No, honey, your *own* words."

I quietly said, "Those are my own words." Surprise, some of us dumb-assed lay people from U of G actually understand that stuff. Not to mention I've read about it for years in search of face-pain relief.

As I left, she admonished me for not having the proper milligrams noted on my medical form for two out of the ten drugs I had listed. It was my fault. I gave her that.

P.S. I don't know just how educated she really thought I was. I only had one earring in all day. Just couldn't get that right one in, so left it out.

Holy Crap, the Psychiatrist

Do not *ever* send me to a psychiatrist again. This particular dingbat is Dr. T.

I should preface this blog by saying I met this wonderful, well-published, knowledgeable, greatest-bedside-mannered psychiatrist (who, darn it all, only diagnoses and doesn't treat) who sent me to this new dingbat. So there are some good ones out there. Psychs are supposed to be neuropharmacologists—that's why I went. This #$%^&, Dr. T, was not. Why are the ones with a good bedside manner similar to my Sciencegirl more into research than people?

First, I spent hours filling out forms, which were sent to me before my appointment. Being truthful on the forms made my eyes leaky. I was being so nakedly honest. How would I handle the appointment? I was actually warned by a friend that this guy was an arrogant prick. I thought to myself, *I can't fight this one*. (This is very unlike me.)

Well, he won. I lost. I battled him in the beginning, but guess what his third question was? "What is your highest level of education?"

I replied, "I left it blank for a reason."

"What's your reason?"

"Because people shouldn't judge me on my degree. Perhaps you could just judge me on how smart I am by talking to me?"

Okeydokey, I put this appointment in the Dumpster straight off.

Later on in the painfully long appointment he said, "I see you've tried ecstasy."

"*I most certainly did not.*"

"Well, you checked here that you did, and more importantly, you signed it at the bottom stating all the above statements are true."

I said, "I think we should go build a cross and nail me to it. I made a mistake. I've never tried ecstasy. Though I appreciate you pointing out how I made a mistake."

In the end, he diagnosed me with "Sarcasm."

Please, my blog readers know that. And I have a PhD from the University of Google telling me exactly what's wrong with *him* (he's an arrogant prig), and exactly what he needed to prescribe for me, so screw him. Have a good day, buddy. I kind of hate you. He prescribed shit that I won't fill.

Timely call from Libbylicious. She and I are sending him a book on neuropharmacology, since he didn't have a clue what drugs I was referring to with my migraine meds (even though I gave him the brand name, the generic name, and, um, maybe the Latin name). Our note will say, "To keep up with your profession."

In Sarcasm,

Little Miss @#$%ing Sunshine

The Waiting Room

Now that I've slept on yesterday for a day (!), I can remember the waiting room from my trip to the batshitprig psychiatrist, Dr. T. From way down the hall before anyone walked into the tiny waiting room, I could hear a repetitive *thud, click, swoosh*. About every other *thud, click, swoosh*, came a grunt. It was enough of a sound to make me wonder if someone needed help. As I was about to go see if someone needed assistance, an elderly man turned the corner of the long hallway with a white-haired, miserable-looking woman. He had an oxygen tank on a three-legged pole along with his regular cane.

I smiled at them and went back to my reading. By the time they made it into the waiting room, he huffed and puffed out to me:

Man: I like those boots you have there. Women don't know how to dress anymore.

Me: Oh, thank you.

❦ MiraLAX® Dissolves in Vodka, Ya Know ❧

Man: You look mighty fine. I watched Victoria's Secret the other night and went through two tanks of oxygen.

Wife: Shut up, quit talking. You can't even breathe.

Man: What do you know? She looks nice.

I looked at the wife and smiled. She didn't smile back.

Then another man walked in who, I kid you not, was a replica of that guy from the *Bob Newhart Show* who went for treatment, Elliot Carlin—toupee and all. Actually, now that I've looked up recent pics of him, maybe it was him!

(Go to Google Images and look up Elliot Carlin. My attorney said I couldn't put my perfect picture I found of him in my book. Poo.)

He came up to the oxygened man and said:

Elliotman: I lost my brother to smoking, you know.

Man: I don't wanna hear about it. (He turns to me.) I got hooked on cigarettes in the war.

Me: Yeah, they gave them to you guys like candy back then, didn't they?

Wife: Shut up, leave her alone. Stop talking to her.

Man: What? She doesn't have holes in her jeans, she looks nice. Nobody dresses nice anymore.

The wife then talks to Elliot Carlin, who had the same mannerisms as the character on TV, I swear.

What the hell was I doing there? Then my doctor called me in. With twenty-twenty hindsight, I'd have been better off staying out in the waiting room with the normal kookadoodledoos, since he was Dr. Evil.

I'm going back to bed, even though he asked why, if I'm so fat, I don't do something about it? He's got that "depression" lingo down, doesn't he?

Cocaine with Your Surgery, Madame?

I hate to say this, but this was my second-highest "hit" day on my blog. That was a pun. Must be that catchy title. (My largest hit was the one about Salt Lake City—don't know why.)

I've never done any type of illegal drug. Never. I can't even say, "I didn't inhale," because, well, I just didn't. Clinton was so silly, wasn't he?

As of right now, my alarm will go off in four hours. Tomorrow morning, I go under the chisel and mallet. Not kidding. I'm having my deviated septum fixed and having those nasty turbinates taken away so they will no longer encumber the path of breathing through my nose. I made the mistake of watching the surgery on YouTube. YUCK. All my other surgeries I feel I could have done myself; I could have taken my own gallbladder out, my own Madame Bovary out, my own adhesions out, my own breast lump out, put my own screws in my feet, fixed my own shoulder. But this one has me freaked. Someone's actually going to banging on my face with a mallet. That's the stuff you see Daffy Duck doing. Or the Roadrunner.

The biggest complaint after this surgery is that they have to pack your nose with a gazillion feet of gauze-type packing, which proves to be painful. Taking it out is apparently not only disgusting, but uncomfortable. Well, my doctor said he doesn't use it! He uses *cocaine,* as it's a great vasoconstrictor. Great, the first time I could "trip" without guilt, and I'll be asleep for it.

A lot of my friends have had the surgery, and they all suggest I have plenty of Chapstick around, since I'll be breathing out of my mouth for three days or so. I can remember my sister telling me to shut up when we would watch TV because I was breathing through my mouth, way too loudly, apparently. I've never been able to breathe really well through my nose. (It is obnoxious when you can hear someone sitting next to you breathing.) Screw you now, Sissy.

All this is done in hopes of making a path of clear sailing up to my brain. New evidence shows that migraines could come from a lack of oxygen, causing the vessels in your head to constrict. We always knew I lacked oxygen to my brain (seems obvious?), but maybe there's actually something to it. Plus, those darn turbinates apparently are giving off negative ions. I kid you not. That's the study I took into my ENT doctor. I refuse to give it up.

So think of me as you're reading this. I'll have a nice, straight septum; you, most likely, will not. My swollen and inflamed turbinates will be gone; yours, most likely, will not. And I will be enjoying pain medication; you, most likely, will not.

P.S. Don't know if you noticed I left one major surgery out that I know I could not have done myself. Just can't reach there, ya know?

Surgery, Cocaine, and Lima Beans?

I know, I know, you're all waiting to hear if I "felt" the four hundred milligrams of cocaine up my nose, right?

❡ MiraLAX® Dissolves in Vodka, Ya Know ❡

I did not. All I remember feeling was that old-man anesthesiologist who slurred his words and stabbed me with what he claimed was their smallest needle to start my IV.

Starting IVs are always the worst part of surgery for me. I'm not an easy vein person. The inserter tends to infiltrate, or my blood pressure is so low that the veins just flatten like a wet Slip 'n Slide. Not fun—lends itself to lots of jabbing around. Of course, I had to *zing* back at him, "That *can't* be your smallest IV needle in the hospital. They sometimes use children's needles on me. Don't you have any children as patients here?" Aren't I a snot? He said nothing in return, thank goodness, because you know I wouldn't have backed down. (Yes, I know this is a flaw of mine.) Why would he say something so foolish? Had I embarrassed the elf-skinned barnacle by covering my mouth with my spare hand and saying "Yikes!" when he stabbed me? I hope so. You shouldn't just go around stabbing people. You should go around inserting, not stabbing. Just don't mess with me. *But*, he was my gas man, so why was I trying to fight with him? He was supposed to be giving me extra antinauseant, and here I was sparring with him? Dumbass.

Down three hallways and to the right I was given my "cocktail" and an oxygen mask. I woke up without all the dreaded, painful packing they usually jam up your nose, so the cocaine stopped the bleeding! This must be the reason I feel about the same right now as when I had my nose cauterized years before. Or maybe I'm feeling fine because of the codeine. Hmm.

Interestingly enough, the doctor not only cleaned out my sinuses, turbinectomied me (I just made up another word), and straightened my septum, but he also found four roguish polyps. Might they have anything to do with my #$%^ migraines I've had for three years? One was the size of a *lima bean* he said, and the other three were the size of peas. I was growing a dark, dank vegetable garden up there—gross. Huh!

So I've been sitting up in bed. I have to stay in an upright position, which is probably why I can't sleep, on top of my normal premenopause inability to sleep. Not complaining (this time). I've got my computer, book, and TV, and no Marty snoring at the moment.

I have no idea if four hundred milligrams (of the cocaine) is what he said. I think that's what he said. But I also saw kitty cats sitting on mantels and bugs crawling the walls when I woke up. Whatever.

Love, Little Miss Lima Bean

… Sarah Berardi …

I Smell

Well, I used to smell. Since my little sinus surgery, I've lost my sense of smell and taste. This has had an interesting effect. I usually have this (fattening) craving for popcorn with butter on it, 24/7. I've thought about my popcorn out of habit, I guess, but I haven't gone and made any. It's not worth it if you can't taste it. I might as well be eating cardboard.

Can you imagine not smelling coffee, gasoline, red wine, sewage, magic markers, or worms on the driveway? Popcorn at the theatre. That pine scent I spray on my fake Christmas tree. I wonder if it will come back. My family calls me "sonar nose." I'm the weirdo that would smell a gas leak on the way to take the kids to school, call and report it, and on my way home find six bulldozers tearing up a gas pipe on some poor soul's front lawn. (I'm petrified of gas leaks, and how could the neighbor not bloody well smell it?)

I can smell BO from a mile away. I can smell Florida when I land there. I can smell smoke from afar. I was a devout smeller. Now I can't smell sh#t. Literally.

I also can't taste. I was eating some cracked-pepper crackers today. Nada. Zilch. No pepper taste, but my mouth is sort of burning from the pepper. I've lost four pounds with this no taste/smell thing. Maybe I should hope it never comes back!

What is the thing you would miss most if you couldn't taste it ever again? Or what smell would you miss most if you couldn't smell it again? My quick answer without thinking too deeply would be my beloved popcorn with real butter—for both my taste and smell.

And to think, I just paid a gazillion dollars to have a venting machine put in my basement so it didn't smell like an old person's basement. I bet Marty wishes I would have had my surgery before I found this company that makes these venting machines. I have no idea if it's working now or not. Marty's sniffer stinks—ha! So I don't trust his judgment.

So you people out there, stop taking your senses of smell and taste for granted. So much for my career in taking Padma's place in *Top Chef*.

Are You a Tooter?

Of your own horn? Oy vey, I keep reading things where people are tooting their own horns. Must I keep submitting articles on being humble?

❧ MiraLAX® Dissolves in Vodka, Ya Know ☙

The only ones who should hear it (your tooting, in every form) are your closest of family. Those are the ones you can brag to, not the World Wide Web, 'K? I find it interesting that the people who toot quite often also don't have a problem putting others down—to make themselves look good, no doubt. Hmm, what does my oh so deep Psych 101 say about that? Um, nothing, we only studied those stupid rods and pins in your eyeballs.

If you're good at something, you'll get noticed. I guess we all have that innate neediness to have others pat us on the back. I know I need it 36/7 (not a typo).

So toot to someone who gives a hoot, 'K? And the worst part is that the people who tooted won't realize I'm talking about them.

I Am Not a Freak—So Says Myers-Briggs!

Last night as Marty lay here snoring, I was up doing a Myers-Briggs personality test, just for kicks and giggles. Marty's been "shrunk" by shrinks a gazillion times in his work, so he's pretty well-versed in this personality delving. http://www.humanmetrics.com/cgi-win/JTypes2.asp.

When I shared my results with him, we almost crapped our pants! I kid you not: ISFJ—Introverted Sensing Feeling Judging. I know you're laughing at the "introverted" part, but the girl who used to babysit my kids can attest to that.

"*ISFJs (that's my personality, apparently, according this test), above all else, need to be needed. Often unappreciated, at work, home, and play. Ironically, because they prove over and over that they can be relied on for their loyalty and unstinting, high-quality work, those around them often take them for granted—even take advantage of them. Admittedly, the problem is sometimes aggravated by the ISFJ themselves. They are unwilling to toot their own horns* (I JUST BLOGGED ABOUT THIS!) *about their accomplishments because they feel that although they deserve more credit than they're getting, it's somehow wrong to want any sort of reward for doing work. Because of all this, ISFJs are often overworked, and as a result may suffer from psychosomatic illnesses.*"

Holy crap. Well, I was speechless, for a moment. It usually doesn't take me long to start up again. I just had the exact situation of being taken advantage of happen to me, which was partly my fault, being that I needed to be needed in the first place. Humph.

As for the psychosomatic illnesses, um…I don't know, so far every surgery I've had has pulled out deformed, defunct, dysfunctional pieces of funk from me. Proof is in the pudding, whatever that means. But it might speak more to the "depression" that some people think I have that I don't have—I just prefer to stay safely in bed. Shut. Up.

You have to try this, and then have your mate try it. See why you can't stand each other!

It also says I'm possessive of my family—check. Family is my priority—check.

It also said ISFJs are extremely loyal—check. This is why my nephew, Nick, says, "You don't F with my Aunt Sarah." You just don't mess with me or you go onto my list. But I will protect you, fiercely, if I love you. Sometimes this is not a good thing. Think of Ophelia in *Hamlet*, Melanie in *Gone with the Wind*, Bianca in *Taming of the Shrew*.

Wait, maybe they didn't have enough questions on there about formidableness. Or maybe they covered that section with loyalty? Does it imply an ISFJ goes batshitcrazy *with* their loyalty?

The best part of reading all this is that I am not a freak. Do you hear me, children? Well, child? (Just one thinks I'm a freak.) I am not alone. In fact, there's a huge, whole category of peeps like me. I am not a freak. I am not a freak.

Love, Little Miss Freakless Sunshine

I Tried to Tango—Bzzzt—Fail

I went out to dinner with my gal pals tonight. Just two of them. When I arrived alone, no waiter or waitress approached my table. So after ten minutes or so, I moseyed up to the bar to get my drink. First step in ticking me off. Ten minutes is a long time to do e-mails on your phone, waiting.

Our waiter must have been shorthanded for the evening. I had my hand raised all night, to no avail—yes, like a childish schoolgirl. All night it proved to be a problem. What part of the hand being raised did he not get?

Halfway through our dinner, a different type of music started playing. It was Tuesday night in a Mexican restaurant. We saw people changing into shoes they had brought in a bag. Whaaaaaaa? Of course, shy as I am (nowadays, AP—after Prozac), I asked a fella, "What the heck are you doing?" He told us he was tango dancing. He teaches at University at Buffalo. I got his name and number, thinking, *What a cool thing to have private lessons at a small dinner party.* Yeah?

I was fascinated in watching the dancers. An elderly, white-haired gentleman came up to me and asked me to dance. I proclaimed I was a total *non-tango* dancer, never learned a step of it. Totally ignorant. He was game. So was I. Secretly, I thought to myself, *I was a gymnast, a gymnastic teacher, a swimmer, a diver, a swim teacher—I have coordination. In sixth grade I was asked to demonstrate to the rest of the sixth grade how to dance—ha! I'm going to rock this, baby.*

After about four minutes of me reluctantly giving up the lead to him, he gave up. (What the hell was I leading? I didn't even know the steps!) He dumped me at the foot of the dance floor. I was shamed. He meant well, I was just ungiving, apparently. You surprised? I can be a little bossy. Though I felt I was giving *tremendously.*

Whatever.

P.S. Postsurgical checkup today. I didn't know there were stitches in my nose, I thought they were snookies! That's the part that's been a little painful, those stitches. I am hereby allowed to lightly, lightly blow my nose now. Eight days of no nose-blowing—huge for an allergy queen like me. I hereby swear to all my migraine followers that you must have a CT of your sinuses, though we have no idea if this is really my fix. All I know is that I've actually showered every day this week, which is a record in the last three and a half years. I got out of bed every day for the last week. (That would be because of a little mood lift due to no head pain!) That also is a record for the last three and a half years. Apparently, my CT three years ago showed nothing. The doctor said the polyps could have been newer, or they could have been hiding behind my sinuses. Or maybe the butthead doctors could have given me an updated CT scan, like I asked. Please oh please, let this be my migraine fix. Day eight with no migraine and just one headache that Tylenol fixed. No triptans. Amazing.

Botox (for Migraines, of Course)

I was actually up early yesterday to go for my three-month Botox shots in my head. No, it's not cosmetic; it's for migraine prevention. The shots are preventative migraine shots, and they don't necessarily go in places that would enhance my looks. The shots go into the top of the head, behind the ears from the temples down on both sides, across the back of the nape of the neck, and down the neck/shoulder area where I, in particular, carry the weight of my world. Some do go in the forehead, however.

I fought the shots into my forehead for one reason only. I *earned* those wrinkles on my forehead. *They have names.* Seventy-five percent of them have Lawyerboy's name on them, the other twenty-five percent have Marty's. Migraine pain won, and I succumbed to the wrinkle-free forehead. Damn. Now my eyebrows don't give nearly the crook my crook-eye used to give.

So on Marty's way out to work yesterday, he poked his head in the bathroom where I was blow-drying my hair, and he said (not knowing where the heck they inject the Botox), "If they Botox you like this, will your face Botox-freeze happy?"

THIS IS MY HAPPY FACE

He must be tired of it being frozen like this:

❡ MiraLAX® Dissolves in Vodka, Ya Know ❢

MY SAD, NORMAL, GRUMPISH FACE

Love, Little Miss Sunshine
P.S. You can see a little bruising from the injections.

JAN 2012

The Princess and the Pea

Yesterday I was lying on my bed writing on my laptop while Marty was down in his King Tut* recliner, napping. All of a sudden I heard very loud thunder along with the clinking of all our glasses in the house. The lampshades jiggled to and fro. My whole body rumbled and the whole house definitely shook.

As soon as it stopped, I ran down the stairs to ask Marty if he felt that earthquake. He quickly got out of his reclined position and said, "Is that what it was? I thought somebody was throwing something at the back of my chair."

Why oh why, would somebody throw something at the back of his chair if it was only the two of us in opposite sides of the house on two separate floors? (Don't answer that.) I told the doofus it had to be an earthquake (I felt very sure of myself) as I was lying on top of my mattress and felt it, as in the Princess and the Pea. But this pea was a movin' and a groovin' pea, not a regular old pea.

I quickly called Lawyerboy to see if he felt it, as he lives twenty-five minutes from me. He *laughed at me* and told me a snowplow probably had driven by. Nay nay, I said. I told him to ask CoD (Crack of Dawn—see list of characters) if she wanted my news scoop (she's a TV news producer). I called a neighbor. She felt it, too. OK, so I *wasn't* crazy.

❧ *MiraLAX® Dissolves in Vodka, Ya Know* ☙

I scoured the news while Viper Tongue told me on Facebook to put the martini down since it was only three o'clock in the afternoon. I was determined to find truth is this matter, since the last time I called the local police thinking I'd felt one, the dumbasses laughed at me. Nobody laughs at me. (Sure enough, it was confirmed by our University at Buffalo seismic analysis department ** later that day. So there.)

Again, I've been vindicated. Yesterday around 3:00 p.m., an earthquake of 5.0 started in Ohio and went all the way to Batavia, New York. Little old Elma, Terrace Lane, was on its path just a bit down the thruway from Batavia. Never doubt me. *This princess felt the damn pea.*

*It's called the Tut chair because when Sciencegirl was two years old, she was choking next to Marty, who was sitting with his feet up and the newspaper up, and didn't notice until I yelled down the stairs to him, "Who do you think you are, King Tut? Andrea's choking; can you smack her back or something?"

**I used to work for eight seismic engineers—just a fun fact.

My Nice Family Dinner Out

The last time the four of us (Marty, me, Sciencegirl, and Lawyerboy) went to dinner, a family of puttanas, their mother (a puttana herself) and father sat down at the table next to us. I was so flabbergasted at the attire of these three daughters, I think I was gaping, looking like Cletus the Slack-Jawed Yokel. The girls were puttanas I tell you, *puttanas*. And their figures did *not* support the puttana dresses, nor did their ages. The queen puttana, the mother, stared at me so much throughout our dinner, I was ready to do the Therese Table-Flip (*The Real Housewives of New Jersey*), go over said flipped table, grab her by the turkey neck, and ask her if she was lookin' at me. Made for a tasteless dinner.

Puttana *f.* (vulgar) whore.

Migraining—Effexor Withdrawal

Does anyone have a tranquilizer gun? If so, could you come over for…um… coffee with it loaded every day this week?

Sarah Berardi

This isn't a funny blog. It stinks coming off Effexor. Do you know its reputation as being one of the most difficult SSRIs to come off of? It was supposed to help my headaches. But my neuropharmacologist thinks it's a *contributor* to the migraines. *Great*. How many years have I been on this pill?

The only way to go off is *SLOWLY*. Painfully slowly. You can actually watch YouTube videos of people trying to get off it. I was flying high last week, thinking I was doing great at a low 37.5 level without a migraine (from three hundred mg seven months ago), when I hit a brick wall. Bam! Could not stop shaking or crying. I think I cried for *six hours straight*. I wanted to go to the ER to get something to put me to sleep (like for a week). My body shook, and it felt as if I was coming out of my own skin while I kept getting these eerie zaps in my head.

So I'm back up to the seventy-five-mg pill, but I'm extracting one or two beads from the capsule a night (and playing with Silly Putty until I fall asleep—it keeps me from biting my nails).

As for the tranquilizer gun, Lawyerboy used to sit in the back seat of the car on our twenty-two-mile ride to school in the morning. I'd be spewing out my anxiety-ridden rant about something, and I'd hear his verbal "thump" from the back of the car. I'd say, "What was that?" It was Lawyerboy, pretending he had a tranquilizer gun and had shot me in the back of the head with it.

Peace out,
Little Miss Detox

FEB 2012

I Feel Like Frankenstein

Flying home from DC last Friday, I was perpetually spraying my hands with hand sanitizer. Marty kept mocking me, saying, "Do you really think that stuff works?"

"Of course it does, can't you smell the alcohol?"

Saturday, as he was boarding his plane to Tel Aviv, I was boarding the "porcelain bus." Apparently it *doesn't* work. The good news was, A) I lost four pounds in twenty-four hours (darn, water weight); and B) it was a twenty-four-hour bug. Jeez, Louise, it left me like a three-month-old mop. When I tried to change the sheets, it took me five tries. I had to keep sitting down to rest my weary body.

Since I got sick very early Sunday morning, I struggled to get myself cleaned up and ready for three cervical facet joint injections today (Tuesday). It's not really a big deal, just…freaky. The info from the doctor said I would get a calming sedative beforehand. Never got one. He told me to bring my own next time. Oh, I will, baby.

Metrohealth.org HAS A GREAT PIC OF "CERVICAL FACET JOINT INJECTION," IF YOU'RE INTERESTED.

I had the injections as yet another effort to get rid of the migraines, which I get less frequently now, but still get. I have a herniated disc in there, and this procedure will reportedly numb up any pain radiating to the head. Interestingly enough, when I talked to the doctor from Pakistan who did the procedure, he said he didn't think I had *just* migraines, he thought I had migraines *along with* another type of headache. *Great.* I've had this for almost four years now. I just told him that every doctor I see has a different opinion, but if he could fix me totally, he would win my heart. This clearly spurred him into action.

Something I noticed about doctors from foreign countries is that they don't call me "Sarah BerNardi," they call me "Sarah Berardi." How refreshing. And I am *not* kidding how refreshing this is. No incorrect mental prejudice on how to say my last name similar to the people who are from the USA.

After my five-minute procedure, I just lay there rigor mortis-style on the gurney, in the same position they had needled me. They told me I could roll onto my back. I said, "No, thank you."

"You can, you know."

"Yeah, um, no thanks. A little freaked out at those needles that were just in my neck, hearing the crunching going on…what was that noise, by the way?"

"Your arthritis."

"Oh."

"You can really roll over."

"Yeah, I'm gonna stay like this for a bit."

I'm scheduled to go back in two weeks for the other side, with my own Xanax.

Love, Little Miss Sunshine, who is refusing to give the hell up.

HOME

Just arrived home from a quick trip to New York City with Libbylicious. I left home a bit weary from that intestinal bug I had, but the sunshine does wonders as a cure. Whereas I am a limo/cab person, Libbylicious is a walker, tried and true. Ugh. She had no sympathy for me, even though I had just had my neck procedure, and had all fluids leave my body within twenty-four hours. Humph. She sees no reason to get a cab for fifty blocks or so.

We had two glorious days of sunshine, shopping, Lancôme makeovers from our new bestie Singleton (that's not right, what was his name? Singulair? Singletary?), and we actually did some praying at St. Patrick's. I'm not kidding.

Going Home Is Always a Problem

On the way back to Buffalo, which always fills me with dread, I was headed through security. I wore a sweater that is actually a sweater dress, with a zipper all the way up. That zipper is a curmudgeon, so half the time I have to step into it or out of it rather than engaging the zipper properly. It could certainly be worn as a dress with leggings, as I wore it, or as just a long sweater with whatever. I, however, chose to have a shirt on under it (saves on trips to the dry cleaner), though one couldn't see it or know I had said shirt on under it.

When I was stripping down to go through security, which I know how to do in my sleep. (Liquids/gels out, computer out in its own bin, shoes off, scarves off, watches and belts off; I even take my freakin' glasses and hairpins out now because those Brunswick security guards insist my eyeglasses make the buzzer go off. I must have very special glasses, no?) Well, this bozobutt clownboy decides he wants to look funny in front of everyone, but at *my* expense. Um, no. You don't do *that*, to *this* (please picture me showing you my personal self, gesturing an invitation to get a full view of me from head to toe). Nay, nay.

MiraLAX® Dissolves in Vodka, Ya Know

Also, please remember that I don't care if people look at my bits and baubles in their X-ray machines—give 'em a good scare for the day is what I say. Better safe than sorry. I just don't care for over-officious jerks.

So I start to walk up to the scanner in the proper manner (stripped down) and clownboy starts his act. "That's a beautiful…*sweater*, or is that a…*coat*…you're wearing?"

"It's a sweater. I've never had to take it off before." This is true. I do not like to lie. I've also never seen anyone have to take their pullover sweater off if they have a shirt on under it. You see, he wasn't complimenting me, he was making a point.

"I see. Could you take it off please?"

"Really?"

"Yes, ma'am," while rocking back and forth on his toes in his polyester government-issued uniform, hands clasped behind his back Barney Fife-style. *Kiss of death.*

I stomped back to the rollerbars as any two-year-old would, unzipped as far as it would unzip, stepped out of it with great show, threw it on the rollers, walked right past him as he now asked me loudly and slowly, "Now, do you have a belt on, ma'am?" I ignored him and kept walking. "Ma'am, do you have a belt on?" I continued to ignore him. I strode right past him and into the X-ray machine, and I assumed the position. He said, "I guess somebody's having a bad day!" thinking he'd get some laughs from people. Nobody laughed.

In my splayed position I said, "You haven't *seen* my bad day yet."

In reality, during my taxi ride to JFK airport, the news on the TV in the backseat said that there had just been a security breach in Terminal Seven at JFK, and the top-notch security guards that *lost* the fellow were on the lookout for said breacher. So what I really wanted to tell the clownboy harassing me in Terminal Four was, "Go find the breached security problem in Terminal Seven and let me keep my freaking sweater on since I only have a thin cami on under it."

Just all part of coming back home, I guess. Let this be a lesson to everyone: don't try to make yourself look good at my expense. If I need to take something off for security, which is standard protocol, I've got no problem with that. I do have a problem with over-officious jerks.

{ Sarah Berardi }

I Want to Be on a Panel

Somebody said to me today, "I've come to the conclusion that I dislike more people than I like." I kid you not, it was not *me* who said this. But I felt an immediate camaraderie.

When I was watching a play on Broadway (*Seminar*), Alan Rickman's character was assassinating Jerry O'Connell's pompous character and trying to bring his ego into check by telling O'Connell he'd "never be on a panel." I just thought that was the funniest thing ever, as if being on a *panel* is what decides whether you are a success in life. Panel shmanel, right? Everyone laughed.

Fast-forward four days later when I was having lunch with Marty. I asked him how Tel Aviv was and just what he did while there. He told me he was on a panel…

I Feel Like Superman

I don't know who I am anymore. No, I'm not being dramatic and esoteric. (Lawyerboy always accuses me of using *esoteric* improperly.) The last two days have been the most blissful, headache-free days in my last three and a half years. Some weird combination of stuff is giving me energy I haven't felt in the same amount of said years.

Yesterday, I spent six whole hours cleaning and organizing my closet. What's up with that? I've been thinking and thinking about doing it, just haven't had the oomph to do it. Did you know I have ten white, long-sleeved T-shirts and eight black, long-sleeved T-shirts? Of course you didn't know. I didn't know. Apparently, every time I couldn't find one that was inappropriately jammed in between things hanging in the closet, I just went out and bought a new one. Now the bloody things take up a whole shelf!

I filled four large, black garbage bags for charity donations of things that don't fit me. I'm not living in la-la land where I think I might fit into them again someday. Also, if I didn't *love* something, I tossed it. If I didn't look *fab* in it, I tossed it. Hence the many bags. I also had two large garbage bags full of hangers to take back to the dry cleaners. Crikey.

Then I didn't stop. I cleaned my bathroom cabinets. Filled one garbage bag with that chore. Marty came home, saw all the garbage bags strewn in his path, and said we looked like hoarders. He was pleased he could actually open my closet door all the way now.

Yesterday I vacuumed up my computer cord and busted it. Today was no different. I so overzealously cleaned my keyboard, that I now need a new one of those! I'd better get off this cleaning kick—it's getting expensive.

Today, I bought new hoses and a huge fire hydrant-style nozzle to hose out my garage. I KNOW! WHO AM I? I watched a movie until 2:00 a.m. I went to Wegmans. I made soup. Please let this feeling stay!

MAR 2012

Where's My Other Damned Shoe?

Almost every time—and I'm not kidding, *almost every time*—I travel, I seem to lose a shoe. I eventually find it, but we have to tear the whole hotel room up in order to do so. Come to think of it, a lot of the time it's when I'm traveling with Libbylicious. I rarely unpack nicely and put things in drawers, as I figure I'm only going to be there two nights or so. So the shoes usually remain in my suitcase with everything else. The problem arises when I return back to the hotel room and dropkick my shoes off any which way.

When I'm with Libbylicious, we always blame the housekeeper. We figure she steals a shoe until we tip her, and then returns it, hidden under the nightstand or bed where we had already looked the day before. So, years ago, we smartened up and started tipping on the very first night.

When I was in Salt Lake City, I did some shoe shopping. I had been looking for a nice pair of black flats to replace my many-years-old ones that had become very worn and slippery on any hard surface. I found some, purchased them. Then I walked to the restaurant closest to my hotel for lunch. During this lunch at Salsa's, Garcia's, Chi Chi's, something like that, I decided to have a festive lunch by myself, and ordered one of those large margaritas that are as big as your face.

Also during this lunch, I decided it would make sense to walk back to my hotel in my *new* shoes, as they would be safer than my slippery shoes.

So I surreptitiously put my two new shoes on and slipped my old shoes into the bag where the empty box of my new shoes had just been.

The next day it was time to pack up to go home, and I could only find one of my old shoes. One. Marty said, "When was the last time you saw it?"

"I don't remember. I bet the housekeeper took it, they always do." (Poor innocent people.)

Marty said, "I doubt she would take just one shoe, Sarah. She'd take the pair if she liked them and they fit."

I texted Libbylicious and told her I couldn't find my blasted shoe. She texted back: The housekeeper took it.

I packed up my one shoe, wearing my new shoes, and then it dawned on me: I must have missed the bag when I slipped my old shoes into it under the table while sipping my large margarita. What do you think the housekeeper at that restaurant thought when she was vacuuming up that night and found just one lonely shoe under that table? Did she think someone must have had one too many and left with just one shoe on? Are you getting a visual of someone leaving a restaurant, tipsy, wearing only one shoe? It's probably happened before. And if you know it has, keep it to yourself.

My Vacation Home That Has Yet to Be a Vacation Home

The following started from a Facebook post I made:

I say: Should I mind that I've arrived at my vacation home and the new owners next door are parked in one of my parking spaces, their yippy dog woke me at 7:00 a.m., and there is dog shit all over my front lawn? Someone has awoken the *nonsleeping* giant down here in Georgia.

A says: You're so lucky to have a vacay home. LOL I'm jealous…but home or vacay home, dog poop all over the lawn is not cool in my book.

C says: I'd ring the doorbell, smile sweetly, and introduce myself. You could let them know you will do the first round of poop cleaning on your property, but you'll be placing it in your parking space. They might want to move their car.

Viper Tongue says: Oh hell no!

{ Sarah Berardi }

J says: Do what I did to my old neighbors: I picked up all the dog shit (which was a lot, quite frankly) and made a nice, neat pile smack-dab in front of their garage door, and when they backed out, LOL, crap all over their tires.

JS says: After reading the comments above, I'm lovin' your fb friends!

C says: Sarah used to babysit me. I learned from the best.

I say: OK, just went over to knock on their door—their car clearly out there, as it's a big-ass Chevy suburban (sitting in my spot). The dog is nippin' at my heels and screaming at me. NO ANSWER AT THE DOOR. I left a very kind note: Hi, I'm your neighbor next door, could we talk re: the dog and my parking spot? Thaaaaaanks.

C says: You had me going there, then did the about-face I was waiting for!

Viper Tongue says: I'd like a primetime interview with "C," please and thank you.

I say: Well, at least you gals have me laughing, as I just found my fridge has been leaking out of its water and ice spigots on its door; rusty bubbles down the door! YAY!

J says: You're far too kind, I would have given them a wakeup call, *Mob Wives* style, LOL, with my German shepherd on one side of me and my girls on the other. Aw hell, fly me down there and problem solved Sarah.

I say: Booking stat, my BIKER CHICK friend.

I say: Plus, I flew down here having forgotten my keys to the car and the house! Ha! I found my hide-a-key, got in, but have no car without the damned car key, which is with the house key. Went to pump up my bike tires, that little valve keeps falling inside the tire tube so I can't blow it up. I had to blow up Marty's and ride his. This is a little dangerous for me. It's too large.

CoD says: Enjoy the vacation while it lasts, because your Lawyerboy has a pile of stained dress shirts and ties deemed for Sarah's Laundering Service ASAP :)

JHD says: Oh dear Sarah, ONLY you!!! This definitely should have been a blog. Don't you wake up every morning afraid of the sh!! that is going to happen to you each day?!

I say: @ JHD—Yes, that is why some days I never get up.

I Am Walking Blog Fodder

After a lovely week-long trip in England hunting for Colin Firth and visiting with my girlfriends who live there, Marty and I started our flight home from London, Heathrow to Dulles, to Buffalo. With about an hour left of our flight

MiraLAX® Dissolves in Vodka, Ya Know

from London to Dulles, I felt pretty barfy. I collected those little barf bags from Marty's seat and mine. There wasn't turbulence, and I had only taken one measly Xanax. I did eat the lunch they served on the plane. So was this a stomach virus or food poisoning?

By the time we landed, I couldn't walk a straight line I was so faint. The girl walking up the ramp next to me asked if I felt OK. I told her I did (I didn't) and that my husband was with me. Turns out Marty being with me didn't really help. What could he do but keep people out of my way? I barfed in each and every restroom from our gate to the United Club (a step up from the regular terminal waiting areas). I continued to get sick there.

PUKEY

Sarah Berardi

I made about eight trips back and forth to the restroom, getting sick every time. I finally told Marty that I was so weak and sick that I didn't think I could take the next leg of our flight home, Dulles to Buffalo, even though it's less than an hour long. One of the security guards saw me and suggested I call the paramedics. We did, and they came. People stared at me, but I was so sick I didn't give a fiddler's fart. Hell, it must have been pretty entertaining for them.

They wanted to take me into the hospital for antinauseants and fluids. "Nay, nay," I said. I was going to see if it subsided any so that I could make it home, since my husband was keen to get back (as was I). He said, "I have a feeling we'll be seeing you in a bit." I am a stubborn, billy goat bitch.

Pffft. He was right. But before we knew to call them back, I had to have Marty walk me to the restroom because I was too weak to walk. Pathetic. Darn it all, I didn't make it to the women's room, and in front of the whole glorious, uppity United Club, I fell to my knees and stuck my head into a cute little designer wastebasket. Marty then called for the paramedics again and carried me and the designer wastebasket into the restroom, along with the nice supervisor lady from the United Club. She rubbed my back and blotted my forehead, just like a mom would do.

Away I went in the ambulance, strapped to that gurney, continuing to get sick on the way out. No more designer wastebaskets for me, just a big, yellow, Rubbermaid tub. The ambulance even had its sirens on for me (how important I am). To make things worse, when my blood pressure dropped due to dehydration, my veins collapsed (this is typical). I warned the guy my IV would be hard to start, as I'm hard to start even when I'm not sick. Indeed, it didn't work. It's very easy to infiltrate (poke straight through the vein). The other guy tried the other arm. It worked.

❧{ MiraLAX® Dissolves in Vodka, Ya Know }❧

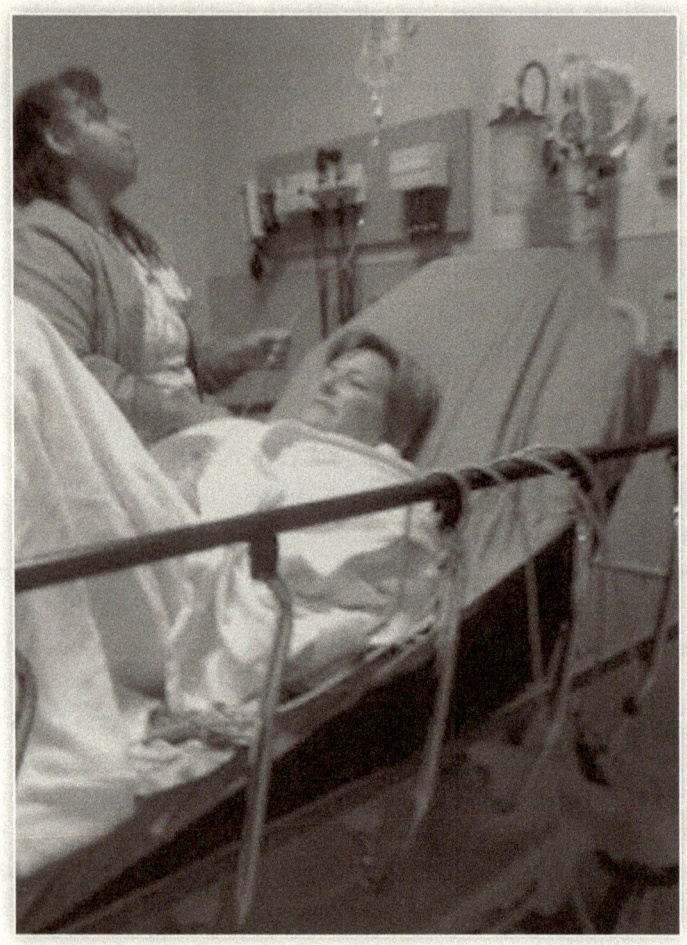

AHHHHH, DRUGS

At the hospital, they checked for various things and found nothing. But they also still couldn't control my barfing! Crikey!

After three rounds of an antinauseant and then a pain medication for my Betty Big Belly, I was able to keep down a whole bottle of that CT scan contrast. Yay.

So we are now rebooked to fly home today (Sunday) after spending the night dozing in the Emergency Room. I cannot wait to get home to my bed, which I clearly shouldn't have left in the first place. (Does anyone ever listen to me?)

Seems there is a twenty-four-hour bug going around. I already had it twice now, thank you very much. No need for a third time, 'K?

{ Sarah Berardi }

My Beloved Bed

When I was talking with my friend, she knew how glad I was to be back into my bed after my trip. She also knew I probably wouldn't get out of it for a few days. You see, my bed has special meaning to me. It means safety, security, quiet, peacefulness, reading, online shopping, and *The Big Bang Theory* reruns.

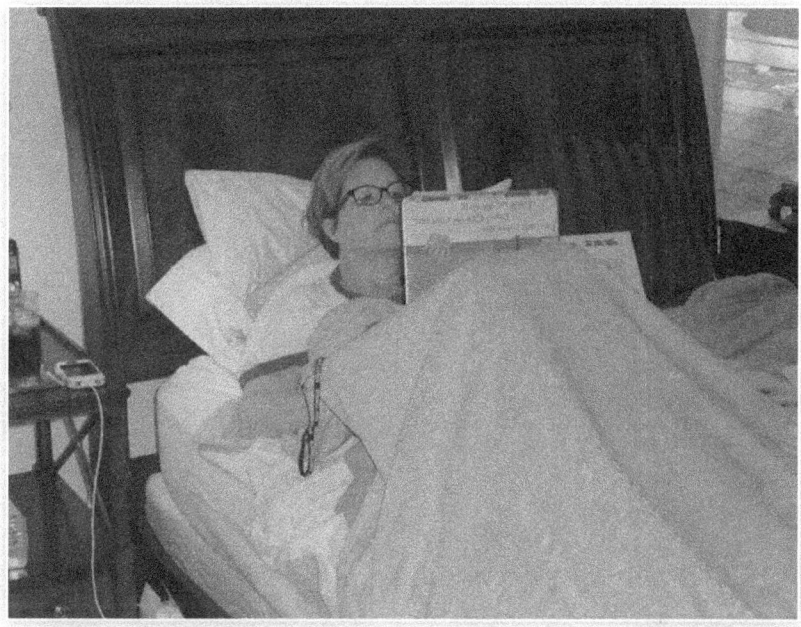

Things that won't happen when I'm safely tucked into my bed:

Idiot drivers won't give me road rage or give me hand signals that mean, "You're a vajayjay."

I won't say something stupid to someone, and they won't say something stupid to me.

I won't volunteer for anything I shouldn't volunteer for.

I won't say I'll go to something I really don't want to go to, and nobody will say they're coming with me.

I won't get into any arguments with the drugstore people (Marty will).

I won't get mad at moron cart drivers at Wegmans and hear that clickity-clack of those brick floors, and they won't have to put up with a batshitcrazy fifty-two-year-old banging people with her cart because they invaded her space.

MiraLAX® Dissolves in Vodka, Ya Know

You see, when my friend gave my bedroom a makeover, she knew it was going to be my safe haven. She knew I was going to be doing just about everything from my bed. So I naturally buy good quality mattresses, but they keep going concave where I sleep. I've had one replaced for free and bought another one all within three years. You see, you can't flip a pillowtop; you can only change it end to end. What would really make me happy now is if we could upgrade to a king-sized mattress, as my paperwork and books need their own spot when Marty is in town.

DON'T EVER SAY I'M VAIN

{ Sarah Berardi }

I'll Choke on It

Sometimes Marty is a big ol' baby. Because sometimes I inadvertently leave things in the bed that shouldn't be there when he finally crawls into his side at bedtime. Have I told you about the things Marty finds in our bed? A nectarine pit stuck to Marty's face (I had looked in vain for that dang thing during the middle of the night), pens, handwritten important notes, nasal strips, random TV and fireplace remotes, lonely single socks, bills that should have been paid, cellophane Weight Watchers snack wrappers (they stick nicely to Marty's face, too), and wire hangers. None of these things are unusual. I know there are more…

Time and time again, he has *lividly* told me, "Do *not* leave things in the bed. I have nightmares that they get stuck in my mouth and I choke on them!"

But this time, he said I had provided the straw to break the camel's back. I am a bad wife. It's as if I'm taunting him, but I'm really not. I just lose things in there.

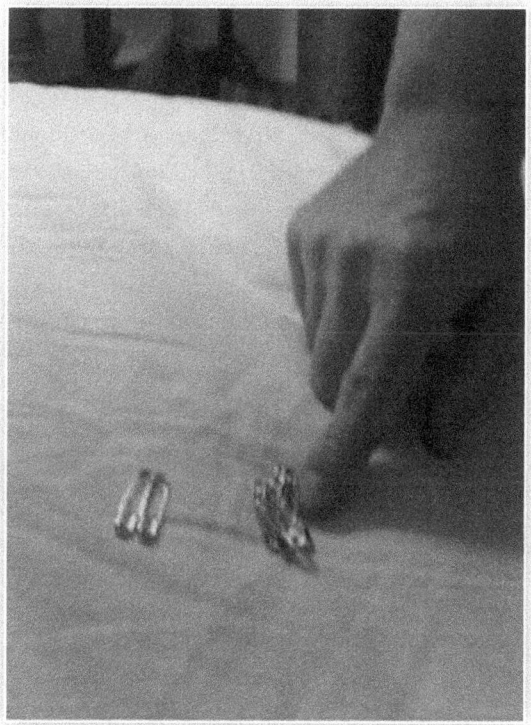

FROM THE DRY CLEANING

I can't help it. I live in my bed, *live* in it. I think I am depressed.

My Post from My Facebook and the Comments That Followed

DAMN IT, WHERE DID I PUT MY ANGER MANAGEMENT BOOK?
1. Hahahaha…I may have borrowed it.
2. U returned it remember, cuz it didn't work…LOL.
3. Maybe you threw it at Marty. Look behind the couch.
4. In the library, with Col. Mustard and the rope.
5. I have it.
6. When you find it, can I borrow it?

I'm Crooked?

I was having lunch with my lunch buddies and asked them if they thought my glasses appeared crooked. They all studied them, and said no. But my glasses *felt* crooked on my face. I had fallen asleep with them on not too many nights before.

So I went to my optician after we finished eating and laughing, and asked for a straightening. The woman looked at them; studied them, actually. I told her they always have to be adjusted to my crooked ears. She said, "You don't have crooked ears, you have crooked eyebrows."

I said, "Nuh-uh, no, I don't!" For years, every optician has said my ears are not level. I know I have one eye that droops, but this was the first time someone accused me of having crooked eyebrows.

I'm a Little "Off"

Today, as I was on my way out, I realized just short of the car door that I literally had one shoe on and one shoe off. Now that's got to mean something's not quite right. I'm chalking it up to…well, any number of my maladies. I have a bevy to choose from.

{ Sarah Berardi }

Returns, Exchanges, and Shopping Online

I do almost all my shopping online. I'm pretty adept at getting the correct sizes by now, but when I try a new catalog or company, I venture into the unknown. This is one of the return slips I was making out. I find that *almost all* return slips have a "reason for return/exchange" choice missing. Why don't they have a "Doesn't fit correctly," "Makes me look frumpy," "I have a Betty Big Belly," or, "I have a Betty Bundt-Cake Belly," choice on them? I really hate to lie. So today I decided to make my own reason and let the company know they should add one more choice.

The Cup

My nightmares have returned. Marty is back to sleeping with a cup on.

Brain Fog

I've been in a horrible brain fog. I just spent a week showering with what I thought was body wash but was, in fact, hair conditioner. I've been squeegeeing the shower before I turn the damned water off again. I also made a seldom-made trip to the grocery store. When Marty came home, he noticed we had food in the fridge and was delighted, to say the least. Until he went to throw something out. Treading very carefully, he asked me:

Marty: Did you buy steaks today?

Me: Yeah, they're grass-fed, hormone-free, yada yada, expensive. Thought we'd have them tonight.

Marty: Do you typically store them in the garbage can instead of the fridge now?

They had been in the trash for about five hours.

Here's to hoping the fog dissipates.

I Was Compassionate at One Time

Text between me and CoD (Crack of Dawn—Lawyerboy's girlfriend):

CoD: My dad ran into someone who used to work with you and Marty. He said you were the most compassionate person he ever met!

Me: ME?

CoD: Yes

Me: Ha, must have been before I turned into Cruella De Vil

CoD: His name is xxxx xxxxx

Me: OMG I LOVE HIM

CoD: He said that your stickies saved his life? Whatever that means.

Me: He took my place as a secretary when I got pregnant with Lawyerboy; I left a notebook of instructions and sticky notes for him. (Are you surprised?)

CoD: Oh, that explains the stickies.

Me: Yeah, that was definitely before I turned to the dark side. But it's made my day, thanks.

At least I admit I'm on the dark side. It was nicer on the other side.

{ Sarah Berardi }

The End

Well, today was hard. Hard to hear. We are in the process of looking into some long-term care policy or something that Marty's getting for me because I'm so broken. We need to cover our asses for the kids' sake. I keep telling him I'm going out in brilliant, wild flames, but he thinks I'm going to linger and make it as painful as possible for as long as possible for everyone.

INSURANCE GUY TO MARTY: Do you have plans to travel out of the US?

ME: Hardee-har-har, name a country he hasn't been in. He'll be traveling until he retires.

GUY TO MARTY: That's a yes?

MARTY: Yes.

GUY TO MARTY: Are you planning on partaking in any risky business, such as piloting a plane, skydiving, scuba diving…

ME TO GUY: No, he is not.

MARTY: Apparently not.

GUY TO ME: What medications do you currently take?

MARTY TO GUY: How much ink do you have in that pen?

ME: Shut up, I'm off six drugs now. Go to hell. It was a mountainous climb, I tell you. Actually, it was a descent to hell. You were probably in a different country.

GUY TO ME: Do you have anxiety, depression, cysts, asthma, migraines, weight gain? (He names lots of others.)

ME: Yes, yes, yes, yes, yes, and yes. Who doesn't?

GUY TO ME: Have you ever been convicted of a felony?

ME: Not yet. But I throw poop at my neighbors in Georgia who let their dog poop on my lawn. I just haven't been called in yet.

The conversation went on with the poor guy laughing (I think) at the other end, and me and Marty bickering on our end.

❦   MiraLAX® Dissolves in Vodka, Ya Know   ❦

Sarah Berardi

Written by my Auntie Mim:

> I see a wave come rolling
> Toward my toes on shore
> I feel it splash and bubbling
> And then I wait for more
>
> The next one rises higher
> I feel it on my knees
> And I turn to run to Daddy
> For a comfort of his squeeze
>
> We catch the next together
> Our toes upon the sand
> But this one does not scare me
> I hold my daddy's hand

—Mary Ann Carroll Funk

BETTY CROCKER® is a registered trademark of General Mills Marketing, Inc.

IN-N-OUT BURGER® is a registered trademark of In-N-Out Burgers Corporation

MIRACLESUIT® is a registered trademark of A & H Sportswear Co., Inc.

MIRALAX® is a registered trademark of MSD Consumer Care, Inc.

SPANX® is a registered trademark of Spanx, Inc.

WEGMANS® is a registered trademark of Wegmans Food Markets, Inc.

All other trademarks and trade names as may be used herein are the property of their respective owners. Author and publisher disclaim any and all rights, title, and interest in and to any such trademarks or trade names. All other rights reserved.

www.ingramcontent.com/pod-product-compliance
Lightning Source LLC
Chambersburg PA
CBHW022354040426
42450CB00005B/169